THE TENT BOOK

THE TENT BOOK

E. M. HATTON

Houghton Mifflin Company   Boston   1979

Line drawings by Jane Tenenbaum

Library of Congress Cataloging in Publication Data

Hatton, E   M
  The tent book.

  Bibliography: p.
  Includes index.
  1. Tents.   I. Title.
TS1860.H37   728   79-9047
ISBN 0-395-27613-9
ISBN 0-395-28264-0 pbk.

Printed in the United States of America

A 10 9 8 7 6 5 4 3 2 1

Book design by David Ford

For   Chris and Earl   Laura and Francis

ACKNOWLEDGMENTS

Invaluable assistance was given me by my agent Heide Lange, my editor Frances Tenenbaum, and Don Perdue, Clay Jones, Pat Ethridge, Mablen Jones, Joan Miller, and Alix Elias. If it hadn't been for them you might not be reading *The Tent Book*. But so many others were extremely helpful — Diane Matthews, Joseph Padial, Abel Cruz, Leonard Sprung, and Lee Black were generosity personified, along with Thierry Demogue, who translated copious correspondence into French, and Alice Lundoff, who helped me out while she was in France. Charlie Savage with Dr. Bill Murtaugh lined me up with those wonderful tents in Krakow, Poland, Barbara Greenberg helped, and Dr. Jerzy Szablowski, Director of the Wawel Collection, went beyond the call of duty to supply me with photos. The architecture section was made possible by the generosity of Horst Berger of Geiger Berger Consultants, P.C., the four partners of Vela/Future Tents, Ltd., along with Ron Kinnius at Irving Industries, Robert J. Sheldon at Birdair, Jim Schmiedeskamp at Owens-Corning Fiberglas Corporation, and Professor Charles P. Graves at the University of Kentucky. Mary Burczyk and Stu Waugh at the Canvas Products Association International shared their resources with me, as did Bill Moss of Moss Tent Works. And special thanks go to Jim Thompson, Carleton Howe, Jean Demogue, Peter Stamberg, Jill Charlton, Robert Adzema and Joel Kopp for donating photographs. Raymond Prestia provided me access to his fine collection, and Ellen Johnston's library was quite helpful. And special thanks, too, to Katherine Sokolnikoff, Janice Byer, Gail Hayden, Kai Lofton, Lois and Ian Alsop, Bunny Bodman, Christi Hatcher, Rosalind Heinz and, last but not least, Jeffrey Aronoff.

This book has relied strongly on photograph archives, and I am indebted (both figuratively and literally) to those that furnished me with the photographs. The New York Public Library Picture Collection, the

Library of Congress, the Smithsonian Institution, and the Lincoln Center Library for the Performing Arts were treasure troves, and extremely helpful.

There are others not specifically mentioned who provided me with leads and general assistance in my quest for material. I thank them as well. *The Tent Book* is the culmination of a great deal of energy . . . and it wasn't all the author's.

Hap Hatton

CONTENTS

Acknowledgments vii
Introduction xi

Part 1 The Tent in History

1 Europe and Asia 3
2 America 41
3 The Nomads 61

Part 2 The Tent as Art

4 Architecture 113
5 Tent Art 138
6 Stage and Screen 151

Part 3 Tents for Campers

7 A Consumers' Guide 165
8 Sources 222

Bibliography 235
Index 239

INTRODUCTION

The tent: versatile, durable, practical, beautiful, portable, economical, liberating, and fun! Bedouins and backpackers, scouts and soldiers, mountain-climbers and circuses, you and I, have used tents of every description all over the globe since civilization began. This is a book about tents — an adventure in tents — that covers all aspects of them.

Millions of people in this country and abroad are camping out in any of hundreds of styles of tents, which range from super-lightweight backpack tents to more permanent, beautifully designed and furnished, summer home–substitute tents. Thousands more are building their own from the kits and instruction books that are available. Nomads on every continent still migrate with tents ingeniously designed to enable them to live and go virtually anywhere from the Sahara to Siberia. And young people have taken the nomadic designs and developed them for their own use here in this country. Tents have always been present in our literature, cinema, and theater. Now tents are showing up as sculptural art forms and tent architecture is beginning to serve as a superb alternative to rigid right-angled steel and glass.

When you get right down to it, tents are everywhere — in every shape and form. The photographs in this book illustrate their rich history, contemporary use, and limitless future. You will find here the ceremonial tents of Alexander the Great and Napoleon, the Eskimo summer tent, and tent cities like the Field of the Cloth of Gold (considered the Eighth Wonder of the World when Henry VIII summit met with Francis I in 1502) and the San Francisco Earthquake. You'll see Rudolph Valentino's sheik tent, the circus big top and how it's put together, plus the world's largest tent building, which is 5.5 million square feet of Fiberglas yarn coated with Teflon covering 105 acres. And, last but not least, all the latest tents available to the camper (with information on where to find them).

In tents the romantic and practical are combined, making the practical even more alluring. Tents are still associated with freedom and the excitement of living and sleeping in the great outdoors and you'll see how everyone from nomads to royalty has been doing it . . . and how you can do it yourself.

PART 1

THE TENT IN HISTORY

1 EUROPE AND ASIA

Are those my tents where I perceive the fire?
— William Shakespeare, *Julius Caesar*, V.iii.13

The tent, man's oldest known artificial dwelling and the portable shelter par excellence, dates back to prehistoric times when people stretched animal skins over trees. In the next logical step either the tree or its limbs was made into support poles, and then the shelter could be moved and pitched anywhere. In areas where wood was scarce, mammoth ribs and tusks served as a framework.

From these humble beginnings tents grew into incredibly huge and magnificent pavilions — sumptuous portable palaces with walls lined with priceless tapestries, the ground covered with exquisite Oriental rugs, and the tent poles encrusted with precious stones.

Probably the oldest tent on record is that found in Egypt in the tomb of the twenty-first-Dynasty princess Isimkheb (1000 B.C.). The tent ceiling is sky blue with multicolored stars appliquéd to it; red and black checkerboard squares with colorful animals and flowers cover the inside walls.

Prehistoric campsites discovered in Moldova, Russia, date back to 40,000 B.C. Remains of animal bones and tusks, which at one time supported hides, have been found, and small embankments or earth berms still exist where early Cro-Magnons anchored their tents by placing rocks, bones, and earth around the bottom. (These can be compared to the tipi rings found in the western part of the United States which mark the sites where tipis stood and rings of stone were used to anchor them.) The remains of a 28,000-year-old tent site were found in southern Russia. The tent measured some ninety-eight feet long and probably sheltered several families as it contained a row of hearths down the center, perhaps one to a family.

The tent remained in this rough form for approximately its first 10,000 years. Cave paintings dating back 10,000 to 20,000 years are the first pictorial renderings of early tents.

When these early Cro-Magnon nomads moved on they might have abandoned the old tent, only to build a new one at their next stop, since one of the ancient taboos (which still exists) among many races strictly forbids both inhabiting an abandoned dwelling or using the material from the old one to build a new one.

When weaving was discovered, possibly some 10,000 years ago, woven fabric was incorporated into the tent, as was felt when it later came into existence. It is strictly conjecture what the early fabric was woven from — possibly it was wool, which was definitely used in the days of Christ. Another possible material is ramie, the flaxlike fiber from the stem of a woody Asian plant of the nettle family, which has been in existence for at least 5000 years.

Up to 10,000 years ago several Aryan tribes were living in skin tents. These people were primarily herdsmen and moved as the seasons affected their livestock's grazing areas. The Turkomans of Asia Minor were isolated from the influence of neighboring civilizations and the type of circular tent or yurt they occupied in the early twentieth century was the same their ancestors used more than 8000 years before. The Lapps are another example of a culture's development isolated from all outside influences.

Until the present day, the support poles of tents have been, for the most part, trees, either in the form of wooden poles or as live trees with or without their leaves. Incorporating a living tree into the structure of the tent itself provides maximum stability, so when felt or pelts were spread over the tree and firmly anchored to the ground, these tents could withstand anything the elements had to offer.

The idea of the tree-tent has not altogether disappeared. Before the Ute Indians were moved onto reservations at the turn of the century, they would rest the poles of their tipis in the fork of two tree branches and integrate the trunk of the tree into the structure of the tipi. Apache girls still participate in an elaborate puberty ceremony which utilizes an uncovered tipi made of live tree branches. And the Altai Turks of south central Asia, in a sacrificial ceremony that takes place in the clearing of a wood, erect a special yurt with the leafy top of a young tree emerging from the smoke hole. An interesting point, too, is that among some peoples the words *tree* and *house* have the same meaning.

The earliest recording of the tree-tent was made by Herodotus (*The Histories*) when he traveled from Greece to Persia in the fifth century B.C. He observed the ancient Scythian tribe of the Argippaei dwelling "each man under a tree, covering it in winter with a white felt cloth."

In the summer they uncovered the trees and lived under them.

TENTS IN THE BIBLE

Our very earliest references to tents come from the Old Testament and date back to c. 4000 B.C. In Genesis 4:20, "Adah bore Jabal; he was the father of those who dwell in tents and have cattle." In those ancient times the way of life was mostly pastoral (the first mention of tents is connected with the keeping of cattle) and the tent is the only form of shelter that can sustain that lifestyle. The black desert tent now used by the Arab nomads on the same terrain is considered the closest in design to the ancient model. Abraham himself, the first of the patriarchs, was considered to be a Bedouin and only in this century have the character and habits of these people undergone change. King Solomon (c. 972–932 B.C.) sang of the Bedouin in Song of Solomon 1:5. "I am black, but comely, O ye daughters of Jerusalem, as the tents of Kedar, as the curtains of Solomon," Kedar being a biblical name for the Bedouin.

From the Bible we also learn that "Abram dwelled in the land of Canaan, and Lot dwelled in the cities of the plain, and pitched his tent toward Sodom" (Genesis 13:12, c. 2080 B.C.). In 2054 B.C. we are told that Abraham "sat in the tent-door in the heat of the day" and saw the angels. At this time of day the external shade of the desert tent is much cooler than the interior of the tent. And among Bedouin tribes it is the duty of the chief or sheik to entertain strangers. His tent is usually pitched on the edge of the encampment toward the trade route or highway from whence strangers usually approach. This custom accounts for Abraham being the first to see his visitors.

Esau and Jacob are described in Genesis 25:27: "Esau was a skillful hunter, a man of the field; and Jacob was a quiet man, dwelling in tents." Numbers 24:2–3,5, referring to the tribes descended from Jacob, adds "And Balaam lifted up his eyes, and saw Israel encamping tribe by tribe. And the Spirit of God came upon him, and he took up his discourse, and said, 'The oracle of Balaam the son of Beor, the oracle of the man whose eye is opened . . . how fair are your tents, O Jacob, your encampments, O Israel!'"

In the common Arab tent of today, the women have separate apartments that are made by attaching curtains or carpets to the supports. In the Old Testament several women had their own tents: specific mention is made of the tent of Sarah, Abraham's wife; those of Leah and Rachel, the wives of Jacob; as well as the tents of their maidservants.

After the Flood (3156 B.C.), Noah is mentioned in Genesis 9:21 when

Esau and Jacob. Jacob is considered the traditional ancestor of the people of Israel and the tents he used are the same as those used today in the Arabian desert. (Copyright de Brunoff 1904)

"he drank of the wine, and became drunk, and lay uncovered in his tent," and prophesied the destiny of his family. He is quoted as saying, "Japheth shall dwell in the tents of Shem" (Genesis 9:27). Psalms 84:10 states, "I had rather be a doorkeeper in the house of my God, than to dwell in the tents of wickedness." And in I Kings 12:16 — "And when all Israel saw that the king did not hearken to them, the people answered the king, 'What portion have we in David? We have no inheritance in the son of Jesse. To your tents, O Israel! Look now to your own house, David.' So Israel departed to their tents."

THE TABERNACLE

The most famous tent of the Old Testament is the Tabernacle and it is described in the book of Exodus (Chapters 25–27, 30–31, and 35–40). The Tabernacle was the portable sanctuary constructed by Moses as a place of worship for the Hebrew tribes during the period of wandering in the wilderness that preceded their arrival in the Promised Land. It was finally placed at Shiloh and disappeared into oblivion after the erection in 950 B.C. in Jerusalem of Solomon's Temple, which used the proportions of the Tabernacle in its design.

The Tabernacle of the Old Testament. In this rather stylized drawing, the components of the Tabernacle complex are visible. Cattle are being led through the crowd toward the Tabernacle for sacrifice at the altar which can be seen through the parted curtains. (Sonzogno, Italy)

The Tabernacle was set up in the center of the camp at every halt and the Tabernacle complex — whose specifications were dictated by God to Moses, according to the Bible — consisted of a large court of about 75 × 150 feet surrounding the rectangular Tabernacle tent. The court was enclosed by linen hangings and had the shape of two adjacent squares (or a rectangle with a length twice its width). The eastern half contained the altar of sacrifice for burnt offerings and a copper and bronze basin holding water for ritual ablutions. In the middle of the western half, in the Tabernacle itself, was the Ark of the Covenant, which contained the tablets of the Ten Commandments. The Ark, the sacred wooden chest of the Hebrews, was overlaid with gold inside and out and was always veiled; the high priest alone could look upon its uncovered surface.

The Tabernacle tent was formed of ten curtains, in two sets of five, of fine twined blue and purple linen with interwoven colored figures of cherubim. All of the forty-eight tent frames were made from acacia wood overlaid with gold. The interior was divided into two rooms, "the holy place" and "the most holy place" (Holy of Holies). The outer room, or holy place, contained a table on which blessed bread was placed, an altar of incense, and a Menorah, the seven-branched candelabrum of the Jews. The inner room, or Holy of Holies, was separated from the outer by a veil of blue, purple, and scarlet with more cherubim, and was considered to be the actual dwelling place of God Himself, who sat invisibly throned above a mercy seat or propitiatory, a slab of gold resting upon the Ark of the Covenant with a cherub at each corner.

The Tabernacle must have been a staggering load to lug through the wilderness — the metal alone weighed in at some 12,000 pounds, fabric and hides measured well in excess of 1500 square yards, and there were also forty-eight gilded support poles as well. This doesn't include the hangings and framework for the outside wall.

THE KAABA AT MECCA

While the Tabernacle of the Old Testament is considered the first and most sacred shrine of the Jewish and Christian religions, the Kaaba at Mecca is equally revered in the Moslem religion and is the place toward which Moslems face when praying. The Kaaba, like the Tabernacle, is covered with fabric. Annually a tent city of pilgrims — sometimes numbering as many as 200,000 — encamp on the Arafat plain outside Mecca.

Interestingly enough, the world's largest tent building (tension structure) is being constructed near Mecca at the Jeddah International Airport. The structure is in keeping with the pilgrim tent cities nearby. It is composed of two identical roof systems made up of 210 tentlike units. Five and a half million square feet of Fiberglas coated with Teflon will be used and an area of 105 acres will be covered. According to projections, by 1985 the airport will accommodate some 8.6 million passengers annually, and by the year 2000 the number is estimated to reach 16.5

million. At maximum capacity, 100 flight operations per hour will be handled. As would be expected, the commerce of the city depends almost completely on the pilgrims as little else is manufactured except articles of devotion and souvenirs of the holy place.

At the center of Mecca is a large mosque, the Haram, which encloses the Kaaba. Many legends surround the origin of the Kaaba (from Arabic for "cube"), but it is traditionally believed to have been built by Abraham at the command of God (just as the Tabernacle was built to God's order). In the case of the Kaaba, it was intended to be a replica of God's house in heaven. Frequently destroyed by floods and reconstructed, it is believed to have retained its original shape of a double cube, being twice as high as it is long and wide, enclosing a room, the "holy of holies" (like the inner room of the Tabernacle), the access to which is gained by a single door. It is here that the sacred stone rests, worn hollow by centuries of ritual kissing; it is held together by a wide band of silver. From the roof is suspended the *Kiswa* (holy carpet), which is renewed annually at the pilgrimage. It completely covers the holy place except for gaps at the eastern corner where the Black Stone, which pilgrims kiss, is exposed and the southern corner with the Yamani Stone, which they touch in passing as they perform the tawaf, or sevenfold circuit of the sanctuary along a road which surrounds the Kaaba. Next to the Kaaba is the Zamzam, a holy well used for religious and medicinal purposes.

The custody of the Kaaba has been keenly sought in the Islamic world. In the fifth century it passed to the Koreish, an ancient Bedouin tribe to which Mohammed belonged. After acquiring the Kaaba, they became one of the most powerful tribes in Arabia. Then in the tenth century, the

The fabric-covered Kaaba in Mecca is the chief goal of the Moslem religion and the site toward which the Moslems face when praying. At the left of the Kaaba is a structure covering the sacred well, and at the right is a large tent. (Smithsonian Institution)

Karmathians, an independent communist community in lower Mesopotamia, after conquering all of Yemen, carried away the black stone in the Kaaba and kept it for ten years. And as late as 1932, an Afghan attempted to steal it.

Up until recently, there was a ban against unbelievers visiting Mecca, but as early as the nineteenth century, the holy city was visited and described by others, such as the explorer Sir Richard Burton, whose tomb is a marble tent.

Tomb of Sir Richard Francis Burton (1821–1890), English explorer, writer, and linguist. Burton was one of the first Westerners to journey to Mecca and Medina and his travel writings and translations (especially the sixteen volumes of the *Arabian Nights*) are remarkable works. His wife, Isabelle, was as Christian as Burton was not. Upon his death, she had extreme unction performed on his body, then she took his priceless unpublished works into the garden and burned them because she felt they were blasphemous. It is surprising that she would allow not only her husband but also herself to be buried in this tent tomb. (Mansell Collection, London)

OLD TESTAMENT TENT MURDERS

There are two tent murders in the Old Testament and both of them were committed by women against army generals — Judith killed Holofernes and Jael killed Sisera.

The Old Testament book of Judith probably was written by a Palestinian before 100 B.C., although some scholars date it later. It tells of an attack on the Jews by an army led by the Assyrian general Holofernes. Bethulia, a besieged Jewish city, is about to surrender when Judith, a beautiful widow of the tribe of Simeon, appears on the scene. Wearing rich attire, she goes over to the hostile camp, where she is conducted to the general, whose suspicions are disarmed by the tales she invents. After four days, Holofernes is smitten with her and, at the close of a sumptuous entertainment, invites her to stay the night with him in his tent. When Holofernes falls asleep, Judith takes his sword, beheads him, and gives the head to her maid. Both leave the camp (as they had previously done, ostensibly for prayer) and return to Bethulia with their trophy. After great rejoicing the Israelites rally against and defeat the enemy. The story is told with a spirit of God's interest in His people and Judith is portrayed as a woman of great self-sacrifice, courage, and nobility.

The story of Jael and Sisera is found in Judges 4:18–24. Sisera was a Canaanite captain who was warring with the children of Israel. Deborah, a prophetess, was judging the Israelites at that time. She and Barak, a leader from northern Canaan, routed Sisera and his army. Sisera left his chariot and fled on foot. Barak pursued his army and put them all to the sword.

Meanwhile, Sisera came upon the tent of Jael. "And Jael came out to meet Sisera, and said to him, 'Turn aside, my Lord, turn aside to me; have no fear.' So he turned aside to her into the tent, and she covered him with a rug. And he said to her, 'Pray, give me a little water to drink; for I am thirsty.' So she opened a skin of milk and gave him a drink and covered him. And he said to her, 'Stand at the door of the tent, and if any man comes and asks you, "Is any one here?" say, No.' But Jael the wife of Heber took a tent peg, and took a hammer in her hand, and went softly to him and drove the peg into his temple, till it went down into the ground, as he was lying fast asleep from weariness. So he died. And behold, as Barak pursued Sisera, Jael went out to meet him, and said to

Judith, the Jewish heroine, seduced and decapitated the Assyrian general Holofernes and saved her people. This painting by Mantegna, done around 1495, shows Judith placing her grisly trophy in her maidservant's bag in order to carry it from the camp. (National Gallery of Art, Widener Collection)

him, 'Come, and I will show you the man whom you are seeking.' So he went in to her tent; and there lay Sisera dead, with the tent peg in his temple.''

ANCIENT MILITARY TENTS

Assyrian

Tents have been used by armies in all ages. The earliest renderings of tents are the ancient Assyrian bas-reliefs dating from around 700 B.C. They were discovered by Sir Austen Henry Layard at Nineveh (Iraq) between 1842 and 1851. The forms of tent and tent furnishings are similar to those which still prevail in the East, and it appears that then as now, when possible, it was a custom to pitch tents within the walls of a city. These early Assyrian tents show an affinity to earlier tree-supported tents.

Jael, another Jewish heroine, drives a tent stake through the head of the Canaanite captain Sisera, her guest. As is common in many renderings of biblical and other ancient scenes, the tents are of the same period as the artist, in this case the fifteenth-century Master of Flémalle.

Greek

One of the earliest descriptions of Greek military tents is that of Homer, who described the tent of Achilles in detail. In actuality this "lofty tent" was more a wooden hut covered with reeds "collected from the marshy shore." Homer mentions also that the soldiers in the encampment had skin-covered tents.

The tents of the Macedonians were small, supplying only a necessary covering when needed for two soldiers. These skin tents could also be bundled up and used in fording rivers and were similar to the *tente d'abri* ("tent of cover"), which has passed down through the ages and is still used today. The simplest *tentes d'abri* are improvised by fastening together skins, blankets, or waterproof sheets over a stick. The larger ones consist of a rope stretched over poles and fixed into the ground, over which canvas is thrown and pegged into the earth on each side so as to form a low ridge.

The tents of Greek commanders were pitched in the center of the camp and consisted usually of two chambers — one for sleeping and one for receiving company. The pavilion of Alexander the Great, however, was enormous and resplendent (as described in the fifteen books of the *Deipnosophists* of Athenaeus). Eight pillars gilded with gold supported a roof emblazoned with designs. In the center was a throne of gold from which judgments were delivered. Five hundred bodyguards, or armed court attendants, clothed in magnificent gold-embroidered attire, surrounded the interior entrances and no unauthorized person could enter without complying with strict court regulations. The pavilion is said to have been one of the most fabulous ever seen.

In 324 B.C., a year before his death, Alexander married the daughter of Darius and married off eighty of his chief officers and friends to girls from the highest ranking families in Persia. A marriage tent was erected for the festivities, which lasted five days. The tent was supported by fifty thirty-foot columns of gold and silver and was huge enough to accom-

This Assyrian bas-relief shows a cross section of a tent that an Assyrian officer has entered. Food is being offered him by a slave and another slave is folding down the bed. A waterbag hangs from the ridgepole. In the adjoining tent a butcher prepares a carcass. Above, left, a man reaches into a deep cylindrical vessel. Outside the tents are animals, including two camels, and at the top is a defensive wall with bastions. This representation probably belongs to the Elamite campaigns of Ashurbanipal (668–633 B.C.), then King of Assyria. (Photo: Foto Marburg, from Berlin VA)

modate a hundred couches and 9000 guests. The tent walls were hung with tapestries of mythological scenes. A ceremonial dais draped with gold brocade rested on fifty columns of silver and vermillion. In the back of the tent there were ninety-two sumptuous nuptial chambers. The tent itself covered four stadia and was later dubbed the Cosmic Tent or World Tent of Alexander, so called because the inside of its domed roof was woven, painted, and brocaded with sun, moon, stars, and all the signs and deities of the heavens. This design was adapted by Nero and the Byzantine emperors as a symbol of their imperial power.

In the Greek military encampment, veteran soldiers were placed at the extremities, therefore guarding the weaker, less-experienced soldiers and the commander or king. When the Greeks stayed long in one spot, shrines and altars were erected to their gods and holy services were performed.

Unlike the Roman encampment, which always followed a set arrangement, the Greek pattern varied from state to state, leader to leader, and place to place. And while the Roman camp was strictly quadrangular, the Greek camp was sometimes circular.

In the East, in almost all forms of encampment — the nomad, traveling, and military — the circular arrangement has always been preferred.

When Alexander the Great invaded Persia, King Darius III underestimated Alexander's strength and was defeated by him (331 B.C.). Darius fled and was later murdered during a struggle for power among the Persians. This highly stylized engraving after a seventeenth-century painting shows Alexander pardoning the family of Darius in the entrance to their tent. (Courtesy Prints Division, New York Public Library)

Roman

Much more information exists on the Roman military tent and encampment. Fragments of ancient Roman leather tents have been found in this century and records and accounts that have provided us with much valuable information still exist. Also, renderings of Roman tents appear on the columns of Antonius and Trajan, which stand in Rome and were erected to record the military victories of the two emperors. The tents on Trajan's Column are of three types — those of the rank and file, the officers, and the commanders.

Our word *tent* is also derived from the Latin *tentus,* meaning "stretched," and a *tentorium* or *tabernaculum* was a tent or pavilion. The Latin phrase *sub pellibus,* "under skins," used by Cicero and many others, has been proven beyond doubt to be the equivalent of our expression "under canvas."

The common tent of the legionnaires was called a *papilio* after the butterflies they resembled when the flaps were open and the valances were lifted up and because the tent was unpacked and spread out from a long roll that resembled a caterpillar. Figure 3 shows a *papilio,* which was made of rectangular pieces of leather sewn together in prominent seams. Along the edges at each end was a narrow reinforcing, as well as weatherproofing, piece running down each slope, and under that and attached to it were the tent flaps. These tents covered a ten-by-ten-foot area plus another two feet for the guy ropes, called *incrementum tensurae.* The floors were strewn with newly mown grass or straw on which eight soldiers slept.

The tent fragments found in Great Britain were originally *papilio* and it is interesting to note that calfskin was used. This is probably because these skins are stronger and more pliable: a tent of this material would have been easier to handle than one of cowhide. Also noteworthy is the

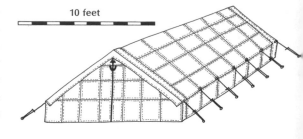
10 feet

Roman soldier's *papilio*

Roman officers' tents from Trajan's Column, 113 A.D.

fact that skin, like wood, has a grain or strain factor. A skin, in order to allow for growth and respiration, is more elastic in the direction of its width and the leather used in these *papilio* has been incorporated into the structure of the tent in such a way as to make use of this quality for a stronger tent. These pieces of calfskin were stitched together in elaborate waterproof welted seams and special knots and stitching provided greater strength in the parts of the tent that took on more stress and strain. Also, the leather was always applied with the external skin outward and pile, velvet, or the internal side inward.

The officers' tent was a taller structure, rather along the lines of a garden tent. Made of the same joined rectangles of leather, this tent had an elaborate overfall. Loops were attached to the overfall, and guy ropes passed through those loops and supported the tent. Leather flaps which could be tied aside provided access to the tents. The floors were covered with sod and furnishings such as dining tables and couches were contained within.

The commander's tent was always pitched first. This tent was larger still and had a marquee of the same kind as the officers — leather roof with an overfall to which guy ropes were attached. But the sides of these tents were of cloth, no doubt to make them easy to transport. These tents dwarfed the others in the encampment — Livy describes one like it as being 200 feet square. Altars stood before these tents, which have been compared to temples. Julius Caesar's tent contained a mosaic floor of portable sections and Emperor Nero's magnificent octagonal tent broke away from the traditional rectangular design.

A French rendering of a Roman encampment showing tents and armies, as far as the eye can see, under the protection of Minerva in her chariot drawn by two screech owls. The uniforms are Roman; the tents belong to the 1600s.

The Roman encampment was a highly organized fortification. An advance guard would choose the site and, with a white flag, mark the location of the general's quarters. Then, using that as a reference point, flags of various colors and designs would be placed to mark that portion of ground assigned to the various legions. When the army assembled on the spot, the boundary was established and, while part of the troops stood watch, the others dug a defensive ditch and made an earth wall atop which was a palisade of freshly cut trees. The arrangement of the tents very seldom varied and the trenches were dug, the mounds built up, and the trees felled even if this was only a one-night stop. Legionnaires sometimes referred to themselves as "Marius' mules" and it was no wonder. After a days' march, laden with more than eighty pounds of equipment (including weapons, armor, cooking utensils, tents or tent stakes, a spade, ax, and food), they had to prepare a fortified camp.

The British army used the same plan for military encampments that the Romans brought to Britain, and now this plan lives on in the armies that obtained the plan from Great Britain during British occupation. See the

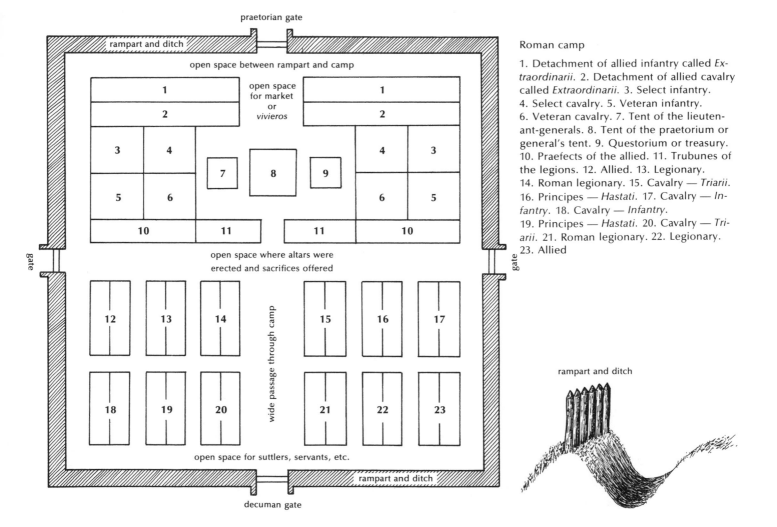

Roman camp

1. Detachment of allied infantry called *Extraordinarii*. 2. Detachment of allied cavalry called *Extraordinarii*. 3. Select infantry. 4. Select cavalry. 5. Veteran infantry. 6. Veteran cavalry. 7. Tent of the lieutenant-generals. 8. Tent of the praetorium or general's tent. 9. Questorium or treasury. 10. Praefects of the allied. 11. Trubunes of the legions. 12. Allied. 13. Legionary. 14. Roman legionary. 15. Cavalry — *Triarii*. 16. Principes — *Hastati*. 17. Cavalry — *Infantry*. 18. Cavalry — *Infantry*. 19. Principes — *Hastati*. 20. Cavalry — *Triarii*. 21. Roman legionary. 22. Legionary. 23. Allied

drawing of the layout of the Roman camp and the photo of the British encampment on page 14, and note the similarity.

It is strictly an assumption on the part of historians, but the Apostle Paul was supposedly a maker of tents for the Roman cavalry. Acts 18:1–3 states, "He left Athens and went to Corinth. And he found a Jew named Aquila, a native of Pontus . . . because Claudius had commanded all the Jews to leave Rome. And he went to see them; and because he was of the same trade he stayed with them, and they worked, for by trade they were tentmakers."

ROYAL TENTS OF ISLAM

Tents of the royalty in the Middle Eastern empires were sumptuously bedecked with colorful precious materials and their interiors were ostentatiously furnished with the spoils of war. Court luxuries were transported about from site to site as the armies traveled so that all the comforts and pleasures of the home court were available. For example, the Persians even carried about boilers to set up hot baths for themselves while in transit.

Persian Tents

Persian tent encampments changed very little in arrangement and appearance from the time of Darius (333 B.C.) until late in the nineteenth

An attack by Kublai Khan is described by the explorer Marco Polo in book II, chapter I, of his thirteenth-century manuscript: "They ascended the hill with alacrity the next morning and presented themselves before the army of Nayan, which they found negligently posted . . . whilst the chief himself was asleep in his tent accompanied by one of his wives." The tents are European, not Asian. (Bibliothèque Nationale, Paris)

The elephant litter of Kublai Khan, thirteenth-century Chinese. Three elephants sheathed in armor were roped together and atop them was placed a huge litter with a tent top. Four men managed the elephants and the litter carried at least sixteen to twenty men.

A depiction of the fabled Ghenghis Khan's yurt. It has all the sumptuous embroidered and appliquéd drapings and hangings (and draped stake fence) suited to the opulent character of the Khans.

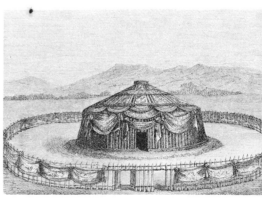

century. The king's tent was the focal point and all other tents and structures were pitched so that every entrance faced the imperial pavilion. Every person — and some encampments numbered 80,000 soldiers and camp followers — was required to bow to the central tent as they exited from their own. Princes' tents were distinguished from those of the viziers and officers by *ser-perdéh* (or royal curtain screens). Tent entrance trappings, such as long upright spears for the horsemen and matchlocks for the infantry, signaled their position in the political and military hierarchy.

"The besotted Iranian camp attacked." Here the Turanians overcome the Iranians in a night-time surprise attack. The Iranians had been making merry and had posted no guards. Two thirds of their army was destroyed. The faces of many of the soldiers are caricatures of universal types, adding comic touches to the tragedy depicted. This painting is from the *Shah-Nameh of Shah Tahmasp* ("King's Book of Kings") from the first quarter of the sixteenth century. The tents are superbly decorated yurts, which were brought to the Middle East by the invading Mongols in the twelfth and thirteenth centuries. (Metropolitan Museum of Art)

"Majunn in Chains Brought by a Beggar Woman to Layla's Tent." This is a scene from the Persian version of Romeo and Juliet where the lovers have resorted to disguises in order to see each other: here the man is the mad beggar in chains. These paintings were so meticulously done in regard to details of everyday life that they are a rich source for historical facts. Portable black shepherds' tents are at top with more commodious and decorated residential tents below. (From the Khamsa of Nizami Royal Safavid Manuscript of the sixteenth century, attributed to Mir Sayyid' Ali, British Museum)

Of course, the shah's tent was the most magnificent of all. For example, Nadir Shah, who ruled from 1736 to 1747, lined the exterior of his tent with fine scarlet fabric and the interior with purple satin encrusted with pearls, diamonds, rubies, emeralds, and amethysts. These jewels depicted figures of all the flora and fauna of the world. His tent poles were similarly inlaid with precious gems as was the set of standing screens surrounding his peacock throne. The whole dismantled tent required seven elephants to transport it. The seven-piece roof fit into two chests carried by one elephant, the screen required another, and the gold tent pins, jeweled poles, and interior furnishing loaded down five other elephants.

Turkish Tents

Prior to the fifteenth century, rulers such as the Ottoman sultans of Turkey and the Negus of Ethiopia maintained power by governing from encampments that were constantly on the move. Though some of these encampments had walls or buildings for harem, nursery, or kitchen, the capital itself was the tents of the monarch and his infantry.

Tents of the Turkish sultans were equally colorful and magnificent as those of the Persians. The tent of Sultan Mahomet IV (c. 1163 A.D.) not only was covered with silk inside and out but also featured gold embroidery on the interior lining (to go with his gold-plated tent posts naturally). The interior arrangement was much like a modern apartment with lodgings for all ranks and chambers for pleasure. There was also a tent for the eunuchs. One of the Turkish tents in Mahomet's encampment, made in Persia as a gift for the sultan, was said to have taken four years to construct. It was lined with a single piece of woven camel's hair and beautifully decorated with festoons and Turkish script.

Sixteenth-century Turkish military tents are seen in this detail from the mural *The Siege of the Battery of St. Elmo, May 27, 1565.* These tents are along the lines of the western European tents of the period, except that they are decorated in the Eastern styles that prevailed. (Frescoes, *Grand Master's Palace,* Valetta)

Turkish Tents in Poland

From the fifteenth through the seventeenth centuries, Poland was more or less constantly fighting the Turks and the Muscovites. The highly efficient Islamic armies forced the Poles to develop and adapt their own fighting techniques, armor, and equipment to match. Poland as the "rampant of Christendom" withheld the Moslem expansion into Europe and at the same time absorbed the Eastern styles. All the trade routes going to the East led through Poland, and commercial trade resulted in an Orientalization of Polish culture that shaped the artistic tastes of the Poles for generations to come. The war booty and trade goods brought back included textiles, carpets, weaponry, pottery, spices, goldsmiths' products, and precious stones — all of which affected art, fashions, military science and equipment, music, horse breeding, and many other aspects of Polish life.

This is a two-poled Turkish oval tent pitched in the Wawel Museum in Poland (opposite page). It was taken as war booty in the seventeenth century by Polish armies. It measures 44 × 10½ feet. Although the exterior is plain, the interior is blue canvas decorated with a mosaic of multicolored satin, canvas, and leather appliqués. Also note that the designs on the tent walls are repeated directly above on the tent top. The wall decorations (see this page) consist of a row of Mooresque arcades with medallions growing out of vases and ornamented with sprays of blooming flowers. The cartouches on the walls contain *Sulus* script invocations from the Koran in gilded leather. The diagonally striped flounce barely visible at the bottom is three-colored. These patterns closely resemble those on the walls of Oriental palaces of the same period. (Wawel Museum, Krakow, Poland)

It was from Persia that the greatest variety of construction and decoration of tents was available. At the battle of Vienna in 1683, several hundred tents were captured, making Poland the second largest repository of Turkish tents, after Turkey itself. The various structural styles were related to function: round or polygonal tents with umbrella-shaped roofs and oblong ones with rectangular walls and ridge or flat roofs were used as stables, stores, or dining rooms for the army; square tents like throne canopies with side walls were used for official purposes; the spectacular ovals were used for councils of war and ceremonial occasions; and garden tents with draped curtains instead of walls were used for shade on very hot days. Special-occasion tents (for parades, monarchs, and so on) often had antechambers. The tent floors were covered with rugs, skins, or boards. Lamps and lanterns provided lighting, and European additions included windowpanes, candelabra, and furniture. The tents themselves were made of thick linen (*musulbas*), laced together by ropes, and supported by poles ending in gilded balls. Although plain on the exterior, on the inside they were decorated with an elaborate wealth of appliqué of glossy satin, velvet, cotton, linen, and gilded leather, all overlaid with detailed embroidery. In the seventeenth century the overall desired impression was that of a garden in the palace, and this was achieved through naturalistic renderings of arcades over lamps, medallions, and vases overlaid with complex flower and plant patterns.

Twelve of these tents exist today in the Wawel Museum in Krakow, Poland.

Moroccan Tents

The tents of Moroccan royalty also varied little between the eleventh and nineteenth centuries. The king's scarlet tent called the *siwan* had a golden orb on top and was always the first to be set up. No other structure in the camp was raised until this task was accomplished. Then a mosque tent and other large marquees for high officials (often joined by passages of covered canvas), the royal stables, and *siwan* were enclosed within an area of about an acre with a nine-foot-high white canvas wall decorated with dark blue designs. The tents of the rest of the king's followers were packed snugly together outside the wall, extending in every direction. They were arranged so close that only a few spaces were left open for camp exits.

Although the majority of his retinue had white tents, the total effect was no less grand than those of the Turkish and Persian camps. Vast quantities of brilliant silken banners brocaded with golden orbs, multi-colored saddles, ornately decorated horse coverings and trappings, scarlet and blue infantry uniforms, the imperial parisols of red and gold, and the nighttime lanterns of colored glass created a theater of color. Standard bearers, acrobats, snake charmers, men with performing monkeys, robed scholars, visiting tribesmen, slaves, dervishes, beggars, merchants, and lepers made up the vast cast of actors.

Tents erected for the circumcision fete of the son of the Grand Vizir in Constantinople in 1864. Photo below shows the Grand Vizir's personal tent used to receive guests. The larger tent was used for the actual ceremony itself, which was a great occasion with much celebration. (*Illustrated London News*)

From *Graphic,* published in 1877 by Illustrated Newspapers, Ltd., this picture is entitled "The Eastern Question — Taking Tickets in the Harem" and was "sketched by our special artist on the steamer from Constantinople to Varna." A simple tent has been erected to provide shelter for the women of a sultan's harem. An attendant collects tickets and the curious passengers look on.

SEVENTEENTH-CENTURY HUNTING TENTS OF THE INDIAN SERAGLIO

Hunting parties of the seventeenth-century Indian sultans were divided up into two separate camps called *Peiche-kanés* ("houses which precede"). One of them kept a constant distance of one day's journey in advance of the other. This was done so that at the end of each day's hunting a fully prepared camp was always ready for the ruler. Each camp required at least 60 elephants, 200 camels, 100 mules, and 100 porters to transport it. The elephants carried the largest tents and heavy poles, the camels bore the smaller tents, and the mules took the luggage and kitchen tools. The valuable light items, such as the royal porcelain dinnerware, gilt-painted beds, and precious furnishings, were entrusted to the porters. The king traveled on men's shoulders in a field throne, by elephant, or, weather permitting, on horseback. The lords usually traveled stretched out on a bed in a palanquin. Sleeping at ease until they reached their tents, when they arrived an excellent dinner was awaiting them since the kitchen and every necessary article had been sent forward the preceding night immediately after supper. Sixty or more elephants carried the various ladies of the court who were protected by eunuchs.

The largest tent (called the *Am-kas*), which was a two-story pavilion, was erected first on the highest platform. It was used for conducting affairs of state. The second one up, a smaller bathing tent (the *goslekané*), was where the king held court every night. The third tent sheltered the privy council, and the rest serviced the attendants, royal ladies, and their domestics.

The royal tent fabric was a coarse striped red cloth with an interior lining of hand-painted chintz ornamented with satin and embroidery of silk, silver, and gold with fringes on the edges. The ground was covered with cotton mats about three or four inches deep and then blanketed with a rich carpet topped with brocaded cushions for seating. The king gave audiences on a magnificent stage seated under a velvet or flowered silk canopy. Other royal tents had similar canopies and also lightweight screenlike booths called *karguas* lined with flowered stain or brocade with gold and silk fringes.

Outside the enclosed imperial square smaller squares with tents housed the lesser rajas and omras, who prided themselves on the loftiness of their tents but had to make sure their tents were not conspicuous enough for the king to notice and, therefore, to command that their tents be torn down. For that reason too, their tents could not be red as that was the color reserved for the king.

Beyond the rajas and omras were tents for officers, other attendants, stables, and a traveling zoo. The procession brought along its own prized animals: birds of prey for show and field sports, dogs, leopards for hunting antelopes, a species of elk, lions and rhinoceros for display, Bengali buffaloes to attack lions, and fighting antelopes for the entertainment of the king. Market bazaars for supplying the needs of the troops were laid out in a wide road through the army in the direction of the next day's travel. Moreover, guards were posted every 500 feet around the whole encampment for robbers were always a threat to this extravagant procession.

CHINESE TENTS (C. 1700)

Emperors' Tents

The emperor and attendants employed the round yurt and cagelike tents similar to those used by Tatar tribes during the yearly hunting expeditions. However, the military used a small marching tent.

Chinese Military Tents

From outward appearances, this tent was a *tente d'abri* (see page 31). However, the Chinese made it quite complex structurally and much work went into erecting it. For this small tent with a height of five feet, five inches, a length of fourteen feet and width of six feet, a framework of eleven pieces and eighty tent pins were required.

The covering fabric was supported by a wooden top piece consisting of two vertical poles connected with a horizontal ridge piece with nine holes in it. Then a nine-piece framework fitted into corresponding sockets was locked in place by iron pipes. Finally the strong linen canvas (about 105 square feet) was stretched over the sloping roof frame and was attached to the ground and along its edges by bark rope loops pegged by large wooden pins.

The tent entrances at both ends had triangular curtains fitted with loops and were made from seven narrow strips of joined canvas. The largest strip was seven feet in height and they progressively decreased in size down to two inches tall. Plain blue linen lined the interior and the tent poles carried ornamental shaped iron crowns. The total weight of the tent hardware and accessories (an ax, spade, shovel, hammer, and camp kettle) was seventeen pounds.

Chinese painting from an early Ming (late-fourteenth-century) handscroll showing the pavilion of a Chinese nobleman. The main tent is a yurt and the lattice wall can be seen inside both the yurt and the tent at far right. Though austere, this encampment has a dignity about it, with its curtained wall and canopy — probably of silk — under which the nobleman held court. (Metropolitan Museum of Art)

This Chinese soldiers' tent was used in the 1800s. Eighty pins were required to join and peg it. Pitching this one was a real undertaking. (From Godfrey Rhodes, *Tents and Tent Life,* 1858)

The Chinese Emperor Ch'ien Lung is carried forth to meet Lord Macartney (at far right), who was sent to China by George III in an attempt by the British to ease trade restrictions imposed by the emperor on the British East India Company September 14, 1793. Macartney refused to kowtow to the Emperor and only in an informal setting such as in front of this gaily decorated tent could this breach of court etiquette be made acceptable to the Chinese. (British Museum)

Chinese "Temple of Heaven," 1877. The plan of the temple complex generally resembled that of an imperial palace with the architectural character varying according to region. The temple shown here is a raised circular terrace, with descending levels and various gateway buildings built along the main axes radiating out from the center circle (see upper right). The ornate canopy is for shade as well as for decorative purposes. (From William Simpson's *Meeting the Sun,* 1877)

EUROPEAN TENTS

British Tents

Early Anglo-Saxon soldiers' tents were made merely of cloth or leather strung on ropes stretched over the tops of long poles and were anchored by wooden hooks driven into the soil. Their sloped roofs shed the rain and some even had doors at their entrances.

By the time of Edward II's expedition to Scotland in 1301 A.D. tent fabric was made of white and dyed linen. Fourteenth-century tournament tents of the nobility were richly colored, emblazoned with coats of arms, and often had turret or garret-shaped windows in their roofs. The tents of Edward III are described as beautifully decorated, lofty, circular, and bell-shaped with a circular ring about two-thirds up the height onto which outside ropes were anchored to the ground. The king's tent resembled the nineteenth-century hospital tent except that its walls were twice as high and ended with a brief sloping top.

In the fifteenth century Henry V used a large blue and green embroidered velvet tent with a gold eagle on top as a rendezvous shelter when negotiating with the French king for a favorable marriage settlement to obtain the hand of the French princess Catherine. His future father-in-

This eighteenth-century engraving is one of a series depicting the victories of the Chinese Emperor Ch'ien Lung. The wall of the encampment is formed by a circular tent structure, and within townspeople are seen paying tribute to the emperor. (Engraving by C. N. Cochin from *Victoires et conquêtes de l'empereur de la Chine*, Paris, 1770–74. Prints Division, New York Public Library)

Fourteenth- and fifteenth-century tents

Tents with conical tops were widely used during the twelfth and thirteenth centuries. This fifteenth-century miniature shows the Crusaders besieging Moslem Ascalon on the coast of the Holy Land. The weaponry shown here, such as the bombards or primitive cannons, are of a later period.

Tents were sited to take advantage of the natural resources and defenses of the terrain. In a siege they were often pitched near to the enemy walls, and could still be out of range of the cannon, which in those days could not fire more than 300 yards. (Bibliothèque Nationale Service Photographique, Ms. Fr. 5594)

Twelfth-century French military tent. Tents of this and the next few centuries were the most superbly decorated in European history since the Dark Ages. (Eugene Emmanuel Viollet-Le-Duc, *Dictionnaire raisonné de mobilier français de L'époque Carlo ingienne à la Renaissance*, 1858–75)

law countered with a pavilion of blue velvet embroidered with fleurs-de-lys. The counselors for the two parties met in a purple velvet tent between the two camps.

Field of the Cloth of Gold

The idea of a summit meeting in June 1520 between Henry VIII and Francis I was considered a turning point in relations between Great Britain and France. Up until then the two monarchs had never met and rivalry and suspicion prevailed between the two countries. The meeting was to be a combination political conference, athletic meeting with tournaments, jousting, and wrestling, and a festival of music and drums, topped off with a series of state banquets. So rich were the costumes and pavilions of both courts that the meeting was dubbed "Field of the Cloth of Gold" and hailed as the eighth wonder of the world.

Five thousand one hundred and seventy-two English men and women and 2865 horses crossed the channel to Calais, traveled to Ardres, and spent a month. The monarchs were housed in a large temporary palace of brick and timber and the chief courtiers were put up in nearby Guînes Castle. The others were accommodated in an encampment of nearly 400 tents that Richard Gibson, "Master of the King's Hales, Tents, and Pavilions," had erected in nearby fields. Gibson's tour de force was a vast,

Tents with dormer windows appeared late in the fourteenth century and disappeared shortly thereafter. These two drawings show tents erected at tournament sites. Top photo shows two contestants being blessed by monks before entering into judicial combat. (From *Barfields Historical Illustrations*, 1938) Bottom photo shows the feat of arms at a tournament held at Inglevere, near Calais. (*Art Journal*, 1868)

highly ornate banqueting tent, covered outside with cloth painted to look like brickwork and decorated inside with gold and silver cloth, interlaced with white and green, the Tudor colors. It was compared to the work of Leonardo da Vinci, who had died at Amboise, France, the year before, and the fairy-tale palaces of Ariosto's *Orlando Furioso*.

Henry's tent, called the "Royal Encampment Tent," was constructed by joining together several large hospital-type tents which were connected by canvas passages at half the height of the tents. The complex was in crimson silk embroidered with gold and crimson and ornamented with fringe. His inscription, which ran completely around the tent in gold letters, read: "DEO:ET:MON:DROET. SEMPER: VIVAT: IN CAETERUS," etc.

The meeting was not entirely a success. As an act of friendship both men had sworn not to shave their beards until the meeting had taken place, but Henry shaved his because his number-one wife Catherine of Aragon didn't like him unshaven (but he was readily forgiven by the queen mother of France who said love was shown in men's hearts and not in their beards). While en route to France Henry aroused French suspicion by meeting at Dover with Charles V of Spain, who was preparing for war with France. Though it was agreed the monarchs would not take part in any joust or combat against the other, once, on the spur of the moment, Henry wrestled with Francis, ended up on the ground, and didn't like it — though Henry later acquitted himself well in the archery contest. To commemorate the meeting a chapel of Our Lady of Friendship was to be built and jointly maintained by the kings; it was never built. A marriage between Mary Tudor and the dauphin was arranged but never materialized. And during the solemn mass at noon on Saturday, June 23, fireworks in the shape of a dragon, intended for the evening's festivities, were accidentally exploded. By 1522 Henry and Francis were supporting opposing sides in the Hapsburg-Valois struggle and were right back where they started. Still, the tents of this conference are the most splendid of the Renaissance, and the Field of the Cloth of Gold remains one of the most fabulous encampments ever.

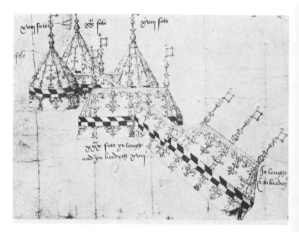

A drawing of some of the 400 tents erected for the Field of the Cloth of Gold. (British Museum)

Field of the Cloth of Gold, where Henry VIII and Francis I held a summit meeting in June 1520. (By Gracious Permission of Her Majesty Queen Elizabeth II)

French Tents

A fourteenth-century tent of the duke of Burgundy was made of wooden planks covered with painted canvas and shaped to look like a castle flanked by towers. Another made of 30,100 ells (37,625 yards) of fabric was built to cover a palace courtyard in Dijon at a fete given for the king and his court, since no hall was large enough to accommodate all the guests. Afterward the fabric was cut up and sold. At a peace conference in 1393, his retinue of 3000 was arranged in lines of tents forming a village with streets. By the fifteenth century the tents of the duke of Burgundy reached heights of grandeur with exteriors of colored canvas and interiors lined with velvet and silk curtains embroidered with golden leaves. The window frames and the duke's throne were of solid gold and the rope stays supporting his tent had gold cords woven into them. The coat of arms over the entrance was appropriately inlaid with diamonds, pearls, and other jewels. Four hundred other grand tents of the nobles were situated around his. On March 2, 1476, the tents of Charles the Bold, then duke of Burgundy, fell into the hands of the Swiss after the Battle of Grandson. Tents were always considered prize booty, and those of the duke of Burgundy were the ultimate in loot.

French military tents of the eighteenth century were single pole structures made from one piece of canvas and sheltered six to eight soldiers. Officers had larger pavilion-shaped tents called marquees, which had bases of six to eight feet and horizontal ridge poles atop two vertical stakes. These were covered with both a canvas roof and inner lining and

Excellent example of fifteenth-century tents. Guy ropes branching into five parts distributed the pull on the eaves of the tent and were typical of that period. The scene here shows "Desir seeking help from Honneur to rescue Coeur" from the *Livre de Coeur d'Amour Esprins*, a chivalric tale from an illustrated manuscript of the fifteenth century. (State Library of Vienna)

A Venetian tent, probably fifteenth-century. This striped yard tent was designed with weights suspended from the unattached sides in order to stabilize them. The occupant could enjoy unobstructed views and breezes and feel more outdoors, while still being protected from sun and rain. (From *Repository of Arts, Literature, Commerce, Manufactures, Fashions, and Politics*, a monthly publication by Ackerman, London, April 1820: title varies)

Venetian galley with a tent. Tents were often used aboard ship as seen on the afterdeck of the Venetian sailing galley below. Frameworks were usually constructed when the ship was built and canvas could be stretched over this when protection from the elements was needed. (Detail from a fifteenth-century woodcut by Bernhard von Breydenbach which appears in his book *Peregrinatio in Terram Sanctam*)

View of Strasbourg in 1744, showing the arrival of Louis XV by the Porte de Severne. The engraving is by M. Mavye after a drawing by J. M. Weiss. These giant tents were set up for the nobility to review the royal procession as it approached the city. (Collection of Raymond Prestia)

June 25, 1807, a defeated Tsar Alexander I meets Napoleon (the shorter monarch) aboard a lavishly decorated barge moored midstream near Tilsit in the Neman River, which separated Western Russia from Napoleonic Europe. The Emperors talked alone for some three hours, and Napoleon later wrote that if the tsar "were a woman, I think I would make him my mistress." (New York Public Library Prints Division)

Wandering Gypsies in France. Camp has been made under the light of the full moon. After supper, the women spread out woolen cloth over the wagons, and the families sleep inside. The next day, the cloth is taken down, and the oxen hitched up, and the migration continues. (Eugene Emmanuel Viollet-Le-Duc, *Histoire de l'habitation humaine depués les temps préhistorique jusqu'à nos jours*, 1875)

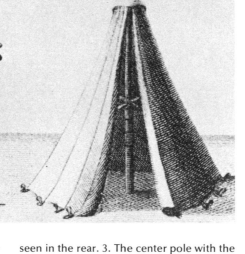

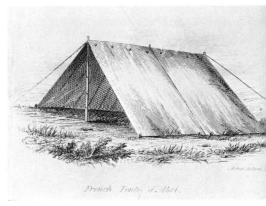

The *tente d'abri* or "tent of cover" is intended to serve as a temporary bivouac for troops on the march. It consists of canvas sheets, a few pegs, and a section of a tent pole. In constructing a tente d'abri for six men, four sheets button together to form the covering and the two remaining sections close the triangular openings at each end. These tents have been used by soldiers of all nations for centuries. (Godfrey Rhodes, *Tenting and Tent Life*, 1858)

"Modern Tents," from Grose's *Military Antiquities of 1801*. His caption reads, "Fig. 1. A bell-tent viewed in the front. 2. The same seen in the rear. 3. The center pole with the cross for supporting the arms."

Grose continues, "Fig. 7. A captain's tent or marquis with a chimney. 8. A captain's marquis shown in a different point of view. 9. A field officer's marquis. 10. His servant's tent in the rear."

The Swedish employed a conical tent for their soldiers during the nineteenth century. The British, French, and other armies used this style in the Crimea. Tents along this line could not be broken down into sections and carried like the *tente d'abri*; they usually were delivered to campsites by horse and wagon. This type of tent is easy to pitch and its conical shape enables it to withstand wind and shed water quite efficiently. (Godfrey Rhodes, *Tenting and Tent Life*, 1858)

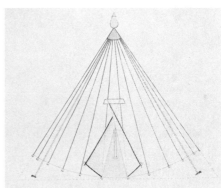

Allied camp on plateau before Sebastopol in the Crimean War (1853–56). Great Britain, France, Turkey, and later Sardinia were fighting Russia over treaty rights of intervention and protection of the Christian Holy Places in Jerusalem, Bethlehem, and Golgotha, all being under Turkey's dominion at the time. Pictured are conical military tents commonly used in the middle of the nineteenth century. (Photograph by Roger Fenton, Library of Congress)

French Officers delivering punishment to a guilty soldier, Crimean War, 1855. Note the striped officers' tents in background with door flap extended and supported as and awning. Size and splendid decoration set apart the officers' tents of previous centuries; striped fabric was the last remnant of this tradition as modern military tents moved into the twentieth century.

Sketch made of Queen Victoria's tent during her visit to Derricunihy, Killarney, Ireland, 1861. This is the famous tent she took with her wherever she traveled. The banner flies from the mast, showing that Her Majesty is present. (*Illustrated London News* and *Sketch*, 1861)

GARDEN TENTS,

As above, 6 ft. by 6 ft., from **£3 10s.** Garden Umbrella Tents, 6 ft., **18s.** Bathing Tents for the Sands, **23s. 6d.**; size 6 ft. across, when open; when packed, only 4 ft. by 5 in.
MARQUEES and TENTS of very best quality for Boating, Camping, Engineering, Prospecting, &c., &c.

KEPT ERECTED ON VIEW AT OUR SHOW-ROOMS. CATALOGUES POST FREE.

PIGGOTT BROS. & CO., 57 to 59, Bishopsgate St. Without, London.

MADE FROM GREEN ROT-PROOF CANVAS.

AS SUPPLIED TO
. H. M. Stanley, | Sir F. de Winton, | Lieut. Wissmann, | Rev. Mr. Ash
. H. H. Johnstone, | Captain Stairs, R.E., | Bishop Hannington, | Rev. Mr. Com
The Congo State Government, The Imperial British East Africa Company, &

H.M. Commissioner, H. H. JOHNSTONE, writes: Surgeon-Major PARKE wrote, March 28, 189
Nothing could be more serviceable or thoroughly good   "I lived under canvas almost continually from 186
those last supplied by yourself, Aug. 16, 1893."   we emerged from Africa with Emin Pasha in Dec
(Order for Tents.)   1890. *Unquestionably yours are the best Tents made.*"

PRICE LISTS ON APPLICATION.

RONG CAMP BEDSTEADS, CHAIRS, AND CAMP FURNITURE OF ALL KIN
For Particulars as to Tents suitable for Travellers in all Parts of the World, apply to

ENJAMIN EDGINGTON, Ltd., 2, DUKE ST., LONDO
FOOT OF LONDON BRIDGE, S.E.

Ads from the *Illustrated London News*, late 1880s. The British developed the fly tent as they ventured into warmer climates. The fly acts as a sunshade and also keeps the interior dry during exceptionally heavy rainfall. "Rot-proof" (right) refers to some of the early treatments of canvas, such as wet-wax, which sealed the canvas and prevented mildew.

Meanwhile, back home, garden tents (left) served the Victorians outside during mild weather. Manufactured in various sizes and shapes, they were usually elaborately decorated.

The wet-plate cameraman at work. (From *Photography in the Field*, 1853)

The wet-plate cameraman set off for field-work with all of his elaborate apparatus, including his darkroom tent, carried if not on his back then by wagon or pack animal. This engraving dates from 1863.

were pegged down in the usual way. This double roof helped to water-proof the tent and insulate it as well. Nineteenth-century military tents were of four types: the six-man *tente d'abri* for temporary bivouac protection, the sixteen-man, oblong and wedge-shaped *tente de troupe,* the twenty-man circular *tente conique,* and the twenty-man walled *tente conique à muraille.*

CORONATION DURBAR OF GEORGE V, KING OF ENGLAND AND EMPEROR OF INDIA

In December 1911, in the old Mogul capital of Delhi, an absolutely matchless extravaganza took place. George V, accompanied by his wife Queen Mary, came to India to be crowned emperor of India. Undoubtedly the royal encampment that accommodated the monarchs was the most splendid in the history of the Western world.

As Prince of Wales, the king had traveled to India in 1905–1906 and, upon ascending the throne in 1910, one of his first royal decisions was to return for a coronation durbar. (A durbar is the gathering of chiefs to pay homage.) The king felt that his visit would "tend to allay unrest and, I am sorry to say, seditious spirit, which unfortunately exist in some parts of India."

There were all sorts of problems — if the king were to crown himself emperor, would this set a precedent and then every monarch have to follow suit? And what about a crown? The king could not take the crown of England, which is also the crown of India, from the Tower of London to India. So, since a new crown would have to be made, who would pay for it? (It was finally decided that the cost would be covered by Indian government revenue.)

The royal yacht dropped anchor in Bombay on December 2, 1911, amidst much fanfare, and after three days in Bombay, their Majesties boarded a train for Delhi. There they were splendidly received. Every ruling prince of the Indian Empire was present. There were 161 in all, each with complete retinue and regalia — elephants, camels, gold and silver palanquins, mace bearers, bodyguards in chain-and-mail armor, horse-drawn drums, riflemen with ancient matchlocks and state swords and banners, in short, all the symbols of power and sovereignty symbolizing centuries of Asian history.

Some 250,000 people in all descended upon an instant imperial capital, a tent city covering forty-five square miles, over twice the size of Manhattan.

There were 475 separate camps — the emperor's camp alone sprawled over seventy-two acres and contained more than 2000 tents for 2140 people. The size of the other camps was dependent upon the rank of the chief involved. All the maharajas encamped in competitive splendor on plots of from 10,000 to 25,000 square yards, which housed from 100 to 500 attendants. Then there were camps for military detachments, provincial governors, the governor-general and other dignitaries, as well as camps for the police, the foreign office, and the massed bands.

Tent used by His Royal Highness the Prince ▶ of Wales on a state visit to India in 1905–1906. This tent was pitched in the old Mongol capital of Delhi, the future site of another splendid encampment in 1911, when the Prince returned as King George V to be crowned emperor of India. (Library of Congress)

A British encampment at Agra, India, 1858. The British Army used the same plans for military encampments that the Romans had brought to Britain, just as today the last vestiges of the British in India remain with the Indian Army. (*Illustrated London News,* July 31, 1858)

The Prince of Wales, who was later to become George V of England, sits amid the booty of an afternoon's hunt. (And one wonders why there are so few tigers left in India.)

The tent is the standard British fly tent. Canvas pieces could be attached to guy ropes supporting the fly in order to protect the sides from the heat of the sun, as seen on the right side of this tent. (Library of Congress)

The drawing room tent for the Prince of Wales. On the couch surrounding tent poles, left, and table in foreground are copies of newspapers (top newspaper, far left, is the *Bombay Gazette*), candelabra attached to poles and chandeliers provided illumination. Also note fireplace with clock atop mantel left of center. (Library of Congress)

This photograph of the 1911 Delhi Coronation Durbar was taken by the Underwood and Underwood photographer from the veranda of the viceroy's residence. (Library of Congress)

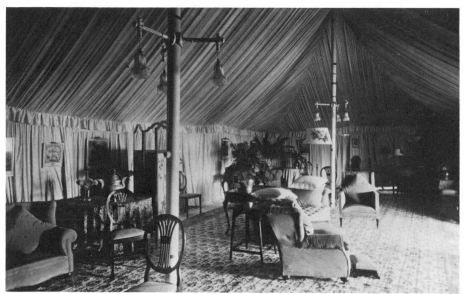

Queen Mary's sitting room, Delhi camp. When George had previously visited India his tents were not supplied with electricity. These in 1911 were — note the light switch on tent pole in foreground. The floors of the tents were made by laying planking, then covering that with carpeting. At lower left can be seen ridges of uneven planking. The decorator here even had pictures hung on the tent walls to make Her Majesty feel more at home. (By Gracious Permission of Her Majesty Queen Elizabeth II)

King George and Queen Mary in their purple, gold, and ermine imperial robes of state (his was eighteen feet long) stand under the homage pavilion at the Delhi Durbar. Over 150,000 attended; the effect upon the emperor was said to be "profound." (By Gracious Permission of Her Majesty Queen Elizabeth II)

The services were complex and extensive. There were forty-four miles of railway line constructed with twenty-nine fully-equipped railroad stations. Within four days, 190 special trains and 256 regular trains converged on the encampment; 75 million pounds of goods and 100,000 parcels were delivered. There were 2832 miles of telephone line, 1000 miles of telegraph line; a main post office with twenty-five substations employing 700 people who handled 5.25 million pieces of mail; six major hospitals and a veterinary hospital; fifty-two miles of water mains, sixty-five miles of distribution pipes providing 3 million gallons per day for people and half a million per hour for animals; a dairy with 2000 milch cows and 500 workers producing 550,000 pounds of milk, 60,000 pounds of butter, and 12,000 pounds of cream for the nine days. And the animals consumed 2 billion pounds of fodder.

Their Majesties spent the five days before the durbar in diplomatic visits. The ruling chiefs were received by the emperor in the throne room of his pavilion. The empress received the ladies of high estate and was presented, in true imperial fashion, with jewels and other extravagant tributes. And there were state banquets, polo tournaments, state church services, and an elaborate presentation of colors.

The durbar itself was held in a gigantic stadium and more than 150,000 attended. In the middle of the stadium were five levels of platforms. The top was fifteen feet above the ground and held two gilded thrones covered by a red and gold canopy, the roof of which was bordered with crimson and gold velvet.

A causeway connected this pavilion to a lower one, which was the homage pavilion onto which the emperor and empress descended from their carriage. After much hullabaloo — gun salutes, national anthems, speeches, and unfurling of banners — the 355 representatives of the peoples of India made obeisance to the sovereignty of the emperor and his consort as the band played, appropriately enough, stately marches from European operas. Then the emperor and empress walked around the platform and ascended the twenty-six steps to the summit and stood before their golden thrones while trumpets blared. Heralds entered on white horses and read proclamations in English and Urdu. This was followed by more trumpet fanfare, more national anthems (played by 1600 musicians), salvos of artillery (first from the east, then from the west), cheers for the emperor, three cheers for the empress, three *feux de joie,* and the national anthem yet again.

The emperor made another short speech in which he unexpectedly announced moving the capital from Calcutta to Delhi. With that, the master of ceremonies was commanded to close the durbar. And then out of the amphitheater went the emperor and empress, followed in descending order of rank by all the notables until 100,000 Indians were left. These people passed silently before the empty throne of the emperor of India. They prostrated themselves before the throne, touched the fringes of the carpets on which their Majesties had stood, and rubbed their heads with the soil the emperor had trod upon. And that was the coronation durbar of 1911. It gave rise to one of the greatest tent cities in the world and marked the high point of the British Empire. It was the best durbar ever . . . and it was the last.

India, July 1925. Mahatma Gandhi, center, presides over the thirty-ninth Indian National Congress. Twenty thousand delegates and visitors gathered under this huge white dome, made of handspun, handwoven *khaddar*.

View of Dacca shanty town where many refugees are temporarily housed. Appalling conditions confronted the government of Bangladesh in 1972, when the new nation came into being as a consequence of a devastating civil war between the army of West Pakistan and the primarily Bengali population of East Pakistan. Fabric, matting, or cardboard structures serve as shelter for the refugees. (United Nations/Wolff PAS)

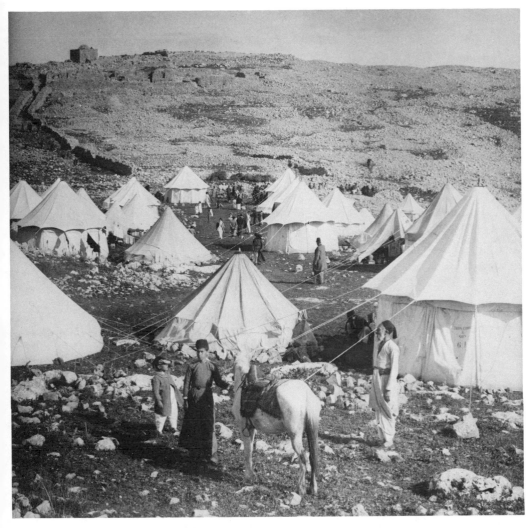

Samaritan camp, Mt. Gerizim, Jordan. Tents house the Samaritans who travel each year at Passover to Mt. Gerizim, the chosen place of God, the only center of worship, and the "navel of the earth." Beyond the tents is the altar where animal sacrifices are still made. Samaritan tradition still holds that the sacrifice of Isaac took place here. The 300-year-old Samaritan temple on Mt. Gerizim was destroyed in 128 B.C. by the Jews, and on the summit are the ruins of the fortified Church of Justinian (527–565). (Library of Congress)

Immigration camp of the Zionist Commission in Palestine, Tel Aviv. These camps were the first homes for many of the Jews who came in the late 1940s to what has now become Israel.

The tents are conical with walls that can be lifted and tied up to provide ventilation. (Library of Congress)

Future king of Jordan Emir Abdullah, center, and his brother Ali, in front of tent with the standard, in Transjordan, 1946. (Library of Congress)

Base camp, Nettilling Lake, on the Arctic Circle in northeast Canada. The members of this 1916 English expeditionary camp built a snow wall around their tents to break the wind just as many nomads erect brush walls around their tents to serve the same purpose. (National Museums of Canada)

Soviet Air Expedition at the North Pole, 1937. The expedition flew in on the plane at right. A party of four remained at the Pole for a year making scientific observations. An insulated black tent served as shelter until a more permanent structure could be constructed. (*Illustrated London News*)

Modern Jews observe the festival of Succoth (from Hebrew *sukkah* meaning "tent" or "tabernacle") by constructing symbolic tents as reminders of the time when the Israelites had no permanent place to live or worship. Pictured here is an interior view of a *sukkah* constructed at Goldsmidt House in Jerusalem in 1937. At that time relations between Jews and Arabs were better, which accounts for Arabic writing lining the fabric walls of this structure. (Library of Congress)

United Nations Emergency Force, Port Said, Egypt, December 1956. A unique style of wall tent shown in the background has windows all around and large vents on the roof. Windows are made of mosquito netting with zippered flaps inside. With vents and windows these tents are more suited for use in dry and warm climates. (United Nations)

Twenty-five hundredth Anniversary of the Persian Empire, Persepolis, Iran, October 1971. A tent city was erected at the ancient ceremonial center of Persepolis. (Embassy of Iran)

2 AMERICA

We're tenting tonight on the old campground,
Give us a song to cheer
Our weary hearts, a song of home
And friends we love so dear.

— Walter Kittridge, "Tenting Tonight," U.S. Civil War song

Let the tent be struck.

— Robert E. Lee (1807–1870), last words, October 12, 1870

The tent has played an incredibly large and vital role in the development of this country. However, our history did not include any of the nobility, royal courts, chivalry, or pomp that depended on sumptuous tents when away from palaces or castles. Instead, America was the frontier, a potentially rich one, yes, but those who were exploiting it depended on simple wall tents to get them where they were going, and when they decided to stay, they built log cabins.

The tents of the American Revolution were almost all oval or rectangular wall tents of various sizes. There were also smaller "bells of arms" tents for the storage of arms (see photos). The tents had central poles with two dowels, which supported the rifle barrels, placed at right angles about four feet from the ground.

The Continental Army followed British patterns and practice as best they could under the circumstances. During campaign season there frequently were not enough tents and soldiers who weren't fortunate enough to crowd into one had to sleep out in the rain and heavy dews. At the end of the 1777 campaign, for example, each field officer of all the regiments was allowed a private's tent. Other commissioned officers were quartered four to a private's tent while noncommissioned officers

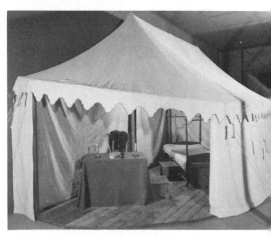

George Washington's field tent. (History and Technology Building, Smithsonian Institution, Washington, D.C.)

and privates were packed eight to a tent. In 1778 in the southern army, there were reports of twelve privates to a tent. The rest had to sleep outdoors. In winter quarters soldiers understandably preferred to erect more permanent log huts with fireplaces and six to eight bunks.

Even George Washington's field tents were modest affairs. While on campaign, when possible, Washington acquired a large house in the area for his headquarters. When no suitable houses were near a chosen campsite, he had at least three tents to serve his needs. The largest, his "dining marquee" (as he called it) and general headquarters tent used three poles, measured 18 × 28 feet, and had pink scalloped edging. It was made of heavy, unbleached woven linen, which accounts for its excellent condition today. Duck boards were laid for the floor, which could be dismantled and transported on a baggage wagon. The tent was returned to Mt. Vernon after the Revolution, and after Washington's death subsequently passed to the Smithsonian Institution. The general also had a smaller eight-foot-long sleeping tent and a baggage tent.

As the settlers pushed west they did so in canal barges or Conestoga wagons. Both had tent tops — the canvas could be adjusted to fit conditions, and on the canal boats the entire tent assembly could be removed to facilitate getting under low bridges. The Conestoga wagon originated in the Conestoga Valley of Pennsylvania in 1725 and was first used by farmers to carry heavy loads long distances before the advent of railroads. Later it was adopted by the pioneers as the "prairie schooner" in the western expansion of this country. Actually the wagon was a tent atop a wagon. The canvas could be raised, lowered, or removed, according to the needs of the occupant. The early pioneers also traveled with the common wall tent.

Emigrants entering the Loup Valley, Custer County, Nebraska, 1886. (Solomon D. Butcher Collection, Nebraska State Historical Society)

THE CAMP MEETING

The life of the early settlers was a lonely and hard one. The desire for social interaction and religious expression was partly fulfilled by the camp meeting movement.

Camp meetings were outdoor religious meetings that usually were held in the summer and lasted for several days. James McGready (c. 1760–1801), a Presbyterian, is generally credited with originating them in 1799–1801 in Logan County, Kentucky. This period also marked a religious revival in this country and camp meetings spread rapidly.

As the name implies, those who attended camp meetings came prepared to camp out, bringing tents, bedding, and provisions. They would come from thirty to forty miles away and sometimes as many as 10,000 to 20,000 people would gather. These revivalist retreats centered around services in large tents or in forest clearings where log benches and a rude preaching platform constituted an outdoor church. People came partly out of curiosity, partly out of a need for social contact and festivity, but mainly for "religion." The meetings would be directed by a number of preachers who relieved each other in carrying on the services, sometimes preaching in different parts of the campgrounds. Activities

C & O Canal boats, late 1800s. Tents served as shelter for barge passengers and the families of the boat captains. These deck tents could also be disassembled easily so the barges could fit under bridges with low clearance. (National Park Service)

included preaching, prayer meetings, hymn singing, weddings, and baptisms. Shouting, shaking, and rolling upon the ground often accompanied the tremendous release that followed "conversion."

Understandably, camp meetings were sometimes occasions of wild enthusiasm and hysteria and they acquired a bad reputation among conservative churchmen. The Presbyterian Church refused to participate after 1805, but camp meetings were enthusiastically carried westward to the frontier by the Methodists, Baptists, Shakers, Disciples, and Cumberland Presbyterians, the latter two being direct outgrowths of camp meetings. The Methodist Church profited most from the camp meeting and gradually incorporated it into its system of evangelism. By 1811, the Methodist Bishop Francis Asbury reported in his journal that more than 400 meetings were being held annually along the frontier from Michigan to Georgia. There was even a National Campmeeting Association for the Promotion of Holiness, which was established in 1867 and was nondenominational. At diverse encampments on both coasts, hundreds of conferees would give testimony of their conversions and their having received the second blessing; then they would return to their local denominational church for the winter.

In a modified form camp meetings have continued to be a feature of social and religious life in the region between the Alleghenies and the Mississippi River, and they still survive as summer Bible conferences and assemblies in other parts of the country, such as the Chautauqua Institution and the Ocean Grove Camp Meeting Association. But, for the most part, their significance passed after 1890, along with the frontier society that created them.

This Methodist camp meeting was held in August 1859 at Sing Sing, New York, so named because that's what the people did there. Ossining is now the name of the nearest town, but Sing Sing Prison is named after the old camp meeting site. (*Harper's*, 1859)

TIPI VARIATIONS

The American Indian lived in one of the most functional and ingenious tents ever devised — the tipi. (For more information on tipis see Chapter 3, The Nomadics.) But the white man went about eradicating both occupant and "pagan" tent with a vengeance. Nonetheless there were two American varieties of tents using the tipi as a point of departure.

Henry Hopkins Sibley, a Confederate general in the Civil War, had the ingenuity to integrate some of the features of the tipi into a field tent for his forces. The Sibley tent was conical and had a very low cylindrical wall which could be raised or lowered. The top of the tent was conical, like the tipi, and there was an opening through which a stove pipe protruded — the stove was also designed by General Sibley. This tent was superior to the wall tents being used by the U.S. army in the Indian Wars and saw widespread use, especially in the West, in the same terrain that spawned the tipi. This is a classic case of taking some lessons from the enemy.

Another tipi variation was the pyramid tent used by prospectors and sheepherders. (See the drawing of a modern pyramid tent on page 173.) The tent was a common sight on the gold fields of California and the Klondike, and it is actually a square tipi either attached to an exterior frame of saplings or tied to an overhead tree limb.

A detachment of the Sixth U.S. Cavalry camped near a Zuni Indian Pueblo in New Mexico (1890s) while on a routine practice march. Pictured here are Sibley tents, named after Confederate General Henry H. Sibley. (Arizona Historical Society Library)

CIVIL WAR TENTS

In the Civil War interesting tent variations appeared in winter encampments. Log walls were erected and then covered with two layers of canvas which served as a roof. Other canvas-roofed structures had log walls and additional outside insulating walls of pine branches. Both of these structures had either fireplaces or wood-burning stoves. In the latter years of the Civil War the Sibley tent also appeared and in cold weather short vertical log walls would be used to insulate the exposed canvas sides.

Winter camp of a detachment of the 50th NYV Engineers, U.S. Civil War, November 1864. These tent houses, complete with chimneys, have been insulated with pine branches. Gaps were left in the design for light entry. (Library of Congress)

Winter officers' quarters of Captain J. R. Coxe and wife at Headquarters, Army of the Potomac at Brandy Station, U.S. Civil War, April 1864. This tent cabin has two layers of canvas — one securely fastened to the structure and the other draped over it. At right the overhang and a vertical piece form a shed. The army took the time to construct these more permanent structures to withstand winter weather. (Library of Congress)

Following the traditional military custom of requisitioning large houses as headquarters, General Meade used the Wallach home in Culpeper, Virginia, as his general headquarters in October 1863. The staff pitched their tents around the house and, therefore, were near at hand and the house could be used for work, dining, and entertaining. (Library of Congress)

THE CHAUTAUQUA MOVEMENT

After the Civil War another social movement that was primarily educational instead of religious began. This was the Chautauqua movement, which started in Chautauqua, New York, at a Methodist Episcopal camp meeting as an assembly for the study of the Bible and Sunday school methods. The purpose gradually expanded to cover the whole field of adult education and included popular entertainment. The programs consisted of lectures, music, entertainment, and later drama. Many distinguished Americans — authors (Thoreau, Emerson, and Beecher, for example), explorers, musicians, and political leaders — contributed and lectured on the Chautauqua circuit. By 1912, the movement was organized commercially, and lectures and entertainment were supplied by the central Chautauqua committees and the lyceum bureau. Tents were widely used, especially in warmer weather, for these meetings. Radio and the movies diverted public attention and by 1924 the circuits ended, although the assembly at Chautauqua continued.

Commemorative stamp of a Chautauqua tent issued in 1974 on the 100th anniversary of the movement in the United States. (United States Post Office Department)

WILD WEST SHOWS

Wild West shows have much in common with circuses except that Wild West shows emphasized displays and events of America's old West instead of wild animals and acrobats. Also, the Wild West show was usually presented surrounded by canvas and not under it — the show took place on an open field surrounded by circus-type seats covered by a canvas canopy. These shows featured events such as an Indian attack on the stagecoach, wagon train, or log cabin of a defenseless family, with a rescue by the U.S. Cavalry; broncobusting, roughriding, roping, Indian ceremonies, and sharpshooting.

William Frederick "Buffalo Bill" Cody organized the first, the best, and the most famous Wild West show in 1883 and it toured the United States and Europe until it closed in 1913. Annie Oakley, "Little Miss Sure-Shot," was one of the star attractions of the Wild West show, and film stars such as Tom Mix and Will Rogers got their start in them. The most recent Wild West show was Colonel Tim McCoy's Wild West of 1938, and since then there have been no more.

Tents of the Buffalo Bill (William F. Cody) Wild West Show. (Circus World Museum, Baraboo, Wisconsin)

Klondike Trading Company Store, late 1880s. Tent stores were a common sight on the frontier. Only when proprietors were assured of a steady flow of business would they abandon their tents and build more permanent structures. (Library of Congress)

Klondike Gold Rush Camp, Alaska, 1917. It took eleven trees to construct a framework for one wall tent — a wasteful use of resources, but it saved the traveler from having to carry the extra load of tent poles. (Photo number 126-AR-4D-5 in the National Archives.)

Main Street, Nome, Alaska, 1899. Tents gradually disappeared as more permanent structures were built to accommodate the steadily increasing business and population of the new town. Already a couple of these tents had semipermanent features, such as wooden doors (left of center and left of Behring Saloon). (Library of Congress)

Actresses bound for the Klondike, at Happy Camp, October 1897. Guess which women are wearing corsets. (Library of Congress)

Detention camp for yellow fever victims of Spanish-American War, Franklin, Louisiana, 1899. American battle losses in the war amounted to 487 men; deaths from disease were 1995. Half of the army in Cuba was afflicted with yellow fever and various forms of malaria. The tent is a standard wall tent with winglike flaps attached to the fly. In harsh weather, both door and overhead flaps could be secured to provide complete protection within. (Photo number CN-5117 in the National Archives)

San Juan Hill terraced for tents of U.S. Army encampment, Cuba, Spanish-American War of 1898. The tents shown here are along the simple lines of the *tente d'abri*. Note brush shelters built over some tents (third and fifth terraces up). (*Harper's pictorial history of war with Spain*, 1899)

Below: Yellow fever in Santiago de Cuba. In the three years following the Spanish-American War, when Cuba was under U.S. military rule, U.S. sanitary engineers under Major William Gorgas wiped out yellow fever and malaria. Entire city blocks were covered with tents and fumigated with cyanide derivatives to kill disease-carrying mosquitos. This technique and the use of live virus vaccine for immunization later made possible the building of the Panama Canal. (Photo number 90-G-10A-7 in the National Archives)

CIRCUS TENTS — THE LARGEST NOMADICS

As America moved into the twentieth century a rather formidable departure in tents took place — and that was the circus big top. The circus itself is associated historically with the circuses of ancient Rome; however, the modern circus is derived only from the Roman amphitheater, which gave our circus its shape, if not its size. (The Circus Maximus, for instance, is said to have had a seating capacity of 350,000.) The Roman circuses were sometimes covered by canvas, which they also have in common with the modern circus. (See page 114 for a picture of the Colosseum vela.) The Roman circus was a round or oval structure with tiers of seats for spectators enclosing a space in which horse racing or bloody and brutal spectacles took place. This is the antithesis of the display of human endeavor, skillful management of animals, and tragic buffoonery of clowns found in the modern circus.

The modern circus got its start in the latter half of the eighteenth century with performances of equestrian feats in horse rings strewn with sawdust and, for the most part, under canvas. Philip Astley (1742–1814), an English trick rider, discovered that centrifugal force enabled him to keep his balance if he galloped in a circle and, in so doing, he traced the first ring. Trick riding shows became the rage. The clown entered the circus at this point in Philip Astley's show as a comedian on horseback. The tent, being the most adaptable structure to accommodate a horse ring, went on the road with these traveling shows as they covered Europe. In 1793, circuses were opened in New York and Philadelphia and horses continued to be the main attraction of the program until the early 1800s when wild-animal trainers appeared with their animal acts. In 1859, with the invention of the flying trapeze (by Jules Léotard) and Charles Blondin's numerous crossings of Niagara Falls on a tightrope, acrobats found their way into the circus and by the turn of the century they had become an integral part of it.

The first circuses in this country performed without a tent in the open. But this made it difficult to charge admission so canvas walls promptly appeared to make the circus a profitable show — those who didn't pay to get in missed it. Then Aaron Turner and Seth B. Howes added tent roofs to their mid-Atlantic traveling circuses in the 1820s, which also enabled them to perform year-round in any kind of weather. Thus the big top was born. Portable seats for the audience were also introduced at this time. "Dr." Gilbert Spaulding, whose circus started off traveling by riverboat, is said to have invented the quarter poles that support the big top between the central king poles and the side poles. And the big tops started getting bigger!

Another factor that contributed to the growth of the American circus was the railroad. In 1872, Barnum, Coup, and Castello made the change from horse and wagon to train, and all the other circuses that wanted to keep up did the same. The age of the giant railroad circus had dawned, and by 1941, "The Greatest Show on Earth" was transported on four trains made up of 107 seventy-foot railroad cars. Also, W. C. Coup of Barnum, Coup, and Castello, introduced a system whereby the gaps

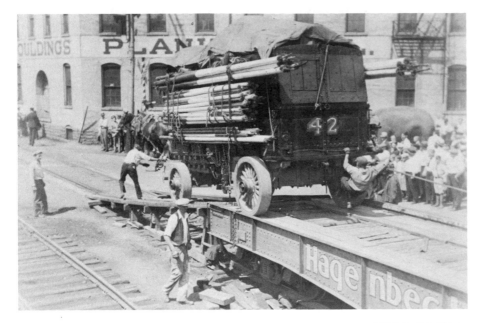

Elephants were used to raise the canvas big ▶ top and when the circus was on the road the tent was pitched and struck daily — sometimes as many as 100 times — as they moved from town to town. (Photo by Lew Merrim, Monkmeyer Press Photo Service)

Circus laborers or "roustabouts" of the Hagenbeck-Wallace Circus roll a load of canvas and tent poles off a railroad car, 1932. (Circus World Museum, Baraboo, Wisconsin)

After the center poles were positioned and secured with guy ropes, the tent canvas was spread around the poles and fastened to pole rings so that it could be raised. The sides of the tent were then raised so ropes could be run underneath the canvas to the poles. (Circus World Museum, Baraboo, Wisconsin)

Elephants were then hitched up to raise the big top canvas. (Photo: Elizabeth Hibb, Monkmeyer Press Photo Service)

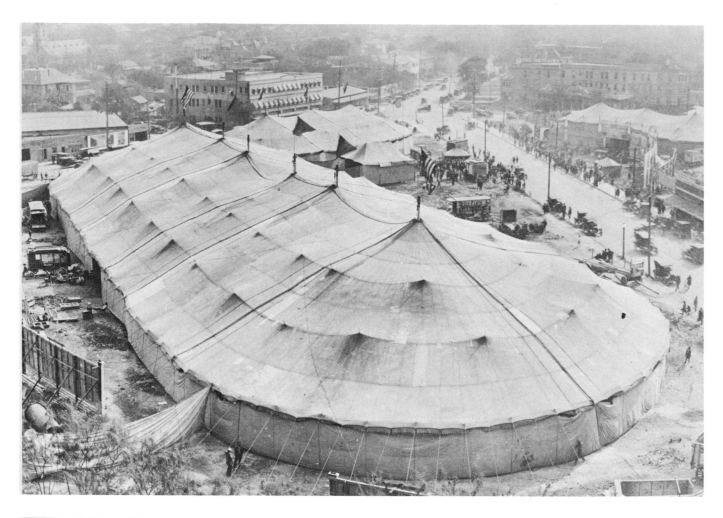

Above: Sells Floto Circus, 1921. Seams in tent canopy can be seen where the roof sections are joined together. The joining is done with the canvas on the ground. Once it is raised auxiliary poles are placed underneath. Finally a wall curtain is attached. (Circus World Museum, Baraboo, Wisconsin)

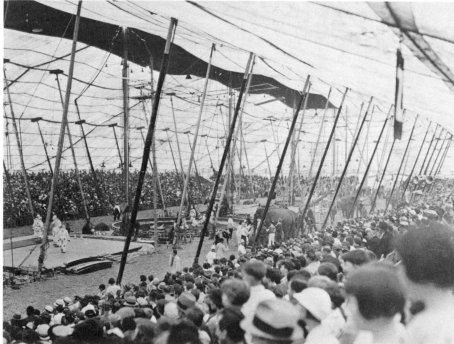

Big top interior during performance, Ringling Brothers and Barnum & Bailey, 1934. (Circus World Museum, Baraboo, Wisconsin)

Air billowing up big top during teardown. (Circus World Museum, Baraboo, Wisconsin)

Ringling Brothers, Barnum & Bailey big top fire of July 6, 1944, Hartford, Connecticut. The wax waterproofing treatment of canvas was a fire hazard and there were several major tent fires during the circus history. This one was the worst — 168 people were killed. Many of these deaths were a result of panicked people clamoring for the exits when they could have escaped by lifting and going under the canvas sides of the big top. (Circus World Museum, Baraboo, Wisconsin)

Ringling Brothers and Barnum & Bailey Circus World in Florida. Circus World is a permanent fixture and the circus can still be seen there.

between flatcars were bridged so the trains could be loaded from the end and each fully loaded wagon could be pushed down the entire length of the train. The modern system of rail-truck freight is based on the highly efficient technology of the old railroad circus.

In their heyday, from 1880 to 1920, the great American tented circuses performed in what could be called canvas colosseums. The big top of the Ringling Brothers and Barnum & Bailey Circus was supported by sixty-five-foot-high ridge poles for canvas which accommodated 10,000 to 12,000 people and covered more than two acres. Most of the other big tops were somewhat smaller, accommodating about 5000. This was never the case in Europe where circuses maintained the one-ring format and met the highest standards. In Europe, in order to expand the area under the canvas and maintain the one-ring design, the tents were set up with four center poles forming a square instead of poles in a single-file line as in the American big tops.

Big business was the impetus that gave America the fabulous spectacle which became truly The Greatest Show on Earth. From 1840 onward, circus combines and amalgamations became widespread and by 1929, the Ringling Brothers, who already controlled six circuses, including Barnum & Bailey's Greatest Show on Earth, bought out the Circus Corporation of America, bringing a total of eleven major circuses under one owner. In Europe, this was not the tradition. The circuses were predominately family owned and tended to split up rather than combine.

Circus day itself was one of the highlights of the year in towns across the U.S.A. The town would have already been "papered" by a mass publicity campaign, which included advertisements in the local papers, posters, banners, and hand-distributed printed bills. The first train to pull into the town would be the "flying squadron," which brought the cook tent, horse tents, menagerie, and steam calliope. This train would have departed while the circus was in progress in the preceding town. Next arriving would be the "canvas train" and then the "lumber train" (bearing construction materials). Wagons would be pulled by horse teams to the showgrounds, always directed by arrows chalked on posts and trees by advance men. The lot was a scene of mad activity: acres of canvas and a forest of poles were assembled before masses of curious people, called "lot lice" by showmen. Elephants (and later tractors) would raise the canvas of the big top and the circus would take form. Then parade call was trumpeted — this was usually about eleven A.M. The free parade was a spectacle in itself and all activity in the town came to a standstill for it. After two shows daily and the teardown, which took place at night, the wagons and teams returned to the trains and disappeared into the night.

As the shows got bigger, in order to make them pay, the 10,000-spectator-tents were erected for one day in each town on a circus schedule. The ring, traditionally Philip Astley's forty-two foot diameter, had to be flanked by other rings with stages between them to fill the larger tents. The Ringling Brothers and Barnum & Bailey Greatest Show on Earth at one time had three rings and five stages surrounded by a hippodrome track. This completely changed things — the show could not be limited to single acts and became an extravaganza that included aerial ballets and spectacular processions for mass effect. Traveling became more and more difficult as well, and, in 1956, increased freight rates and labor problems forced The Greatest Show on Earth to give up tenting. On the Heidelberg Raceway outside Pittsburgh, at John Ringling North's order, the last big top came down. (A discount house now stands on the site.) From then on the circus has appeared only in permanent metropolite buildings such as exhibition halls or their winter quarters. The popularity of television also contributed to the decline of the circus — even though it introduced the skill of the performer to a much larger audience, the actual attendance at performances fell. By the 1960s there were only thirty small circuses still touring the country, most of them traveling by road instead of rail. Motorization has enabled the canvas-tent circus to survive. In Europe the circus is alive and relatively well. In the Soviet Union, the circus business is booming: there are more than a hundred permanent and tenting circuses playing annually to about 22 million people.

THE TWENTIETH CENTURY

In the first half of this century, tents were widely used in times of cataclysm, world war, drought, and depression. The wall tent provided most of the shelter, though many people were too poor to afford even that and erected lean-tos and shanties in forms determined by the materials at hand.

On April 18, 1906, a violent earthquake, followed by disastrous fires, destroyed most of San Francisco's central residential and business districts. Building losses were approximately $100 million and total property loss was three times higher. Hundreds of people were killed and thousands were left homeless. Survivors camped in tents amid the ruins on the dunes west of San Francisco and in Golden Gate Park. Others fled to outlying towns and by staying there gave impetus to the twentieth-century suburban growth around the San Francisco Bay area.

In Oklahoma in the 1920s, recurrent droughts burned the wheat in the fields, and overplanting, overgrazing, and unscientific cropping aided the weather in making northwest Oklahoma part of the Dust Bowl of the 1930s. A great number of tenant farmers were compelled to leave their dust-ridden farms and go west as migrant workers. Hard times uprooted many Americans and a large segment of the population became nomadic, traveling in a grim search for work.

During the depths of the Depression, impoverished veterans of the First World War marched on Washington demanding bonus relief. They lived in squalor under conditions comparable to the frontline trenches and were finally forcibly evacuated by U.S. Army troops under General MacArthur.

With the end of the decade, war broke out and war brought jobs. Migrants and other unemployed workers descended on factories where jobs were available and tent cities served as living quarters.

Tent shelter, Union Square, aftermath of San Francisco earthquake of April 18, 1906. (Library of Congress)

Left: August 4, 1916. City kids under an improvised tent shelter on the fire escape of their building on Allen Street, New York City. The tenting instinct is a strong one, and children of all ages in all parts of the world have improvised play tents. (Photo by von Hartz, Museum of City of New York)

Right: Fighting tuberculosis on the roof, New York, early 1900s. Until 1909 tuberculosis was the chief cause of death in the United States. A major factor in its prevalence was the overcrowding, poor hygiene and nutrition rampant in large cities. At this time fresh outdoor air (even in winter) was thought to be beneficial. (Photo by Jacob Riis, Museum of City of New York)

Singing "Over There," the Bonus Expeditionary Army celebrates the news that Congress votes to act on the Patman bonus bill, June 15, 1932. Approximately 7000 veterans erected a tent city near the Capitol in Washington under conditions comparable to those of the front line trenches. The World War I veterans were protesting their inadequate war-relief benefits. It was considered shocking to the U.S. population at the time that veteran soldiers were living in conditions of penury and neglect. Congress didn't agree and defeated the bill. (Library of Congress)

Motor hospital, World War I. This mobile hospital consisted of two tents extending from each side of a truck in order to triple the functional space. (*Scientific American*, 1914)

The Bell Stretcher Tent in opened and closed positions. This World War I stretcher enabled wounded soldiers to be carried over long distances while being completely protected from harsh weather that might worsen their condition. The tent is equipped with flaps that roll up and down over mosquito netting. It also folded up in one piece and required no assembly. Modern methods of evacuation of the wounded (such as by helicopter) have phased out the Bell Stretcher Tent.

Migrant Workers, American River Camp near Sacramento, San Joaquin Valley, California, July 1935. These were former Tennessee coal miners following in the wake of relatives. When they arrived in California they found conditions no better than they had been in Tennessee. (Library of Congress)

Japanese-American detention camp during World War II. (Library of Congress)

A tent camp that accommodates workers from the gunpowder plant in Childersburg, Alabama, May 1941. World War II brought with it jobs, and the tent came through as quarters for workers flocking to locales where jobs were available. (Library of Congress)

Tent street, Forrest City, Arkansas, February 1937. A street of modified square Sibley tents, all with stoves inside, in this camp for flood refugees. Again the tent provides instant shelter for the homeless. (Photo by Edwin Locke, Library of Congress)

This contented carpenter's wife in Mission Valley near San Diego, California, December 1940, is quoted as saying, "We're living in a tent because we wouldn't pay anyone thirty or thirty-five dollars for a two-room bug trap." (Photo by Russell Lee, Library of Congress)

A tent serves as a first aid area for New York City Marathon, October 22, 1978. Some 9800 people participated in the five-borough run of twenty-six miles; of the 1212 who didn't make it to the finish line, those who collapsed were treated in emergency units and temporary tent hospitals set up along the route. (Photo by Rhoda Galyn)

Also with the war came the relocation of thousands of Japanese naturalized citizens and native Americans of Japanese descent to detention camps for the duration of the war. These people lost everything — their homes and jobs — when they were evacuated.

After the war times were somewhat better, though impoverished migrant workers continued to roam the country and use rough tents for shelter. In 1968 tents also housed the Poor People's Campaign on the Mall in Washington, D.C., in a nonviolent protest of the form espoused by Dr. Martin Luther King. Spring rains quickly turned the ground to mud and facilities were primitive, but the unifying spirit of nonviolent protest made the venture an inspiring statement for the cause of human brotherhood and justice. The Mall was also the scene of another protest encampment in 1978 when five hundred American Indians and other ethnics marched from San Francisco to Washington in what was called the Longest Walk. The march was in memory of the tens of thousands of Indians who perished on forced marches as they were driven from their homelands in the east.

Fortunately for the most part, tenting today is a happier pastime — the Woodstock rock festival in August of 1969 was a tent city, Boy Scouts continue to have their annual Jamborees, and one in four Americans will go camping this year.

Tent city, Boy Scout Jamboree, August 1977. This is an international summer camp, held approximately every four years since 1920. It is a gathering of thousands of scouts representing their countries in the spirit of world brotherhood. From the beginning the scout movement has been nonmilitary, non-political, interdenominational, and interracial. There are also international camps for scoutmasters (indabas) and handicapped boys (agoons). (Courtesy Boy Scouts of America)

3 THE NOMADS

To a native place cling not, where folks oppress and hold thee in scant esteem,
But depart the land that exalts the low above the high in dignity,
And take thy flight to a safe retreat, although it were on the skirts of Mount Kaf,
For know full well that a free-born man in his country meets but with disregard
As the pearl within its shell is slighted, and underrated its preciousness.

— Maqamat of Hariri

They think me unworthy
My Mide brethren
but look and see
the length of my wigwam.

— Chippewa Song

The most time-tested and enduring tents are those of nomadic herdsmen and hunters. These tents are feats of engineering, having been perfected to totally support the nomadic way of life and provide complete protection from the most severe environmental extremes. The women, who are in complete charge of the household, design, construct, pitch, and strike them. Various styles of nomadic tents have been used since ancient times.

The nomadic way of life is deeply ingrained, and nomads all over the world have always been skeptical if not frightened of permanent housing, though they are presently being forced into it against their will by unsympathetic rulers. Nomads have been settled onto reservations or in ugly housing developments. Sometimes the tent is still pitched next to the house, though as it wears away with age, it is not repaired and gradually will be done away with.

Nomads have always had their own laws and have never heeded other rules and regulations; local governments consider them a nuisance and a sign of underdevelopment. Also, in order to wander freely the nomad uses much more land and therefore is an inconvenience to nations that prefer to develop their land.

The nomads have taken the specific climatic conditions of their terrain and have tailor-made efficient and ingenious tents to combat the prevailing elements. For instance, the tipi of the American Indians has assumed several structural forms, each dependent upon the wind conditions and pack animals available to carry it. Eskimo and Lapp tents are very individualized and efficient Arctic dwellings — the Lapps even have a summer and a winter tent, both of which serve them well. The black tent provides optimum shelter from sun and sandstorm on the desert, and the Mongolian yurt keeps its occupants warm on the bleak Siberian steppe.

The nomad's mobility has been his salvation. Nomads have been able to survive simply because of their ability to travel and search out food for themselves and their herds. And when war or famine has prevailed, they've simply moved on.

Even a few decades ago nomads wandered freely in their ageless migrations. In fact, for centuries in Mongolia the yurt was the only dwelling known besides the Buddhist monasteries. The nomadic way of life has been a delicate balance of animal husbandry, trade, and perhaps some crop cultivation. The technological age has upset that balance, perhaps irrevocably so. One of the most romantic and imaginative ways of life is disappearing from the earth and unfortunately the vast amount that could be learned from it will also disappear as we become more and more dependent on our permanent dwellings.

TIPI

"You have noticed," the Indian Black Elk has said, "that everything an Indian does is in a circle and that is because the Power of the World works in circles and everything tries to be round. The life of man is a circle from childhood to childhood. Our tipis were round, like the nests of birds. But the white men have put us in these square boxes. It is a bad way to live for there can be no power in a square."
— John G. Neihardt, *Black Elk Speaks*

Tepee, teepee, or tipi: It is the ideal dwelling of nomadic peoples. It's easy to set up, easy to take down, and easy to shift. Spanish explorers in the early 1500s first reported the existence of tipis to Europe, but they've been used for time immemorial by Indians from New England to northwest Canada. The tipi is ingeniously designed and engineered to provide an extremely comfortable, well-ventilated home in any weather this continent can whip up, including tornadoes, the scourge of the southern plains; strong winds cannot pick up its inverted surface. The tipi is really one of the most superb nomadic tents ever to be developed. The Mongol yurt is also a remarkable achievement; however, the tipi has the advantage of being lightweight and easy to transport while the yurt is cumbersome. But the Mongols have camels as beasts of burden and the Indians used only dogs and horses.

This photograph, which looks like a scene from a Western movie, taken on January 16, 1891, shows General Miles and his staff viewing "the largest hostile Indian camp in the United States," near Pine Ridge, South Dakota. (Library of Congress)

Flathead Indian encampment in the Salish Mountains in the central plateau of northwest Montana c. 1940. This photograph shows the typical open-ended camp circle, which usually faced east. Hanging on a tripod frame in foreground is jerky, a staple of the Indian diet. (Library of Congress)

Prominent tribal leaders — chiefs, leaders of war parties, and medicine men — occupied superbly decorated tipis, such as this Arapaho tipi which was "Tent of the Keeper of the Sacred Pipe" used at an Arapaho sun dance in 1900. These painted or "medicine" designs usually originated in dreams and visions and were handed down from generation to generation. They were highly symbolic, representing the supernatural powers that looked after the owner of the tipi. In proper ceremonies, the designs could be purchased and the "medicine" and rituals "passed" from one owner to the other. (Photo by J. Otis Wheelock, courtesy of the American Museum of Natural History)

Some tipi designs were heraldic and painted to proclaim the heroic deeds or war exploits of their owners. These two Sioux tipis deal with the war with the white man. Note American flag painted on left tipi and tassels of rawhide strung with beads and bone hanging from smoke flaps of all three tipis. (Library of Congress)

The darkened area at top represents the darkened sky and the similar border at bottom earth, with what could be sun wheels in the white area. This tipi is from the Piegan Indians (a branch of the Blackfoot) of Montana. Medicine tipis were supposed to protect the owners and their families from misfortune and sickness and bring good luck and success in hunting and war. (Library of Congress)

Piegan Indian child's painted tipi. Dark area represents sky above with white discs that represent constellations; the shapes emerging from the lower border, representing the earth, could be those of ancestors. Child's tipis were rare and reserved only for the sons of the most prominent family in the tribe. (Library of Congress)

Northern Arapaho, 1893. A common practice in extremely cold weather was to construct a windbreak to protect the tipi from the freezing winds which drive the temperatures down to −40°F and lower. (Photo by Mooney; Smithsonian Institution.)

These Ute Indians incorporated the trunks of trees into their tipis. This is reminiscent of the first tents of early man, which were skins thrown over bushes and small trees. (Western History Collection, Denver Public Library)

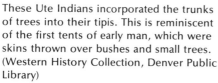

Crow Lodge of 25 Skins, George Catlin, oil on canvas, 24 × 29 inches. (Courtesy National Collection of Fine Arts, Smithsonian Institution)

Sun Dance, painting by Short Bull, Chief 1901(2) of Oglala Dakota Sioux. (Courtesy American Museum of Natural History)

Interior of tipi of Yellow Kidney and Little Plune and squaw, Sioux or Piegan. Those who owned medicine or painted tipis were also entitled to decorate their tipi lining. The lining helps insulate and cut moisture inside the tipi. Note cleared patch on ground midway between fire pit and clock. That is the altar for the tipi. And slightly to left of Yellow Kidney (the older Indian) and partially visible is a tripodal tent seat composed of three poles, two of which are carved and support a tapered mat of peeled willow rods or, as seen above, a hide. Part of the lower end of the mat is laid on the ground and acts as a seat. (Library of Congress)

Many people in this country, being brought up on Saturday afternoon matinees at the local movie theater, are not aware that as an art form painted tipi covers easily rank as the most expressive and imaginative esthetic achievement in the long history of Native American nomadic hunting cultures. Needless to say, we never saw dazzling, superbly decorated tipis in the Hollywood cowboy and Indian movies. It's true that most of the Indian population lived in plain tipis; however, prominent tribal leaders such as chiefs, leaders of war parties, and medicine men always lived in beautifully painted ones.

A real Indian tipi is always a tilted cone, the back made steeper than the front in order to brace it against the strong prevailing west winds of the Great Plains. This tilt also makes for more headroom in the back of the lodge, where most activity is carried on. The entrance traditionally faces east — toward the rising sun. Also, the interior is egg-shaped, not circular.

Women were responsible for everything related to the tipi — designing, sewing, selecting campsites, erecting, and furnishing. The man would paint history, war records, tribal relationships, or religious symbolism on the tipi covers, but it was the woman who decorated the inside lining and owned the tipi itself. In fact, in some tribes, all she had to do to divorce her husband was to throw his possessions outside and that was that.

There have been changes made in the tipi in the past few centuries. After the introduction of the horse in the seventeenth and eighteenth centuries, larger tipis were made by the central tribes since transporting them became less of a problem. Also, the obliteration of the buffalo by the white man in the nineteenth century forced a radical change in Plains Indian technology. Canvas replaced buffalo hide and the custom of painting tipis, which had been handed down from generation to generation, gradually faded into the past as the ranks of the Indians were decreased and their spirit broken on reservations. Before the bison were nearly exterminated, however, some Indians had already switched to canvas. It weighed much less and there was not as much work involved with it, as canvas required no tanning or curing, was easier to sew and to handle, and enabled the tipi to be made even bigger. Also, when the Indians obtained wagons and transporting the tipi was no longer a problem, the diameters of some tipis increased to as much as twenty-eight feet.

There are three- and four-pole tipis and those in the know can instantly tell one from the other. These two types are determined by the number of poles used in the first stage of tipi erecting. Either three or four poles are tied together some four feet or so from their upper ends and then a tri- or quadripod foundation is made. The other poles, usually numbering fifteen or twenty, are laid in the crotches. The poles are approximately twenty-five feet in length. The three-pole tipi can withstand high wind better so it was used for the most part by Indians of the open prairie; the four-pole tipi was used by those in the northwest who lived nearer to the mountains. The four-pole is less tilted than the three-pole and has the smoke flaps set farther apart as there is a larger number of poles to be accommodated on the four-pole. In areas with high winds, the poles usually are set a few inches into the ground in order to add stability to the tent.

The last pole to be fitted in place is called the lifting pole, so called because the cover is tied to it and rolled around it, and pole and cover are set in place at the center of the back of the tipi, opposite the door. Next, the cover is stretched around the wooden framework, on both north and south sides, to overlap at the entrance. Wooden pins (lacing pins) are then inserted horizontally through holes over and under the doorway to hold the cover securely in place. The tipi cover is firmly anchored by stakes driven through holes or loops in the bottom edge of the cover. Before the white man introduced the steel ax to the Indians, the tipi cover was held to the ground by placing stones around the bottom. "Tipi rings" of these stones are still to be found in many parts of the West, and when storms approach rocks and logs are still placed atop the stakes and along the cover to anchor them more securely.

One of the truly ingenious features of the tipi is its smoke flap system. Smoke flaps are used to keep out snow and rain and to regulate the draft and smoke from the fireplace, which is slightly forward of center in the tipi. They are nearly triangular skin flaps that provide an opening starting slightly above the highest lacing pin used to fasten the tipi cover to the

Handling smoke flaps

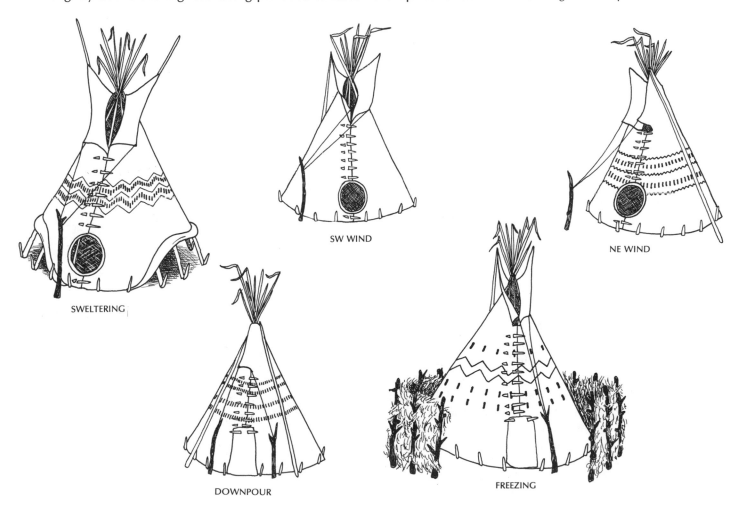

SWELTERING

SW WIND

NE WIND

DOWNPOUR

FREEZING

poles. On a three-pole tipi the ends of the flaps are made into little pockets or ears into which the upper ends of two additional poles are inserted. On four-pole tipis, there is usually a hole or eyelet through which a pole is inserted. A person standing outside the tipi can adjust the flaps as wind or weather changes.

Doors vary — some are quite elaborate and ornate, others are only an old blanket hung to the lacing pin above the doorway. The hides or cloth from which the door is constructed are usually stretched by a transverse stick or a hoop frame. Sometimes doors are decorated with beaded stripes and fluffy feathers; other times the skin of a large calf or steer (or bear or buffalo in the old days) is used, with the hair left on to increase water repellency.

Another unique feature of the tipi is the inside lining. Also referred to as a dew cloth, the lining keeps dew from condensing inside and therefore keeps the interior reasonably dry — drier than any other tent. The lining also insulates the tipi in cold weather, especially when hay or brush is piled between it and the tipi cover. The lining sections are from 6 × 8 to 6 × 12 feet in size and are hung all the way around the tipi, with the sections overlapping. Like decorated tipi covers, only certain women of the tribe were allowed to decorate their linings; however, the patterns did not vary as much as tipi cover decorations and there was some uniformity throughout tribal nations. The linings were vividly colored and beaded, with dangles made of thongs with colored cornhusks or tassels made of fluffy feathers, dyed hair, or buffalo dewclaws. (A dewclaw is a vestigial claw, so called because it only reaches the dewy surface of the ground.)

One other function of the lining in times gone by was its ability to prevent the casting of shadows from the fire onto the wall of the tipi. This was important for safety's sake — so no lurking enemy could see a shadow at which he could aim and therefore injure the occupant.

The tipi was furnished only with boxes, rawhide cases, pouches, saddlebags, pillows, robes, furs, beds, and backrests. The latter are made from a tripod of willow rods four or five feet high, usually handsomely carved and decorated, from which a decorated tapered mat (smaller at the top) made of peeled willow rods woven together would hang. The mat would be about five feet long, two feet wide at the top, three feet at the bottom, and could act as the back of a chair for anyone sitting on the ground.

The lives of the Indians revolved around spiritual symbolism. The floor of the tipi represented the earth; the walls, the sky; and the poles, the trails from the earth to the spirit world beyond. There was also an altar inside the tipi which was usually a little patch of bare earth, with all grass, roots, and stubs removed.

Earlier, and smaller, tipis were transported by dogs. As previously mentioned the horse made it possible to enlarge both the tipi and the household. (And by the time the Indians obtained wagons their nomadic existence was practically at an end because the buffalo were gone and many of the old trails were fenced up.) The tipi poles weigh from fifteen to twenty pounds each and anywhere from fifteen to twenty poles were needed. One horse could drag eight to ten poles. The scanty household gear, wrapped in a bundle in the tipi cover, lay across the trailing ends. An Indian camp, with men, women, children, and household effects, was able to travel greater distances and with more speed in one day than could the most well-equipped army of the day. Camp could also be struck in minutes. Other gear not carried in the tipi cover was carried on a drag, or travois, which consisted of a platform or netting supported by two trailing poles somewhat shorter than the tipi poles, the forward ends of which were fastened to a horse or dog.

Also, sometimes the wounded, the aged, the very young, or puppies and other pets rode on the travois. When it carried passengers usually a dome-shaped structure of willow branches was erected to provide protection either from the elements or in case it overturned.

On the average it took three horses to carry the household — two dragging tipi poles and one dragging a travois. Of course, this varied. Sometimes as many as five horses were needed to move a large tipi and its accoutrements. Dogs were also used as beasts of burden.

Cooking Tipis

During hot spells, the Indians sometimes had special cooking tipis which were simply old tipis with the bottom two or three feet of the cover cut away to provide ventilation; so worn tipis were still used, in a less important way, instead of being discarded. Also, old tipi coverings were used in making moccasins, bags, and ground cloths.

Squaw Coolers

Brush arbors (or *ramadas,* as the Spanish called them) were also constructed when the Indians camped for several days during hot spells. The Indians referred to them as wickies or squaw coolers and they are still common in Indian homesteads. These are constructed by driving forked corner poles into the ground and placing stout poles from fork to fork, then laying cross poles over them at invervals and covering the entire structure with fresh-cut leafy branches. These serve as a structure for eating, lounging, cooking, working, and so on. Occasionally a piece of canvas is stretched and tied to the supports on the windward side.

WICKIUPS

The wickiup is a framework of arched poles and limbs tied together and covered by brush, bark, rushes, canvas, or mats. It is found among the more sedentary Indian tribes in Arizona, New Mexico, Utah, Idaho, and California and was used by those tribes who did not follow the buffalo for their subsistence. This house, too, was erected by the women.

The Apache woman covered her wickiup with a thatch of brush, grass, leaves, or rushes, while the Sauk and Fox used woven reed matting.

Camp scene, Sauk and Fox Indian. This tent is made from woven reed mats stretched over a wooden framework. Canvas is then added on top to waterproof or, on the windward side, to insulate. This is located in a more permanent encampment and a hinged door has been built in. Note squaw coolers at right where Indians are congregating. (Smithsonian Institution)

This photograph, taken by K. T. Dodge in 1899, shows an Apache scout camp in San Carlos, Arizona. By the turn of the century, most of the Apache tribes were no longer tipi dwellers and instead occupied first circular, dome-shaped wickiups and then wickiups and wall tents. Alternating rows of each are pictured above. (Smithsonian Institution)

This photograph of a wickiup was taken in 1880. (N. H. Rose Collection, Western History Collection, University of Oklahoma Library)

Dance ground and tipis at Mescalero, New Mexico, July 1956. The uncovered tipi at left, made from live branches, is a ceremonial tipi built for the puberty rites of Apache maidens. Many ceremonies involving the tent and the live tree exist all over the world. (Smithsonian Institution)

This E. S. Curtis photograph of a sweat lodge shows a lone Apache warrior ready to enter the tent. The entire ritual takes several hours. (Smithsonian Institution)

Sweat tent, Lame Deer, Montana, August 1941. The skull, outside the sweat tent, is "medicine" and part of the ritual. (Photo by Marion Post Wolcott on Cheyenne Indian Tongue River reservation, Library of Congress)

Family of Stump Horn with horse travois, Cheyenne, Fort Keogh, Montana. Young woman with baby in cradle mounted on horse. Two children in travois basket. (Smithsonian Institution)

Two tipi covers and frames are used to construct this windbreak for a Plains Indian communion service. (American Museum of Natural History)

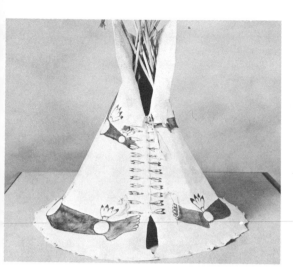

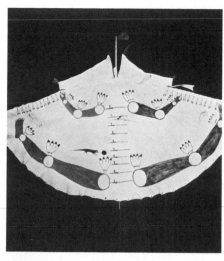

Two views of *Leg Picture Tipi of Fair-Haired Old Man* by a Kiowa Indian artist, 1897. (Courtesy National Collection of Fine Arts, Smithsonian Institution)

Paul Zoñtum painting model tipi, 1897. At Anadarko, Oklahoma, from 1891 to 1904 at the request of James Mooney, Smithsonian Institute ethnologist, twenty-five decorated buckskin models of the tipis of the Kiowa Indians were made by Indian artists with instructions being given by the tipi owners or their close descendants who occupied these medicine tipis before being forced to the reservations. The entire collection was on exhibit at the Renwick Gallery of the National Collection of Fine Arts, Smithsonian Institution in Washington, D.C., for most of 1978. (Smithsonian Institution)

In July 1978, five hundred American Indians and other ethnic supporters marched from San Francisco to Washington, where for nine days they camped in protest on the grounds of the Washington Monument. As they neared the Capitol, after five months of walking, their ranks swelled with members of various Indian communities and other supporters, including blacks in the Washington area. The five month transcontinental protest march was called the Longest Walk, in memory of the forced marches of thousands upon thousands of Indians who were driven from their land onto reservations in the West. Whole tribes were obliterated by disease and starvation en route. (Wide World Photos, Inc.)

Nomads still exist in the United States. One group, besides migrant workers, are Basque sheepherders in the northwest. The Basques migrated to the United States between 1900 and 1930, when there was continuing civil unrest in Spain and when American ranchers were recruiting immigrants from the Basque regions. Now they number well over 70,000. After their sheep are sheared in late May or early June, these sheepherders take their sheep into the mountains where good grazing land is available for two to three months. Several tent manufacturers make sheepherders' tents, which are usually standard wall tents with stove-pipe hole and insulating asbestos ring. (Photo by Russell Lee, Library of Congress)

Whatever the construction, canvas was usually stretched over the windward side for insulation or over the top to keep the inside dry. An opening was left at the top to allow smoke to escape from the fire pit within and the doorway was simply a low opening over which a blanket or piece of skin was stretched. The house was reasonably comfortable, but compared to the tipi it was a rude shelter. Smoke inside the wickiup was a constant problem and total protection from the elements was not possible. Also, it takes about four hours to erect a wickiup and a fraction of that time for the experinced tipi owner to set up a tipi.

Most of the Indians who used wickiups moved outside for the warmer months and erected squaw coolers or ramadas.

To facilitate moving, the furnishings in the wickiup were kept to a minimum. The Apaches used wooden bed frames that raised the sleeping surface some two to three feet off the ground. Brush and dry grass covered by blankets served as a mattress. Kitchen utensils, baskets, and bags rounded out the furnishings. Moving camp was an enormous task for the women. The family horse was loaded to capacity and the women carried the rest.

SWEAT TENTS

Most of the Indians from Alaska to Tierra del Fuego used a sweat lodge as an important part of their religion. The American Indian constructed the sweat lodge by setting long willow shoots in the ground in the form of a circle and then bending them over and twisting and tying them together in pairs, forming a domelike structure which was then covered with canvas. The use of a sweat lodge for purification was highly ritualistic, complete with virgins or medicine men collecting the special stones that were blessed by the holy man of the tribe. Like a small wigwam, the average sweat lodge could accommodate four to six people and temperatures of 140 to 170 degrees Fahrenheit were raised by dousing white-hot stones with water.

ESKIMO

Only a people of great ingenuity and strength could have thrived in a region that lies under snow and ice for six to nine months of the year, and where vegetables are unprocurable and trees exist only in one or two marginal districts — so large areas lack wood of any kind, including driftwood, from which to fabricate houses, tools, and weapons. The Eskimos' adjustment to such a severe environment has been equaled by no other group. They inhabit the arctic and subarctic regions of North America and the Chukchi Peninsula of northeast Siberia; they number approximately 55,000. Despite their wide dispersal, Eskimos are surprisingly uniform in language, physical type, and culture and speak different dialects of the same language.

Sea mammals (four or five species of seals and, in certain regions, beluga, walruses and whales) provide them with food, clothing, shelter, cooking and lamp oil, tools and weapons; the skill required to secure these necessities places the Eskimos among the foremost hunters in the world. Fish and caribou are next in importance in their economy. The word *Eskimo* comes from the Algonquian and means "eaters of raw meat." But it is this practice of eating raw meat that provides their limited diet with the nutrients they need, which cooking would destroy.

In the summer Eskimos live in caribou and sealskin tents. Then, with the darkening days of winter, they band together in small groups in voluntary association, under a leader recognized for his superior ability to provide for the group. Very few Eskimos live in igloos all winter. Although they can provide adequate protection for weeks in severe cold, igloos are used almost exclusively as temporary shelters while traveling and hunting. The Eskimos reinforce their tents or move into either rock igloos or earth- or sod-walled structures.

In order to live in tents through the winter, Eskimos cover them with shrubs and spread a second skin cover over them. In some instances several families join their tents. In the front part where the tents are joined the covers are taken away and replaced by a whale rib which affords passage from one room to another. The rock igloo is constructed like the snow-block igloo but the sides are banked with sod and the roof is covered with grass and the summer tent, and lastly with snow. Earth and sod-walled houses are built on a frame of driftwood, sometimes with large whale bones acting as structural members. In many cases the poles

Eskimo spring tent on ice at Cape Lockyer, March 1915. The passageway at the bottom leads into the tent, which rests on a foundation of packed snow and blocks of ice. This is one of the many variations of the tent used by the Eskimo. Their migration patterns and sources of sustenance, and the time of the year, are directly related to the type of structure they occupy. (National Museums of Canada)

Woman mending Alaska winter tent of sealskin. The Eskimo tent is made of either sealskin or caribou hide, depending on whether the band of Eskimo are caribou herders or seal hunters. (Smithsonian Institution)

from the summer tent also serve as supports. Many of the design features to offset cold and wind are common to these structures — both include an entrance shelter, snow vault, or storm shed, frequently long and narrow, to keep out cold and wind. Inside there is always a raised bench (sleeping bench) to keep occupants up off the colder levels of the house. During the long winter nights, this bench also is the center for many other activities such as eating, making tools, and mending equipment. The windows of these habitations are made from intestines of seal or walrus and are translucent, not transparent.

The snow-block igloo, on the other hand, is illuminated with a skylight not of gut but of translucent freshwater ice cut expressly for that purpose. When the drifting snow of winter is piled over and around these houses, they can be quite comfortable. But in spring, many of them flood with water or the roofs cave in and they become uninhabitable. At this time

Chuckchi Eskimo tent, Plover Bay, Siberia, July 1899. This tent is secured by ropes tied to large stones and strung over the tent (at lower right). The large floats of inflated sealskins are used with the retrieving harpoon when whaling. Fastened to the long line leading from the harpoon head, they offer enough resistance to exhaust the wounded animal. Furs and fur garments are hanging over lines at sides. (Smithsonian Institution)

the occupants move back into their tents of seal and caribou skin and go their separate ways, hunting and fishing until the winter.

The summer tents of the Eskimo vary as much as their houses. The framework consists of numerous poles, usually lashed together ingeniously. These tents are usually not high and are well built and shaped in such a way as to resist gale winds that whip down from the mountains. The covering is held down on the outside by a ring of heavy stones or by ropes (or rawhide strips) wrapped around the tents and attached to rocks. These various configurations are more or less dependent on the shape of the wood that is available. Dogs and dogsleds are used in transporting the tent and household gear. The Eskimos are a littoral people who rove inland in the summer for freshwater fishing and game hunting, and in the winter move to the coast where the temperatures are slightly higher and seal are available.

The Eskimos have mixed to a great extent with the white man and many of them are giving up the old ways and are being encouraged to move into houses.

Another variation of the Eskimo summer tent, this one is made of caribou hide. Fish is drying on the small rocks at left. (Smithsonian Institution, photograph taken before 1931)

LAPP

The Lapps are found in the northernmost part of Europe in Norway, Sweden, Finland, and Russia, in an area within the Arctic Circle that is generally referred to as Lapland. They number about 30,000 and are concentrated mainly in Norway. The Lapps are thought to have originally migrated from central Asia, arriving in Norway before the Viking age, as hunters and fishermen. In northern Norway and Sweden, Lapland is quite mountainous. In the northeast, in Finland and the Soviet Union, it is composed mostly of tundra, although there are also extensive forests and many lakes and rivers. The climate is arctic and vegetation is generally sparse, except in the forested southern zone. The Lapps have a milder climate and therefore enjoy more physical comfort than the Eskimos.

The Lapps are the shortest and most roundheaded race in Europe and from ancient times have had a great reputation among the Finns and other neighboring peoples for skill in sorcery. This, along with behavior the Swedes and Norwegians consider unclean, has prejudiced the Scandinavians and the Lapps are not allowed to remain permanently in any of the towns, nor has there been interbreeding between Lapps and Scandinavians. The Eskimos, on the other hand, are no longer pureblood since there has been much interbreeding with the white population moving into the frontier.

The Lapps may be roughly divided into two classes — the sedentary, or the Sea Lapps, and the nomadic, or Mountain or Forest Lapps. The former are fishermen, the latter are hunters and herdsmen. The Mountain and Forest Lapps live in tents year-round. Like the Eskimos, they live in small encampments that seldom contain more than half a dozen tents. The reindeer furnishes them with food, clothing, and shelter. Their tents

By way of introduction, the Lapps are proficient skiers.

are conical and some say this Eurasiatic occurrence may have been historically linked with the conical tents of the North American Indians.

The Forest Lapps build tents that very much resemble the tipi and they cover it with bark and bank it with snow or earth in winter. When they move their reindeer herds on to new pastures they abandon the bark-covered tent and rebuild at new pastures. The Mountain Lapps, the more northerly peoples, carry their tent poles and coverings with them as they follow the reindeer on the treeless tundra. They move from Sweden over into Norway during the short summer. There is a special treaty in force between the two countries to ensure pastorage rights. The Forest Lapps stay in the forest year-round. Their reindeer are larger than the mountain peoples' reindeer, and they also fish and farm.

The Mountain Lapps use different types of tents in winter and summer. The summer tent is conical in shape and is constructed by placing poles, some forked at the ends and some not, around the circumference of a circle. The ends come together at a height of eight to ten feet and this

Like the Eskimo, the Lapps use several types of tents. This one is a summer tent in Norway. (Isefilm, Stockholm)

Lapp family outside winter tent.

Serving coffee in the Lapp winter tent. (Coffee grinder is at left atop box.) Logs in foreground mark pathway into the tent. The floor is covered with twigs, left, over which hides and blankets are spread. Cheese hangs on small platform suspended from the beams. Chain suspended from roof beams normally supports pots over fire. (Courtesy Swedish Information Service)

framework is covered with either fabric or hide. The Forest Lapps utilize this design year-round, always covering it with bark.

The winter tent of the Lapp is more complex. It is more like an American Indian wigwam than a tipi. Against two large parabolas with holes, a crossbeam is inserted. Fifteen or twenty poles are then rested against this framework to form a perfect cone, open at the top (the smoke hole is five feet in diameter), and some fifteen feet in diameter at the base. The tent is covered with layers of hides and canvas; sometimes insulation of dirt, grass, or twigs is placed between the layers. And the tent is always banked. The smoke hole can be covered if the weather demands it.

The floor is covered with an eight- to ten-inch layer of fresh twigs; several reindeer-skin bags on the floor serve as chairs, and birchbark cases, somewhat like our suitcases, are used for storing and carrying various articles. A central pot is suspended over the fire from the cross-

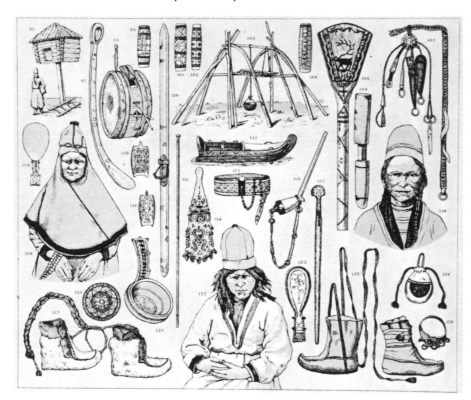

Accessories of Lapp life. The Lapps are quite gifted artistically, as can be seen by the profusion of detail work on the items pictured here.
96. *Njalla,* pantry of the wilderness
97–98. Portable cask and ladle
99, 101, 102, 104. Knife handles
100, 113. *Suksi* and long stick of the skater
106. Knife in sheath
103. Mounting of a kata (Lapp tent)
105. Fragment of a crook in form of spade
107. Female belt with sewing equipment completed by 110, 111, 120
108, 123. Small ladles
109. Woman of Luka
112. Winter sled
114. Ear pick
115. Male belt
116. Pipe of glazed earth
117. Sled driver's stick
118. Daughter of Swedish Lapp
119. Winter boots
121. Soup ladle
122. Lapp of Lulea
124. Pocketbook
125. Summer boots
126. Gold ring

This *Illustrated London News* drawing of 1877 shows a winter tent being taken down by Lapp women. Some of these *kata* are equipped with doors, such as the one above. Sledges, reindeer dogs, and reindeer are seen in foreground.

beam connecting the parabolic frames, and the baby crib, when there is a baby, is also suspended from tent supports above. Reindeer skins are unrolled for beds — one side of the fire is for the family, the other for guests. Like the inhabitants of the tipi and the yurt, the side of the fire opposite the door is considered sacred. In the Lapp tent food is also stored in that place.

A few of the winter tents are fitted with raised benches and storm sheds (like the Eskimos' winter dwelling). Also, some tents contain separate boxlike sleeping shelters within the main tent, each shelter being used for several occupants. Like the Eskimo summer tent, the design and interior furnishings of the Lapp dwelling vary throughout Lapland.

During a reindeer migration, when the Mountain Lapp is on the move, every adult member of the family carries part of the tent. The tent poles are dragged by reindeer. These poles are drilled with small holes near the larger end and are then laced to a wide leather strap attached to the cinch and pack saddle. Then poles are fastened one above the other, letting the small ends drag on the ground. This method was also used by some American Indian tribes when they were on the move. The remainder of the Lapp household is loaded into sleds, which are pulled by reindeer.

THE BLACK TENT

The black tent is the primary shelter for nomadic tribes of the entire coast of North Africa, the Middle East, and Asia (even to the eastern borders of Tibet). It is so named for the darkness of the pure natural goat hair used in its fabric even though it is not always black. When the goat hair is blended with sheep and camel wool and plant fibers it is often dyed other colors as well. However, some amount of goat hair is always used for strength because the other materials are shorter, weaker, and stretch too much.

Although this tent is primarily suited to hot dry climates, it has migrated from its biblical Mesopotamian origins to a wide range of environments. Mountain peoples have raised the pitch of its roof steeply to shed rain and have closed off the sides to insulate the interior. On the other hand, nomads of the hot deserts have flattened and lowered their roofs and have opened up the sides to provide ventilation. The dark color is surprisingly functional for residents of both temperature and moisture extremes. Although the dark hue absorbs heat, the loose weave both allows hot air to escape and also insulates with air pockets. It shields the interior from both heat and cold like a wool blanket. The black tent is actually cooler than light-colored canvas tents which reflect sunlight. The wet fabric swells to close the holes and lanolin of the hair repels rain, but it will leak in extended storms. However, the nomads using this structure rarely live in extremely wet areas. If this tent does become totally soaked its weight increases so much that it cannot be transported easily by pack animals. Moreover, because the loose weave lets winds blow through the fabric, the tents' owners must erect wind barriers made of brush, mats, or other environmental materials, and also choose sheltered sites in winter.

The black tent is one of the earliest examples of modular architecture. It is composed of rectangular fabric panels that can be multiplied to increase the tent size. Each year new sections are added at the middle, so that by the time a panel is worn out (in five or six years) it has reached the outer edges and can be removed. The women spin and weave the material for the panels, which are often sewn together by the whole family.

The black tent is also an efficient tension structure that requires very little wood framing. This is because the heavy weight of the woven fabric and all stresses are concentrated on a few vertical compression points on the poles. This is the opposite of the freestanding frame structures of the tipi and yurt where the cover and frame are totally independent.

The two major styles of construction follow the differences in geography and climate. These two basic types — the Eastern (or Persian) and Western (or Arab) — are both made from the series of joined rectangular panels with sewn loops at their margins for attachment to the stays. However, the historically earlier Eastern tent found in Iran, Afghanistan, and Tibet places the main rope pressures in the same direction as the seams (so that the panels don't pull apart) with the poles under the seams. The Western tent found in Arabia, Iraq, Syria, and west of this area adds strips across the line of joined rectangles so that the stresses are across the seams, and the pressures of these tension bands, poles, and rope stays are independent of the tent fabric itself. The development of the tension band system was an adaptive response to the attempt to reinforce the tent fabric against the high desert winds. The Bedouin of Arabia, the Sinai, Jordan, Syria, Israel, and Iraq have refined this later design to its height of development for desert use.

Bedouin Black Tents

And the night shall be filled with music,
And the cares that infest the day,
Shall fold their tents, like the Arabs,
And as silently steal away.
— Henry Wadsworth Longfellow, from ''A Psalm of Life''

In Arabic Bedouin means desert dwellers. The Bedouin people are the nomadic tribes of Arabia, Syria, Jordan, Iraq, and North Africa. The Bedouin represent about one tenth of the population of the Middle East, but inhabit or utilize almost nine tenths of its land area. They are of the same Semitic stock as their sedentary neighbors and, with them, share a devout belief in Islam, but they are distrustful of any but their own local traditions and way of life. The Bedouin are full-time tent dwellers and must move constantly from place to place over the bare and empty desert to find what little grass there is to feed their sheep, goats, and camels. When the sparse grass is gone, or when the people hear that rain has fallen elsewhere, they pack up their black tents and travel on.

The tribe is a community of equals headed by a sheik to whom all members of the tribe are related by blood or through marriage. Large tribes are divided into clans, and clans into sections, and each section is composed of a group of families. Each clan, section, and family has its own chief. The land is divided into recognized tribal orbits within which these family groups travel. These territories may cover hundreds of miles and only when there is a drought and no grass or food available can these boundaries be crossed, and then only with permission of the tribes who inhabit the area.

Occupationally they are roughly divided into three classes: camel herders, sheepherders, and goat herders. The camel herders are the first in prestige and historical importance.

The food supply of the Bedouin includes dates, coffee, flour, and sometimes dried fish and spices. Occasionally plagues of locusts descend and the Bedouin fills bags with them for consumption during periods of famine. Goats and sheep supply them meat and wool, and goats and camel provide them with milk and cheese. Bread is made from millet or wheat and fried or roasted, not baked. Wild game like gazelle is always shot and eaten.

The nomadic way of life of the Bedouin has evolved over thousands of years to sustain existence in the harsh desert environment.

The black tents of the Bedouin are made from goat hair spun into thread and woven into long pieces of cloth. The tent is primarily a sunshade, a roof rectangle supported by poles and offering protection from blazing temperatures that average 120 degrees Fahrenheit. But, when required, it must serve as a protective shield against up to one-hundred-mile-per-hour winds mixed with sand. Sometimes during the summer the three front posts are not used, and the tent is supported only by the middle and hind poles, thereby providing more protection from the intense sun and heat outside.

The average Bedouin tent is eight or ten yards long and half as wide, but there is an extreme variation in size, depending, of course, on the wealth and rank of the occupant. The smallest tents are supported by nine poles altogether — a high row running lengthwise down the center with shorter rows at each side. The height of the taller poles, which creates a slope in the roof to shed water and facilitates entering, is seven to ten feet, but the height of the tent at its sides seldom exceeds five feet. The ropes extend outward from both sides and from the center of each end.

To pitch the Bedouin tent, first it is spread out on the ground, guy lines are drawn, tent pegs are driven home with wooden mallets, and the long tent poles are properly spaced and inserted under the roof strip. Then, by lifting and pushing, up goes the structure; first one pole in place, then the next, and so on until the whole goat-hair structure rests securely on its supports.

Detachable goat-hair curtains form the sides and ends of the tent. They are fastened to the tent with wooden pins and secured in the ground

A Bedouin nomad with his camel photographed at Rabach village in Israeli-occupied Sinai, Egypt, April 1973. (Courtesy United Nations/Nagata)

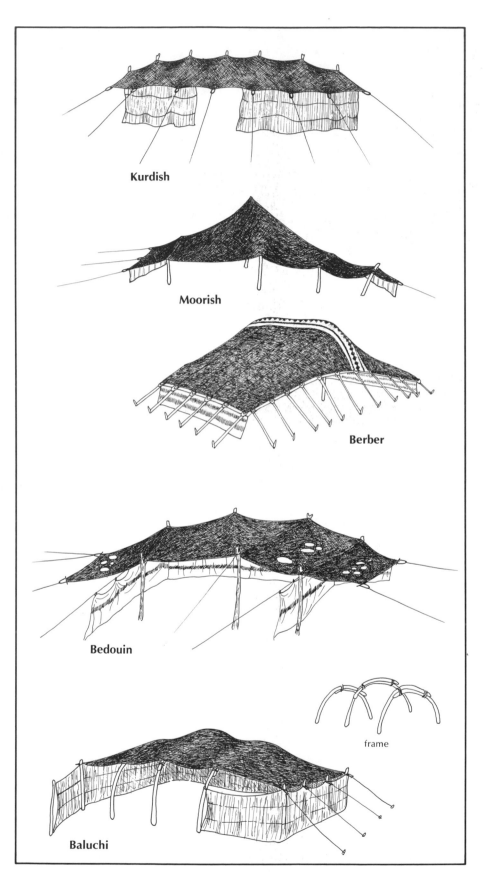

Kurdish

Moorish

Berber

Bedouin

frame

Baluchi

Black desert tents

A Bedouin tent set up on the desert near ▶
the town of Hofuf in eastern Saudi Arabia.
(Courtesy Arabian American Oil Company)

Bedouin encampment in the desert of Wadi ▶
Rum, Jordan. This is a small encampment
compared to those of the past, when encampments of hundreds of thousands of
tents were annual occurrences for the Bedouin. (From the film *Lawrence of Arabia*,
courtesy of Cinemabilia)

Though not frequently built anymore, when the Bedouin were in an area where reeds were available and they planned to stay awhile, the women would put together a structure resembling the wickiup of the American Indian. These four photographs illustrate its construction: 1) Suitable papyrus reeds are gathered; and 2) woven into mats on an ingeniously constructed loom; 3) A framework is then built by placing limbs in the ground opposite each other, then tying the tops together; and 4) the mats are fastened to the framework. This hut does fall into the tent category as it is constructed from woven material stretched over a framework. (Photos Library of Congress)

Sultan El-Atrash and retinue — taken in men's side of a Bedouin tent at Wadi Sirhan Desert between Jordan and Saudi Arabia. The coffee hearth is seen in the foreground, also note hunting falcon at lower right. This photograph dates to the early 1900s when the Bedouin nomad was still at large on the Arabian desert. Now their numbers have diminished due to local government interference. (Library of Congress)

This Bedouin sheik has been given land and ▶ a house in a settlement area being developed by the World Food Programme (sponsored by the United Nations and the Food and Agricultural Organization). However, he prefers a tent, which at the moment he shares with his sons. His wife lives in the house. As the Arab world moves toward becoming a modern industrial society, many of the Bedouin are leaving their tents. Note how tent roof has been repaired. (United Nations/Rice/RE)

Street scene in Cairo. The traveling litter is called a *bethab* and is the riding tent of a wealthy tribesman. The interiors of the *bethab* are adorned with costly silk and cashmere; the seats and backs are lined with rugs and padded with soft cushions. Truly a luxurious way to travel. (Photo courtesy of Trans World Airlines, Inc.)

This tentlike contrivance is a *howdah* and is used to carry the nomads from campsite to campsite. In some Bedouin wedding processions, the bride is brought forth concealed in a covered *howdah*. (Library of Congress)

with iron pegs driven through rope loops. The tent is pitched with its back to the prevailing winds and storms. The shape of this tent has been likened to that of the hull of a ship turned upside-down — an interesting comparison as a ship's hull is so formed to displace water and the Bedouin tent is aerodynamically designed to resist sandstorm winds of up to 100 miles per hour. Sometimes bushes are buried and the guy ropes of the tents are attached to them if the Bedouin doesn't think the tent stakes will hold.

A curtain woven in elaborate geometric patterns is secured along the center pole in order to divide the tent into the women's and men's quarters, called, respectively, the *harem-lik* and the *salaam-lik*. Cooking utensils, supplies, children, animals, bedding, and clothing are stored in the *harem-lik* and the fire pit for cooking is also here. Guns, spears, camel saddles, cushions, and rugs are kept in the *salaam-lik*. This section also contains a coffee hearth and it is here that male visitors are received and an elaborate ritual of coffee serving takes place.

Some of the Bedouin tents are quite large and luxurious and are up to 120 feet long. These tents are referred to by the additional number of central, or *wasit*, poles used to prop them up. A four-, six-, or ten-*wasit* tent means the same to the Bedouin as a four-, six-, or ten-room house does to us. The male sections can be quite luxurious, with Persian carpets and a profusion of cushions propped against beautifully inlaid and decorated camel saddles. And exquisitely woven dividing curtains separate the quarters. The women's section will also be divided since the desert chieftains occupying large tents will usually have more than one wife, and these wives with their families occupy separate quarters.

It can take over a dozen camels just to transport the tent. One camel alone carries the ropes, another the iron pegs used to anchor the main guy ropes, and so on. It is the women who make, pitch, and strike these tents.

When a section of a Bedouin tent becomes worn, the woman rips out that portion and replaces it with new cloth. Goat clippings are always saved and used to weave new material to mend the tent. The old piece that comes out of the tent roof can then be used to replace part of a side curtain. After a Bedouin tent is made — and this is only when a youth with his wife or wives leaves his parents' home and sets up housekeeping on his own — it is neither old nor new, since it is constantly being patched.

Transport of Bedouin tent

The fate of the Bedouin is uncertain. As the Arab world moves toward becoming a modern industrial society, many of the proud desert wanderers are being absorbed into a different way of life. Trucks now travel the old caravan routes and oil pipelines crisscross the desert. Also, since the First World War, the establishment of countries and borders has subjected the nomads to control by the governments of countries in which their wandering areas lie.

Already in areas like southern Jordan, 30,000 of the 70,000 Bedouin have accepted the homes and settled agricultural life the government has offered them — many times pitching their tents next to the houses. And most of the Bedouin are staying; they have no alternative.

Moroccan Berber Black Tents

The seminomadic Berbers herd sheep and till agricultural areas of the North African coast along the Mediterranean and Atlantic coasts from Libya to Morocco. Sedentary Berbers using the black tent move up into the Atlas Mountains every spring and summer. Since this area has considerable rainfall they waterproof their tent canopies with pitch. They also make black tents for ceremonial events.

At the *Moussem* celebration the people trade, sing, dance, ride horses, shoot off their old muzzle-loaders, pay homage to Moslem leaders, and worship. Above, riders with their rifles. (Moroccan National Tourist Office)

Musicians in front of festival tent. (Moroccan Embassy)

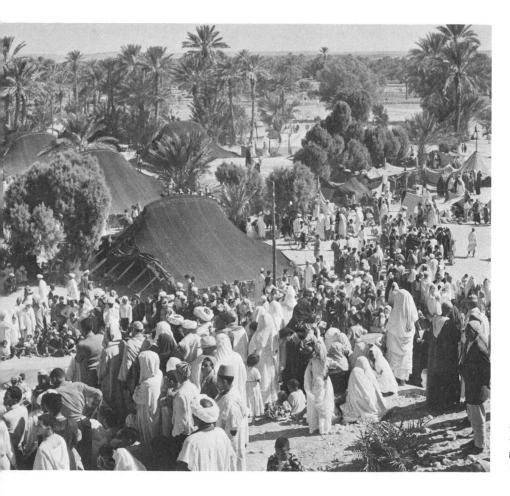

These tents are set up near Marrakech, Morocco, for a *Moussem,* a local religious celebration at which the people of a tribe or the tribes in a region congregate to observe religious holidays. (Moroccan National Tourist Office)

City-dwellers in Morocco own tents which ▶ they bring by car to camp grounds where *folklorique* get-togethers take place. (Moroccan National Tourist Office)

The decorations on these tents are a simplified and repeated Moorish order design, and the tent liners that they fasten to the interior walls usually have the same design but are more colorful — typically red and green. (Photo by Jim Thompson)

Moroccan festival tent, on the plain north of Marrakech. (Photo by Jim Thompson)

This version of the black tent, called the *alaarba* tent, is a Western type with the tension band system adapted from the Bedouins who invaded their lands. Three subsidiary bands and one large central strip called the *triga* are used in building these tents. Berbers stretch their fabric over a curved center ridgepole which is supported by two nearly vertical upright poles. The *triga*, which holds these framing elements in place, molds the distinctive, high curving ridgeline profile of these tents. The undersides of the poles, which are exposed to the interior, are carved and painted with geometric designs and hung with protective religious charms.

Women weave the rectangular panels (four or five feet wide) on upright rug looms and then dye them in a mixture of pomegranate skins and copper sulfate to blacken the material. Here the men sew the sections together, but the women always erect the tent, which is never pitched in the same location twice. Finally the wall panels are pinned to the roof edges with iron pins. In winter, reed or rush mats and stone, brush, wood, or sack walls are added outside for insulation and as wind breakers. The tent is renewed each October with new sections added at the middle.

Annually in the Souss area of southern Morocco in Goulimine a large religious festival gathers all the nomads of the area. There are horse and camel races, a "Guedra" dance under the tent, the sacrifice of a she-camel for the saint, and the trade of commodities varying from wheat to rare or unique products brought from distant lands.

This occasion provides the nomads, normally scattered by the conditions of the environment in which they live, to become reunited. This picture shows the encampment, looking down a row of tent posteriors on left and open fronts at right. These striped tents are prevalent in the southern part of Morocco and variations of this desert tent are used from Tibet to the African Atlantic. (Courtesy Moroccan National Tourist Office)

The Berbers arrange their tents in a sacred *douar* circle made up of between fourteen and twenty family units around a mosque tent in the middle which is called the "center pole." This central structure is used as both a religious school and traveler's sanctuary. They also arrange brush between each outer tent to form a nighttime corral for their animals.

Moor Black Tents

The Moors, ancient distant relatives of the Berbers, intermarried with the Spanish and later with the Arabs after they were expelled from Spain. They settled in the coastal towns and plains of Morocco occupied by Arabs while the Berbers lived in the mountainous parts of that country.

The Moor black tent is different from all other North African black tents, not only by its omission of the Western tension band system, but also because it is supported by two crossed vertical center poles set into a short ridgepiece. It is smaller than most other black tent designs and has little height, except under the peak which is supported by the center poles, to provide resistance to the desert winds.

Their woven panels are also very narrow in width — sixteen inches wide for the roof sections and eight inches wide for sections reinforcing the front and back edges. Distinctive seam stitching is done in light-colored yarn which contrasts with the dark goat-hair fabric. Since new panels are periodically added to the middle, the exterior shows graded shades of color from the darkest brown to blonde. Wooden stay fasteners are sewn to the narrow edges hemmed around rope and iron pins attach the side wall panels, which are then weighted with stones on the ground.

The Moors often cover their interior walls with an inner lining of white cotton for warmth and illumination. Cotton sheets also serve as room dividers for areas designated for couples or single women. Their furnishings consist of decorated leather pillows, floor mats of grass covered with rugs, and lashed shelves to store blankets and belongings. The Moors adopt the Arab tradition by arranging their individual tents in a line about forty feet apart instead of in a circle as the Berbers do.

Iranian Nomadic Black Tents

The Iranian nomadic black tent has been progressively disappearing. The government of Mohammad Reza Shah Pahlavi tried to systematically destroy the nomadic cultures. Use of the black tent by the Lurs, the Basseri, the Bakhtiari, and Qashqai nomads was outlawed in the 1930s as an attempt to eliminate these independent tribes. The Kurds in the Zagros Mountains of Iran survived most successfully in their mountain strongholds. Although the shah's government was forced to revoke the antimigration law because of the mass starvation of people and flocks, it still tried to force nomads to join permanent settlements. Many of the people live in stone houses in the winter and migrate to the higher mountain pastures in the spring and summer with their tents. However, now they are sending their flocks to the pastures with only a few herders

Interior of the men's section of a Moroccan tent. (Photo by Jim Thompson in desert east of El Aaiún, Spanish Sahara.)

Lurs tent in the vicinity of Khorram-abad, Iran. The framework of this tent consists of three T-topped poles (forked poles with crosspieces). These account for the wavy shape of the roof. Woven matting is placed around the tent on three sides to act as a wind break and provide privacy. (Musée de l'Homme, Photothèque, Paris)

who sleep outside under shelters of poles and branches instead of black tents.

Iranian black tents (and their ropes), made of pure goat's hair, are constructed in two parts. This allows the weight to be distributed to two pack donkeys when traveling. Each half is joined to the other by sewn loops and corresponding toggles on the matching hem edges, which are reinforced with a band. Supporting guy ropes then tie to the large loops attached to the ends of the band in a fan-shaped pattern to distribute the stress. Straight or T-shaped center poles under the center seam and short straight poles along the outer edges support the fabric.

Although the principal tent structure is similar among the various tribes, the tents look different because the types of center poles vary between the straight and T-topped types. Moreover, only certain parts of the tents are erected at different times of the year. Single side walls may be set up as a windbreak while traveling, a roofless box during the summer, and the complete form with the steep roof in cold weather. The Lur, Bakhtiari, and Qashqai have wavy roof lines because of their T-shaped center poles and the Kurds have a peaked silhouette due to their straight center support.

Kurd Black Tents

The Kurd black tent differs from that of the other Iranian nomads by its multiple peaked silhouette. The many straight center poles extend right through the tent ridges. Like those tents of the other tribes, large Kurd tents are also made in two halves that join together with a rope loop and toggle system sewn into the edge hems. After the halves are joined the

October 1965. Milder climatic conditions enable this Iranian nomadic tribe to build higher tents, though the form follows the basic black desert tent. Forked poles are used (see tent on left) to anchor the tent top. The guy ropes fasten to one side of the fork, the tent to the other. The sides also are resting on ropes fastened to these poles, providing more room within the tent. (United Nations/PS/PAS)

Kurds pin cloth over the gap between the sections and down the sides. Reed mats are set against the exterior perimeter as exterior walls and again inside to divide the men's and women's quarters.

The Kurds are traditionally nomads, dating back to before 2000 B.C., and Kurdistan is their unrecognized state (despite the many attempts by the Kurds to be acknowledged). Kurdistan is divided among the mountain areas of Persia, Iraq, Turkey, and the U.S.S.R., with a population of approximately 1 million. The Kurds have resisted tribal destruction by these governments more successfully than many other nomads. Iran has supported Kurdish uprisings against Iraq, and vice versa. Now each government has focused its attention on the Kurds within their boundaries and are trying to settle them in villages. A sedentary population is easier to control than a nomadic one. Many Kurds are seminomadic, living in villages during the winter where they plant crops and in summer moving out into the mountain valleys with their tents and flocks.

Kurdistan, Iraq, 1958. Kurdish women have more freedom than the neighboring Arab women. They go unveiled, speak freely to strangers, and participate in the activities of the tribe, even to the point of becoming tribal chiefs on the death of their husbands and serving on electoral boards. (Photo United Nations/vb/jf)

NOMADS IN AFGHANISTAN

Afghanistan is one of the few (if not the only) countries in the world in which the number of nomads is not decreasing. By some international standards this makes Afghanistan one of the least developed countries of the world. By others it makes Afghanistan one of the most romantic and colorful countries of the world. More than 2 million Afghani nomads wander from the mountains in the center of the country to the lowlands along the borders, and then back again, always searching for grass for

Nomads on the road between Kandahar and Kabul, Afghanistan, 1970. (Photo United Nations/B. Legelle/NJ)

their sheep and goats. These nomads exist outside the structure of society and travel with impunity across the borders of Afghanistan into Pakistan, Iran, or the Soviet Union, and, of course, they pay no taxes to any of these governments.

Like their counterparts in Arabia, the Afghani live in tents made of goat hair that are supported by nine poles. But in the case of the Afghan tent, the rope supports, which run from the tops of the outside poles to wooden tent stakes in the ground, are inside the tent walls and spread them outward, therefore providing more room inside the tent. The sides are either anchored with rocks and branches or staked. The floors are covered with hand-woven carpets.

The nomad caravans that abound in Afghanistan are an embarrassment to the government, which feels that the nomadic existence of the nomads deprives them of the social and health services that are slowly spreading throughout Afghanistan. Most of the nomads cannot read, the infant mortality rate is a high 190 per thousand, and in some regions there is almost twice as much tuberculosis among the nomads as in the settled population.

Traveling some 100 to 200 miles per year, the nomads provide remote villagers with meat, butter, cheese, and yoghurt in exchange for vegetables, fruit, and nuts. They are also a source of information and news to villagers who are cut off from the outside world. It is also believed that many of the nomads carry opium, which is produced in abundance in eastern Afghanistan.

For the most part things have not changed for these people since Alexander the Great passed through Afghanistan over two thousand years ago. The nomads encamp in the lowlands until spring comes and their sheep have given birth, then they head back into the mountains. The camel is the beast of burden and the women still do most of the work, including tending the animals and setting up and taking down camp. The men do whatever fighting is necessary and for the most part sit around and talk more than work. Traditions of fighting and revenge are strong, having come down through the centuries in legends and poems. An example is this verse in Pashto, the Afghan language:

> My beloved returned unsuccessful from battle.
> I regret the kiss I gave him last night.

But hospitality also prevails and guests are almost always welcomed and regaled with trays of almonds and raisins and cup after cup of sweet, milky tea. This, of course, breaks the monotony of camp life for the nomads and gives the traveler food and shelter.

There are many similarities between the Bedouin and the Afghan nomad. To the existence of the former, technology is a threat. But the Afghan nomad is threatened neither by technology nor the government. Actually the government of Afghanistan has very little control over its nomads and it appears that there will be little change among them for decades to come.

Nomads near their tents at a Koochi camp near Kandahar, Afghanistan. The Afghani nomads trade with inhabitants of remote villages and raise sheep, which they bring from the mountains to the lowlands as winter approaches. Their tents are the black goat-hair tents of the Arabian and north Arabian desert. Note brush shelter to the left. (United Nations/H. K. Lall/NJ)

Hide tents of drought victims in the village of Bume in southern Ethiopia. These former nomads no longer have animals or pastures. Over 1.6 million people in south and southeast Ethiopia have been affected by the drought. Other parts of Africa have been equally hard hit. Annual rains have not fallen for over six years now — 90 percent of the animals have died, there are no crops, people are starving. Emergency assistance provided by various governments and U.N. agencies is being channeled into the affected areas by the United Nations Disaster Relief Coordinator. But it's still not enough. (Photo United Nations/Jerry Frank.)

Afghan nomad camp in the Hindu Kush Mountains, 1973. As can be seen above, level terrain is not necessary for these structures. When they are dismantled, the mats are rolled up and the poles tied into bundles to facilitate moving, though this does not occur frequently. (Photo United Nations/Siceloff/PAS)

MAT AND SKIN TENTS

Mat and skin tents made of light freestanding stick frames covered with skin, bark, or mats are used by hunting and gathering cultures throughout the world. The advantage of this tent is that its lightweight cover can be rolled up for easy transportation. The frame is only taken along when wood for a new one is scarce. Its disadvantage is that the mat or skin coverings are weak and cannot be stretched strenuously. This fact necessitates a complex frame system to support the cover.

There are four basic frame systems: the dome, barrel vault, box, and box with barrel vault. The dome, which is the oldest and most common variety, is constructed by bending light poles into arches across each other and lashing them together. If the arched sticks are set parallel in a line instead of crossing each other in a circle, they form a barrel vault. The rectangular box frame made from straight lashed pieces is often combined with a barrel vault roof so that it sheds rain more efficiently than a flat top.

These original hutlike tents were the predominant shelter throughout the whole Middle East until they were replaced by the black tent. Only a few groups continue to use them even though the mats have been kept for yurt and black tent side walls in a small area bounded by the western Sahara, Baluchistan, and northern Kenya. Some tribes, such as the Tuareg and Baluchi use both types. Mat covered huts are still used as local cheap housing in South America, Africa, and Asia for non-nomadic peoples such as the Marsh Arabs of southern Iraq, the *barridas* squatter towns of Latin America, and Bangladesh.

Northeastern Madagascar, Bezanozano — tent/hut of bent branches, straw, and mats. This dwelling always faces west and is highly symbolic, as are many nomadic tents. The interior walls of the Bezanozano house are associated with the twelve zodiacal signs and therefore with the months. The structure is supported at the center by a center pole which is equated to the center of cosmic space. (Musée de l'Homme, Photothèque, Paris)

Nomadic mat tent dwellers are the original north African native Hamites, descendants of Noah's son Ham. The two major Hamitic groups are the northern mountain Berber Hamites, who adopted the black tent, and the western Sahara Tuareg and southern Sahara Teda desert dwellers who use the mat and skin types. The latter are offspring of ancestral Berbers who were forced into the desert by the Arab invasion of northern Africa in the eleventh century.

The Tuareg culture is divided into a feudal system of noble, priest, vassal, serf, and slave classes. The Tuareg is the only tribe of the Sahara in which the men are traditionally veiled. These herder nobles used to be the ancient pirates and robbers of desert caravans — cowboylike nobles who did no work but were the only owners of camels (the source of their power). Whole tribes were serfs to the nobles by inheritance even though they could not be sold or freed like slaves. The slave class, descendants of war prisoners, are now legally free but still work for their owners since they can get no other employment.

The Tuareg and Teda women, who are superb leather crafters, make the skin tent panels in addition to all other leather accessories and furniture. In contrast to the Arabs these women own their dowry and property (that is, the tent and all its furnishings) and retain them upon divorce. (And the women can dissolve their marriages at will.)

Now that many men work in the oil fields and uranium mines and the flocks have been decimated by droughts the number of tents has been decreasing. However, the Tuaregs and other nomadic and seminomadic tribes still make both types — the mat and the skin.

Seminomads who move only a few times a year use the mat type. The mat panels are made of strips of plaited palm leaves sewn into larger oval sections for the roof; the wall modules are of grass and straw interwoven with leather strips. Wall mats are sometimes positioned underneath the plaited palm roof sections for better resistance to rain.

The frame structure was originally meant to be stationary because it is too heavy for easy portability. Therefore only the mats are taken during migration. The frame is made of long acacia roots. Acacia is a type of ornamental plant that has some varieties that produce gum arabic and others that produce catechu, which is used in dyeing, tanning, and medicine. They curve the arches by heating these roots over a fire, bending them, and tying them down with ropes until the arch is dry and holds its curved shape. Then final cutting and trimming is done. Pairs of curved roots are lashed together into one long piece to make a single arch.

To set up the frame the Tuareg set three arches into the ground in a line. At the ends of this they set boxlike frames made of vertical poles with lashed crosspieces. Finally thinner branches are intertwined through the arch loops and tied to the ends. At last the mats or skins are tied on.

True Tuareg nomads who travel almost every other week prefer skins over their frames. The sun-bleached skins become sand colored and blend into the desert landscape. Although goatskin is preferred for its strength, sheepskin may also be used. Cattle herders are often forced to use cowskin but this shrinks and hardens when wet and also requires tanning and waterproofing with butter. When cowskin is used it is often

Eritrea, Ethiopia — Samhar region nomads. In Africa, where the mat and the black desert tent coexist, a logical development is the black desert tent made of woven mats instead of goat-hair fabric. This tent resembles the Berber tent with its keel-shaped design. (Musée de l'Homme, Phototèque, Paris)

Gabès, Tunisia. Another variation of the desert tent, this one striped and humped. The white stripes mark the locations of supporting ropes sewn into the tent fabric. Short lengths of wood are tied to each pair of the ropes and these in turn are fastened to tent stakes with more rope. Stitching can also be seen running horizontally to the stripes where tension bands are sewn into the tent roof for front and rear support of the tent. (Musée de l'Homme, Phototèque, Paris)

Al Kharj, Saudi Arabia. Type of temporary housing in which an employee of Al Kharj experimental farm lives. The walls are made of stone and branches and the roof is a tent, which could possibly be the tent the worker and his family resided in as nomads. A canvas tent is pitched to far right. (Standard Oil Company)

Women from a nomadic tribe of sheep-herders outside Baghdad, Iraq, November 1965. These people have been resettled in a tent city by the Ministry of Agriculture, with the support of the United Nations, in an attempt to develop small-scale agriculture and animal husbandry. These people, like so many other nomads, have given up their black desert tents for regulation army tents (with and without windows) or small houses, also provided by the government. (Photo United Nations/PB/PAS)

Yuruks, near Lycia, Turkey, August 1977. The Yuruks or seminomadic sheepherders of Yugoslavia and Turkey are a homogeneous tribe of people who preserve in a very pure form the language, economy, and customs, and probably also the physical type, of the old Turks who emigrated from central Asia. Sedentary during the winter months, growing crops and making rugs, these Yuruks travel in the summer months, sell their wares, and graze their goat and sheep herds. (Photograph by Grace van Hulsteyn)

Left: A view of the women's wing of a desert tent, with the Pyramids of Giza in the background, early 1900s. The women's section is the area for cooking utensils, supplies, children, animals. Cooking, weaving, and general housework are performed here. (Library of Congress)

Right: Tuareg mat tent — near Timbuktu, Mali. (Photo by Carleton Howe)

Tuareg mat and skin tents with frame variations

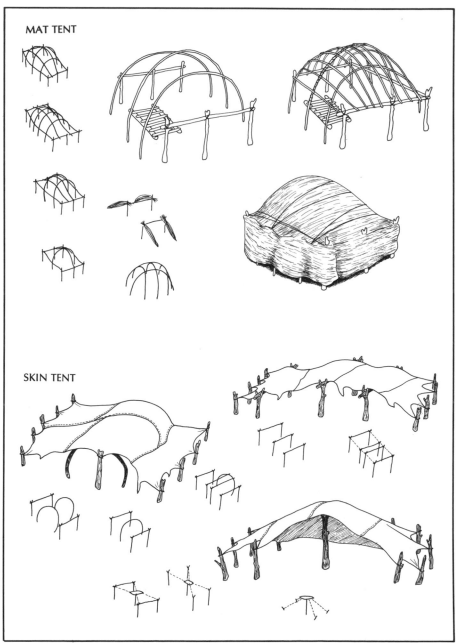

MAT TENT

SKIN TENT

colored reddish yellow with a mixture of red ochre and camel dung.

After roof skins are cut into rectangular panels and sewn together, the Tuaregs add a fringed edge strip along the seams, which dangles into the tent interior. This is considered very attractive. Outer edges of the roof skins are left in their natural irregular shapes so that the extensions (from the animal limbs) can be tied to the outer poles. An average-sized goatskin tent will have thirty-five to forty pelts; a large one averages around 150 of them. The Tuaregs heavily decorate the interior surfaces of these skins with colored leather and fringes that move with the breezes. Woven wall mats, wood carving on the beds, and leather cushions all display colorful patterns.

Other variations of mat and skin tents extend through African areas and tribes such as the Fezzan of Libya, the Eritrea of Ethiopia, the Rendille of Kenya, the Kel Geres of the Sudan, and the Ad Sek, the Danakil or Afar, the Somali, and the Beja of Somaliland. The choice of mat or skin is determined by weather, scarcity of materials, and also preference for decoration. Even though the skins are insufferably warm in the hot season they are sometimes favored because of their decorative beauty. Though the skins are heavier, need more side support poles, and are hot in the summer, mat tents leak and absorb water so that they have to be dismantled and dried out after each storm. Sometimes the more quickly assembled lighter mat tents are covered with skins during the rainy season so that hybrid variations of the two types are created.

YURTS

The yurt is among the most ingenious, waterproof, and luxurious of the many types of portable dwellings conceived by nomadic tribes, and it has provided shelter for the wandering Mongolian, his family, and his animals for thousands of years. These shelters, based on a very light wooden frame, are solid and strong and provide comfort and warmth in some of the highest and bleakest parts of the world — the Siberian steppe.

Genghis Khan (1162–1227) mobilized the ever-warring Mongol princes into a mighty force and by 1260 his sons ruled a far-flung Eurasian empire, composed of eastern Europe and most of Asia, which was divided into four khanates: one comprised all of China and most of east Asia and was later ruled by Kublai Khan; another in Turkistan; one in Persia; and the Golden Horde in Russia, founded by the Batu Khan. It was the gorgeous tents of the Batu Khan that caused his successors to be known as the Golden Horde. This khanate included large elements of Turkic peoples who came to be known collectively as Tatar.

The Tatars decorated their yurts with brightly dyed goat hair which would be pressed into the felt covering to produce intricate designs. They also installed their larger yurts on wagons. Rubruquis (c. 1215–1270), the Franciscan friar who was one of the chief medieval travelers and travel writers, measured between the wheel tracks of one and found the

The Mongol yurt has covered more of the world than any other nomadic tent. (From Henry Yule: *The Book of Ser Marco Polo*)

Interior of a Tatar yurt. The disposition of furnishings within the yurt is regulated by strict ritual and hierarchical order. Drapes over the marital bed form a tent within the tent and provide further insulation against the outside cold. A cradle is strapped to the side of the tent at left. Carved chests contained the family's possessions, samovar held tea, scimitar hangs from roof support at right. (From C. Rechberg, *Des Peuples de la Russie*)

These two photographs show stages in construction of the yurt. The sides are a lattice-work made of willow. The sections fold flat for good portability and the number used may vary, allowing the size of the yurt to change according to the need of the day. Note reed matting (above) and compression band encircling the yurt. A door frame has been lashed into the wooden wall (below) to carry a stout wooden door and the compression band has been lashed to this frame. (Library of Congress)

This photograph, taken before the turn of the century in Russia, shows a Mongol family inside their yurt. Piled behind them are decorated boxes, roped to facilitate being carried by camel and containing household utensils and carved wooden boxes in which the family valuables are kept. Folded rags and bedding sit atop the boxes and roof support poles are visible at top. (Library of Congress)

distance to be twenty feet. The axle was like a ship's mast and twenty-two oxen were yoked to the wagon, eleven abreast. The wagon carried a tent pavilion some thirty feet in diameter, for it projected beyond the wheels at least five feet on either side. It also had latticed windows and the occupants were able to travel within the tent. This practice of carrying yurts on wheels is obsolete now in Mongolia. The huge yurts of the Mongolian noblemen would always be surrounded by smaller yurts, which housed an entourage of wives. And for centuries the yurt was virtually the only dwelling known, apart from Buddhist monasteries, in Mongolia.

Today yurts are still widely used throughout the rich steppe lands of central Asia and in Ulan Bator, the capital of Mongolia. Nearly 50,000 of the quarter of a million inhabitants of Ulan Bator still live in them, though the government is attempting to get the yurt dwellers to move into housing developments. Also, a university recently started in Ulan Bator uses yurts as dormitories.

Actually the words *yurt* and *yurta* are of Russian origin and have become the Westerner's term for the collapsible felt tent of the Mongols. For the Mongolian, the correct term is *ger*, meaning "dwelling." The English word *horde* comes directly from the Mongolian *ordu*, which means a collection of yurts, hence a tribe, so *horde* was applied to Mongol armies.

The Mongols have two types of tents. One is a simple traveling tent that is a ridge-pole tent covered with dark cotton cloth. Their more permanent tent is the yurt. The most practical feature of the yurt is its latticed frame, the sections of which fold flat for easy transporting. This works on the same principle as the child's safety gate. The number of sections used may be varied, allowing the size of the yurt to change according to the needs of the day. Usually, when expanded the sections stand about the height of a man; however, they can reach tremendous proportions. Herbert Vreeland in his *Mongol Community and Kinship Structure* reported in 1927 that a sixteen-section yurt was so large that loaded camels were able to walk through its door and six hundred people were not able to fill it.

To erect a yurt, the sections are expanded and bound together, and a door frame is also tied to them. Then a compression band or rope is drawn around the top part of the wall and door frame. This band encircling the structure at the eaves takes the outward thrust of the roof and therefore supports it. The compression band is that integral component that makes the yurt work. Next, wooden ribs are lashed to the wall lattice and joined to a higher central compression ring or crown. Sometimes there are two pillars holding up the central ring — other times there are none and the roof is self-supporting. On self-supporting crowns, there are two arrangements for connecting the ribs with the crown. One involves having roof pieces tapered at one end with loops at the other. The tapered end fits into a hole in the crown and the other end is looped to the wall pieces. The other configuration works on the principle of the ribs of the umbrella. The roof ribs are hinged to the crown and either branch out to connect with the wall or collapse for transport. In both

A nineteenth-century rendering of a Tatar yurt. Woven mattings of different decorations and color indicated the social position of the yurt owner. Matting is used on the yurts found in Turkestan (a region of central Asia extending from the Caspian Sea to the Gobi Desert and including parts of Russia and China). (*Illustrated London News*, August, 1873)

A carpenter and a nomad talk business. Three compression rings at left lean against lattice framework and a beautifully decorated door is slightly to right. (Library of Congress)

Wealthier Mongolian families had more than just the yurt. Pictured here is a simple traveling tent, set up outside the wall of a town. (Library of Congress)

Yurt Interior — Peoples Republic of Mongolia, 1953. Mongolian worker, his wife and children, at home in their yurt. The brazier of the traditional yurt has been replaced by the new gas stove. Note iron-framed bed, at left, with curtains. Chests with print patterns and suitcases have replaced carved and appliquéd boxes. Mirrors, radios, clock, sewing machines, and photographs of Stalin and other Soviet leaders are now standard items. Urban yurt communities exist throughout Mongolia and the government is trying to move the yurt dwellers into housing developments. (Photo: Eastfoto)

The Council of the Wise, in front of their yurt in the village of Kupre-Bazar, U.S.S.R. Young couples (like the one shown here), department chiefs, and villagers throughout Mongolia can obtain advice from their local councils of the wise. (Photo: Tass from Sovfoto)

Forty-four miles from Frunze, capital of Kirghiz, Southern Russia, 1966. The modern age reaches the Mongolian nomad. These nomads gather around a radio with their morning tea. The two men reclining are brothers whose ancestors had hired herders on a feudal basis. They own about 760 head of sheep each and average about 120 lambs to every 100 ewes. The other man is one of their pensioners. The hats of the brothers distinguish their rank from that of their pensioner. They will all make a winter trek when the weather starts to change. (Novosti from Sovfoto)

cases the number of ribs corresponds to the number in the wall section, plus four to six extra pieces attached to the top of the door frame.

The nomads' herds, for the most part, provide the material for the outer covering of the yurt. Thick felt mats are stretched over the framework and lashed in place or weighted with stones. Occasionally a layer of canvas is used, but only felt can provide the necessary protection from the elements. In severe weather with temperatures of minus 50 and 60 degrees Fahrenheit and 90-mile-per-hour winds as many as eight layers of felt may be required for insulation. Too, the circular shape of the yurt enables it to withstand the high velocity winds and it is easier to heat the inside because there are no corners for heat to get lost in. Dried yak and sheep dung bricks are used as fuel.

Transport of a yurt

The doors to the yurt are distinctly decorated with bright inlaid patterns on front and back. A felt flap is hung over the entrance and put into use when the door is left open during the day, and also serve as insulation in cold weather. Another felt flap is attached atop the yurt and, when weather conditions demand, it can be drawn over the crown. It can also partially cover the opening in order to enable the wind to create a suction to draw the smoke from the yurt.

Again, in the yurt as in other nomadic tents, everything is placed in its traditional position, including the yurt itself, which is always pitched facing south so that the patch of sunlight shining through the smokehole acts as a clock. This plan is firmly established. The household equipment includes cooking utensils, perhaps a samovar, clothing boxes, a storage bin for boots and shoes, and a cowskin in which a variety of milk from yaks, sheep, or horses is stored. Leather bags contain goods like rice, barley, flour, weaving equipment, and extra rugs, mats, or skins. The altar or shrine box above the bags would house lama statues and images as well as a variety of offering trays. In extremely cold weather young or pregnant animals — yaks, calves, and lambs — are brought into the yurt and the body heat generated by them and the Mongol family enables the people to sleep with little or no covering.

Yurt-cleaning is simple — and necessary. The furnishings are moved outside, the felt cover along the vertical wall is removed, and family members take up positions around the wall, pick up, and relocate the yurt to a clean patch of ground.

In summer, the canvas and felt closest to the ground can be rolled up, exposing the latticework and providing ventilation. This is also done with the tipi in hot weather.

The yurt is fraught with religious symbolism, as is the tipi. As the yurt evolved, the Mongol began to recognize a symbolic connection between his dwelling and the universe. The smoke hole became known as the "Sun Gate" and the "Sky Door." Some yurts, though not the ones pictured in this book, have eight braces reinforcing the central compression ring. These are quite similar to the eight-spoked "Wheel of the Law," which is ubiquitous in Buddhist temples. Outside, the piece of heavy cloth drawn over the smoke hole is decorated with a design similar to the ancient Chinese "cloud collar." The flames in the fire pit symbolized the gate to the underworld. Smoke rising from the fire was referred to as the "World Tree" moving from earth to God. Every morning an

Another Turkish yurt, on this one a highly ornate band of cloth is wrapped around two thirds of the circumference and the decorated doors at right identify this tent as the dwelling of a high-ranking personage. The cord draped over the left side is used to pull the felt cover over the smoke hole. (Musée de l'Homme, Phototèque, Paris)

This yurt of the Akcha of Northern Afghanistan has a higher and more conical dome. The shape and coverings of the yurt may vary according to the tribe and region. (Musée de l'Homme, Phototèque, Paris)

offering would be made by pouring tea on the iron grate of the fire pit. The religious man of some tribes would climb a ladder and examine the flow of smoke from the smoke hole in order to obtain omens or messages from above.

An interesting point is that the Mongolian herdsmen were not wood craftsmen and therefore depended on the inhabitants of wooded regions, who were fine carpenters, for the component parts of their yurts. The central compression ring was always a purchased item, and doors and latticework were also available from artisans who earned their living making them.

The yurt could be erected in about a half an hour and dismantled and loaded in about the same amount of time. The parts were then loaded onto one or two camels, with the compression ring being placed horizontally atop one camel load. Having the camel as a beast of burden enabled the Mongols to develop this heavier weight, highly efficient tent.

TIBET

Before Tibet was annexed to the People's Republic of China in 1951, it was known as the land of lamas, and Lahasa, the capital, was the mecca of Lamaism (a form of Mahayana Buddhism). Pilgrims, with their tents, flocked to Lahasa from places as far away as Manchuria, Mongolia, and the U.S.S.R. Now all this has changed; even the Dalai Lama fled to India during a 1959 revolt against the Chinese occupation forces, and tent cities of the pilgrims no longer exist around Lahasa. The main tent dwellers of Tibet are the nomadic herdsmen who compose nearly half of the population.

Tibet itself lies on a high plateau surrounded by the world's highest mountain masses. The lofty Himalayan chain sprawls along the entire southern frontier and blocks off the warm monsoon winds from the Indian Ocean. And Tibet is crossed from east to west by smaller ranges. Even in the eastern portion, which is drained by many of the great rivers of east and southeast Asia (the Yangtze, Mekong, Yellow, to name a few), the valley bottoms are as high as mountain peaks — 10,000 feet and over. Tibet possesses an incredibly harsh, bare, seemingly uninhabitable terrain and is called by its inhabitants "the Region of the Glacier-Snow Mountains." Good soil is seldom found and crops, when planted, are threatened by drought, hail, and sudden frosts. The land sustains a small peasant population. The remainder of the Tibetans who are not lamas are nomadic and pasture their flocks mostly in the uplands at altitudes of more than 14,000 feet, mainly in the wilderness of northwestern Tibet. Other pastoral groups migrate seasonally, spending the winters in the lowlands and grazing their animals on mountain slopes in the summer.

The tents of these nomads resemble the black tents of the Bedouin in size, support system, and shape. But while the Bedouin tent is made of goat hair, the Tibetan tent fabric is woven from only the black hair of yak steers, which has been pulled, not shorn, from their bellies. This makes for a reasonably waterproof fabric that becomes increasingly more so from the smoke and soot of dung fires within the tents.

For the most part, these tents are square in shape and average around thirty square feet and are six to seven feet high in the center. The tent is composed of two sections, with a division in the center running from front to rear. The strips of fabric from which the tent is made also run from front to rear and are anywhere from eight to twelve inches wide. The tent cloth is heavy and each section, with its tent poles, makes a yak load. The tents vary in size due to the fact that they are renewed annually piece by piece, like their Bedouin counterparts. So after a tent has been in use for a year, it is never completely old or completely new. New pieces — one for each side — are sewn on each side of the center division because it is this central division that acts as a smoke hole, and there is a substantial amount of wear and tear over the hearth because a system of loops and toggles (made of horn) forms a two-foot-wide combination skylight and smoke hole. During storms there is a flap that is pulled and fastened over this vent to keep out the rain and snow.

The tent is supported by six poles — two in the center, which are six or seven feet long, and four shorter, one at each of the sides. Eight guy ropes, one at each corner and one midway on each side, keep the tent stretched tautly over the poles. Each of these yak hair ropes (this hair comes from other parts of the yak) is fastened to the tent roof in a three-cord spread, then stretched over the top of an external prop pole, and

These tents of the Tibetan nomads are made from yak hair which is pulled, not shorn, from the bellies of the yak. This tent is supported by six poles (as opposed to the customary nine of the Bedouin) and, unlike the desert tent, has a central vent in the roof. (Photo: Library of Congress)

finally is pegged securely to the ground. In frozen ground iron pegs are necessary, though sometimes boulders serve as anchors. The prop poles may be adjusted in distance and angle to provide any desired pull on the roof of the tent. This enables the tent to be more adaptable to the high winds. The walls also are adjustable — they can hang free or be pegged slightly outward. Of course, there are many variations in the size and shape of these tents throughout Tibet. Some are quite large — constructed from three or four sections. Others are smaller and irregular; however, all are supported with guy ropes and prop poles.

Inside the tent there are two sections. Entering from the front by the center pole, the right side contains the elaborate family altar in the far corner and prized possessions stacked along the side. The Tibetans carry with them yak-hide bags and wooden chests filled with food and with all the normal household items that would be found in any permanent dwelling, including large churns in which tea is mixed with butter to fortify the nomad against the cold. These possessions stacked against the walls also insulate the tent. The open space by the hearth is for the men and guests. The left side is where the women do their work and sit by the fire. That area contains a pile of fuel (yak or sheep dung) in the front corner and kitchen utensils in boxes and bags spread along the back. Butter and cheese making equipment is also kept in this area.

The nomadic Tibetans also have pup tent–like shelters that are used for sleeping on the rim of the encampment or where the herds settle down for the night. Many pastoral families also have smaller tents for travel or picnicking. These are very simple affairs — usually a ridge-pole style, that is conical in shape or a rectangular roofed tent that utilizes the guy rope, external prop suspension system of the black tent.

Less often found among the nomads are ceremonial yurts, or "god houses" for the group. The Tibetans have resisted using the yurt and the black tent is sacred to them; however, it is a status symbol to have a yurt in reserve for use in entertaining high-ranking persons or celebrating special occasions.

The Tibetan wears an oversized large-sleeved felt raincoat that looks like a walking tent and, when riding horseback, this tent covers the rider, all his gear, and half the horse; when seated by the fire it can cover belongings and both food being consumed and half the fire upon which food is being cooked. When the Tibetan beds down, it covers both bed and gear.

The Tibetans make felt from sheep's wool and there is great demand for it. Felt is also made into circular pieces, sometimes as much as ten feet in diameter, and forms a makeshift tent that protects caravan loads, the traveler, and the traveler's gear.

There is a set pattern of placement when the community is on the move and tents are pitched. These patterns can vary from the common "tent circle" or, sometimes, more distance is kept between the tents, in which case the neighborly relationship is retained. As would be expected in a country as rugged as Tibet, the encampments sometimes must conform to the terrain, and tents may be found scattered along valleys or interspersed on level ground on ridges or in ravines.

PART 2

THE TENT AS ART

4 ARCHITECTURE

To accomplish a task with a minimum use of materials is finally the only interesting problem.

— Bernard Lafaille

From their inception, tents and permanent structures have gone their separate and independent ways, both of them reaching incredible heights and extremes. Then a few decades ago, the tent, due to technological developments, began to be considered a feasible alternative to conventional right-angled steel and glass. And now the tent — in the form of air-supported and tension structures — is becoming an integral part of modern architecture.

Before this century, only occasionally did the tent exert its influence on architecture and vice versa. One time-tested example of the tent's incorporation into architecture is the convertible roof or tent top that has provided shade and protection for streets, marketplaces, town squares, courtyards and amphitheaters through the centuries and throughout the world. In ancient Rome the grandest theaters and amphitheaters, among them the Colosseum, had velum tent tops that could be extended and retracted, and, appropriately enough, sailors were in charge of that operation.

From comments in Roman literature, the theater vela were supposedly introduced in 69 B.C. and a fresco in Pompeii dating from 59 B.C. showing a Pompeii amphitheater velum was discovered in a building near the amphitheater in 1869. Little is known of the actual workings of these roofs. They consisted of cables attached to massive beams, and cloth was fastened to the cables with eyelets. Linen was predominantly used, though decadent Rome was, in various theaters, shaded by silk. Some vela were also beautifully decorated — Nero is responsible for two —

The Roman Colosseum under canvas. The vela of the Colosseum above is reminiscent of the roof of the Pantheon (a circular temple constructed in 27 B.C. and still standing in Rome), which has a similarly proportioned round hole in its roof.

Hall of State in the palace of an Egyptian monarch. Again, the fabric roof is applied, this time in the form of pieces of decorated material (probably linen) strung from supporting poles. (From Jacob von Falke's *Art In the House, Historical, Critical, and Aesthetical Studies on the Decoration and Furnishings of the Dwelling*, 1879)

The Agora of Athens in the 1860s. Again a velum, though a ragged one, is in use. Agora is the Ancient Greek term used for marketplace, which was also the popular place of assembly. (From W. F. Ainsworth, *All Round the World*, 1869)

This Pompeian fresco dates from 59 B.C. (ten years after the conception of theater velum) and is the only known pictorial rendering of an ancient theater velum. It shows the Pompeii amphitheater and its velum, which hangs between two towers of the adjacent city wall and partially covers the amphitheater. Note the small fabric structure in the foreground. (Editorial Photocolor Archives)

In 1781, in the midst of civil strife in Sweden, King Gustavus III felt that the Chinese pavilions that composed the palace complex at Haga should be placed under guard and, for guard houses, had erected metal tents fashioned after those used by the Ottoman sultans for large receptions in the sixteenth and seventeenth centuries. Decorated in several colors (one is blue and the other is striped), these guardhouse tents are painted in trompe-l'oeil and decorated with simulated fringes, braid, drapes. The crown of the kings of Sweden is on the roof of the one on the right.

A shopping street in Manama on Bahrain Island, Saudi Arabia. Again, fabric is used to provide protection from the sun. Through the ages fabric has been used to cover outdoor gathering places and transform them into cool and comfortable areas. (Arabian American Oil Company)

and the one in the Pompeii amphitheater was made of sky-blue cloth decorated with stars. The other covered the Pompeii theater in Rome and showed Nero as a deified charioteer against a purple sky with golden stars. These fabric tent tops over buildings reached proportions that remained unequalled until this century.

The vela of ancient Rome covered areas that the existing structural technology was unable to duplicate with rigid materials. And today, even though these areas can be spanned without depending on fabric, cloth remains by far the most practical covering: it can do the job faster and cheaper, and conserves energy as well. The new Pontiac, Michigan, Silverdome stadium's air-supported roof of woven Fiberglas coated with Teflon covers ten acres. The stadium, which seats 80,638, was completed ahead of schedule and did not exceed the budget. Jeddah International Airport near Mecca, Saudi Arabia, which is due to open in 1980, will cover a whopping 105 acres. In the centuries between the Pompeii amphitheater and the Silverdome fabric has been used over everything from Egyptian palaces to streets in Saudi Arabia.

There has been other interaction between tents and buildings. Tents have on occasion been camouflaged to look like buildings: for example, Ptolemy II, king of ancient Egypt from 285 to 246 B.C., had the ceiling of his domical tent painted to look like stone, and, in the Field of the Cloth of Gold in 1520, the walls of one of Richard Gibson's fabulously decorated and designed tents were painted in trompe-l'oeil to resemble brickwork. At the other extreme, there have been buildings constructed to look like tents, for instance, when the Greeks captured the field tent of Xerxes, the king of Persia who invaded Greece in 480 B.C., they were so impressed with it they modeled the theater of Pericles in Athens after it. And metal

Steel tent. Project for the World's Columbian Exposition, Chicago, 1893. Architect: Leroy S. Buffington (1847–1931), drawing by Harvey Ellis (1852–1904). Buffington's architectural business was located in Minneapolis and, in 1885, was the city's largest. He patented a steel skeleton construction technique on which modern skyscraper technology is based, and one of his divergences from that type of architecture was this steel tent. Harvey Ellis, the artist, was with Buffington's firm only two years, during which time he completed this drawing. (Northwest Architectural Archives, University of Minnesota)

tents were built in 1781 at the palace of Haga in Stockholm, Sweden, to resemble the tents used by Turkish sultans for large receptions when the Ottoman Empire was at its height.

More recently tents were pitched indoors, as was fashionable during the Empire period of France (1804–1815). Rooms were also built or decorated to look like tent interiors.

Another interesting and more logical innovation is the tent house, which has enjoyed great popularity in this country. Religious camp communities, state sanitariums, and tourist resorts have used them quite successfully, saving themselves the cost of erecting and maintaining permanent structures and certainly providing more of a sense of adventure for their clientele. Various manufacturers make permanent camping tents designed for platform campsites, and superbly designed tents intended to be used in place of an often-unaffordable summer house are also on the market. As the tent becomes the hottest thing in architectural design for large buildings, it stands to reason that the tent house also has an exciting future.

It is only in this century that the tent has entered the field of architecture and this was, unobtrusively, in the form of air-supported structures designed for military needs. Air-supported structures, of course, are just that — airtight structures supported by slight interior air pressure. Fans or blowers provide the pressure and entrance to and exit from these buildings is usually through an air lock. The air-supported structure is distinguished from the inflated structure by the fact that in the inflated structure the occupied area is not under pressure and the walls of the building are filled with air — like an air mattress.

In response to the U.S. government's need for a means of protecting

A tent house at the New York state sanitarium at Ray Brook in the Adirondack Mountains. The tent house has enjoyed great popularity in this country, especially at resorts and religious communities. At the turn of the century camping was not considered the exciting return to nature it is today. It was still strongly associated with pioneering and the rough lifestyle of the frontier and was, therefore, not genteel. Camping was also difficult for women wearing the Victorian fashions that were in style. Children, however, were encouraged to camp out, and did. And vacationing in a tent house served as the equivalent of camping out for the adults.

and enclosing the large, highly sensitive radar antennae developed after the Second World War on the Distant Early Warning (DEW) line in the Arctic, Walter Bird — who is now recognized as one of the pioneers in the field of design and fabrication of air structures — developed the first large (fifty feet in diameter, forty feet high) air-supported radome in 1948 while he was with Cornell Aeronautical Laboratory (now CALSPAN) in Buffalo. Radio waves could be transmitted almost without resistance through the light neoprene-coated Fiberglas walls, full weather protection of the instruments inside was provided, and transmission efficiencies could be maintained in adverse weather, thereby eliminating snow, ice, and wind factors.

In 1956, Bird and four associates went on to organize Birdair Structures, Incorporated, to promote the development of commercial structures as well as to continue doing military research. Birdair has participated in the construction of practically every important fabric structure since then. In the late 1950s, publicity on air structures resulted in the formation of several other companies that started manufacturing bubbles for use as warehouses, pool and tennis court enclosures, and exhibition spaces — in short, air structures began to find applications when the low cost and portability factors produced a need.

Meanwhile, innovations in tension-supported structures kept pace. Unlike an air-supported or inflatable tent, tension or tensile structures are membrane and high-strength cable structures that derive their stability from their geometric shape of opposing curvatures. Two basic principles are at work in the tension structure: one, the intersecting cables (and there can be a hundred or a hundred thousand of them) must curve in opposite directions to provide equilibrium; two, the cables must be prestressed to the point where the structure will remain stable under the varying loads (such as wind, rain, snow, and so on) to which it might be subjected. Since tension structures do not require airtight construction and therefore use no air locks or blowers, energy can be saved. But, to be considered in the cost of tension fabric structures is a slightly higher initial cost because of cables and other steel supports necessary.

Buildings with tension-supported roofs were the predecessors of modern tension structures. The pioneer of tension buildings is the arena in Raleigh, North Carolina. For years considered the most important large-span cable net structure, it was designed in 1950 by architect Matthew Nowicki and engineered by Fred M. Severud. The building has a cable-supported membrane roof and was originally planned with a neoprene-coated cover membrane; however, building code restrictions then in effect dictated the use of sheet metal instead.

Other early tension structures were designed by the late Eero Saarinen and engineered by Severud. The David S. Ingalls Hockey Rink at Yale University in New Haven, Connecticut (1957–1958), has a gracefully curved roof composed of a web of steel cables stretched, not only between the spine and side walls, but also running parallel with the spine to prevent flutter. The ends of the building are braced with steel trusses. Saarinen's Dulles International Airport in Virginia is the first

Walter W. Bird, one of the leading authorities on air structures, standing atop a radome. (Photo: Birdair)

Pentadome-A, built by Walter Bird for the Air Ballistics Missile Agency, was used as a principal Armed Forces Day exhibit at Andrews Air Force Base for several years. It also served as a rocket workshop. Large objects such as rockets could be air-locked in through the long, cylinder-shaped structure at left and then set up in the large dome. These membranes encapsulated 50,000 square feet. (Photo: Birdair)

The Raleigh arena, one of the earliest and best of the large-span cable-net structures. Steel cables in tension take the roof loads and inclined, reinforced concrete arches in compression take the loads from the cables. The thrust of the arches is in turn taken by concrete tripods with prestressed underground ties to prevent slipping of the footings. The hall is used mainly for cattle shows. (Severud-Perrone-Sturm-Bandel, Consulting Engineers)

Raleigh Arena, suspended roof under construction. (Geiger Burger Associates, P.C.)

Saarinen designed and Severud engineered the reception building at Dulles International Airport in Virginia. Its cable-suspended roof is slung between two rows of concrete piers.

commercial airport designed exclusively for jets and its cable-suspended roof is slung between two rows of shaped concrete columns.

In 1962, architect Victor Lundy and engineer Horst Berger designed the Unitarian Church in Hartford, Connecticut. This building sported a wooden plank roof supported by cables. Berger refers to this structure as the "missing link," but it is a fine example of the kind of innovation and daring tension design that has led to the breakthroughs of today. In 1965, with Fred Severud, Berger engineered the University of Virginia's new Field House which uses a combination of precast and cast-in-place concrete combined with post-tensioning. The architects were Baskervill and Son. Following along the same principles as those at work in the roof of the Mongolian yurt, this structure contains an outside tension ring that was post-tensioned by wrapping it with cable, just as a fabric compression band is wrapped around the yurt. Ribs radiating into a smaller central compression ring were anchored into the outside tension ring, and precast lightweight concrete shells were placed on the framework.

Another architect who has designed some splendid tension structures is Kenzo Tange. His roof for the Shizuoka Convention Hall (1953–1954), the magnificent National Indoor Stadium for the 1964 Olympic Games in Tokyo, the Takamatsu Prefectural Office (1955–1958), and his design for a housing complex over Tokyo Bay are tension buildings. They possess the heavy look of some of the other tension buildings of the time due to the limited number of acceptable lightweight building materials available. For instance, the roof of the Olympic swimming hall is suspended from a pair of fourteen-inch cables hung between twin concrete towers. From each side of this falls the curved metal tension roof, sweeping out to semicircular compression arches formed by the seating galleries within. The striking exterior design of this and the neighboring gymnasium also produces equally arresting interiors.

In the 1950s, Sheldahl built this dome of transparent polyester foil. This tent structure which looks almost like a giant mushroom, rests on a light tube platform at roof height. Entry is from beneath. (Sheldahl)

This air-supported membrane was built by the Sheldahl Company in Northfield, Minnesota, as a grain silo. It measures sixty-seven yards in diameter, and up until the early 1960s was the largest pneumatic structure with radial cables. The wooden wall retained the grain. (Sheldahl)

University of Virginia field house, 1965. Architects: Baskervill and Son. Engineers: Fred Severud and Horst Berger. Built on the same compression-band principle as the Mongolian yurt, the concrete dome, which spans 282 feet, is composed of thirty-two columns arranged on a circle. Precast arch ribs insert against the columns and deliver their horizontal thrust to a cast-in-place, post-tensioned ring at the periphery and a cast-in-place compression ring in the center. The outside ring is post-tensioned by wrapping it with ten layers of wire, just as a fabric compression band is wrapped around the eave of the yurt to support the roof supports. Precast lightweight shells span between the ribs, producing the undulating shape which so beautifully matches the hills of Virginia. (Geiger Berger Associates, P.C.)

Though not a tension structure, this fluted dome designed by Philip Johnson at New Harmony, Indiana, in 1960, appears to be draped over a Jacques Lipchitz sculpture commemorating nineteenth-century utopian communities in Indiana. (Philip Johnson)

Hampton Roads Coliseum. Architects: A. G. Odell, Jr., and Associates; Engineer: Fred Severud. This 6.5-million-dollar colosseum also applies the yurt compression-ring principle. The roof consists of forty-eight two-inch diameter cables supporting ring trusses. The cable is anchored at the top of folded precast panels, which in turn transmit the horizontal forces to the compression ring, which can be seen approximately thirteen feet below the cable anchorage. (Severud-Perrone-Sturm-Bandel, Consulting Engineers)

Unitarian Church in Hartford, Connecticut, designed by Victor Lundy and Horst Berger. (Geiger Berger Associates, P.C.)

Kenzo Tange also designed this model for a 50-billion-dollar urban complex to be built over Tokyo Bay. ("There would be a minimal amount of land speculation," the architect's report is quoted as saying.)

Japan's foremost architect Kenzo Tange designed two magnificent tension structures as stadiums for the 1964 Olympic Games in Tokyo. The three cable networks supporting the roof can be seen in the photo above. First, fourteen-inch cables run from ground level and between twin concrete towers, similar to a suspension bridge. Second, the roof is slung from the fourteen-inch cables to the semicircular compression arches formed by the seating galleries on each side. Third, transverse cables running from opposite points on the semicircular arches further support the welded steel plate deck and stabilize the roof against flutter.

This unique application of stretched fabric provides shelter for a walkway which links the computer center to the main building of the IBM Havant Plant, Hampshire, England. Arup Associates were the architects and engineers for the factory complex.

West German architect Frei Otto is one of the acknowledged experts in the field of lightweight construction. He has designed tension structures to cover everything from ocean bottoms to cities in the Arctic. This aircraft hangar tent was designed by Otto in the mid-1950s and is composed of a membrane with ridge and bracing cables. The tent manufacturer Stromeyer in Konstanz, Germany, manufactured these hangar tents in large series.

Birdair in Buffalo, New York, developed this hybrid radome which combines both single and dual wall construction. The single-wall "curtain" can be raised during critical phases of antenna testing. The surrounding dual wall of the dome is composed of inflated toroidal segments, like those making up an air mattress. (Birdair)

Frei Otto. Project: Medical Academy, Ulm, 1965. These centrally supported radial "cable nets" were, by a strange coincidence, woven in Frei Otto's studio by a spider at the tip of a model for a crane. Lightweight structures comply completely with the laws of nature.

Another of Tange's projects, this one only in the model stage, is a 50-billion-dollar urban complex that would be built over Tokyo Bay. Two suspended highways spanning the bay enclose the business and industrial structures and segregate them from the residential complexes, which sprawl over the bay on each side of the highway system and municipal area. These residential units are subcities composed of tentlike "megastructures" hovering over the water on pylons. Each carved facade would contain fifty stories of apartments with public terraces and playgrounds represented by the cutout areas on the curved surface. Schools, shopping facilities, parking, and monorail terminals would be situated within the cavity formed by the two facades. Tange's plan is to let the people plan their own houses on platforms created within the tent walls. This would provide some personal freedom and individuality within the urban complex. Tange developed this type of building while studying at the Massachusetts Institute of Technology.

One of the tension achievements of the 1960s was architect Frei Otto's West German Pavilion at Expo '67 in Montreal. This really caught the public eye and, with the giant megastructure covering all indoor facilities for the Olympic Games in Munich in 1972, set the precedent for scores of large-scale tentlike structures to follow.

In the mid 1940s, shortly before Walter Bird was developing his radomes, Frei Otto, while in a prisoner-of-war camp in Chartres, was put in charge of a construction team repairing bridges. A shortage of materials and an abundance of labor enabled him to begin experiments in tension structures, and he engineered new designs in bridge-building using tension principles. Twenty-two years later came the West German Pavilion and the Stuttgart Institute of Lightweight Structures, which Otto founded and from whence his diverse and formidable works emerge.

In the 1970s, inflated and tension structures, in order to satisfy building codes as permanent structures, had to use conventional materials for roofing. Until that time all architectural membranes deteriorated in sun-

Fabric roof of the West German Pavilion being fitted into place. The size of the workers gives an idea of the scale of the structure.

The roof of the West German pavilion at Expo '67 in Montreal established Frei Otto as one of the most significant and exciting innovators in contemporary architecture. The roof is made of a prestressed steel-cable network of high and low points in a state of equilibrium with an outer covering of laminated canvas and an underslung roof skin made of translucent polyester fabric.

light and open air, severely limiting their lifespan and rendering them impractical. It was their potential use for traveling shows and exhibitions that sustained and developed the air and tension structures. Being temporary, building permits were obtainable and short-life membranes could be used. Unusual shapes and their unique characteristics attracted attention, and lower cost, easy transportability, and easy removal at the conclusion of the exhibition made them ideal for this purpose.

The U.S. Pavilion at Expo '70 in Osaka, Japan, gave the air structure the impetus it needed. Birdair had developed the Cabledome™ concept, which was an extremely stable, cable-reinforced air dome that could be used to provide low-cost and efficient structures in sizes up to 1000 feet in diameter. Designed as a permanent structure with panels individually replaceable (without deflating the building), this structure was proposed for use as a sports arena or stadium, but no investors seemed interested in taking it on. Meanwhile, Davis Brody, Architects, had been awarded the design commission for a unique dual-wall air structure they had proposed and that Birdair was to fabricate. Then Congress cut appropriations in half and there was a need to maintain exhibit space while greatly reducing the cost of the structure; the cable-reinforced air-supported roof was chosen as the solution to the problem.

The design of the Osaka Expo '70 Pavilion was 250 × 450 feet with sloping earth berms to blend into the roof to provide uniform aerodynamic loading over the full roof. One hundred thousand square feet were encapsulated. This air-supported structure required the circulation of 40,000 cubic feet of air per minute. Osaka is typhoon territory and this low-silhouette structure was capable of withstanding 150-mile-an-hour winds. Also, the earth around Osaka is swampy, making it impossible to anchor the fabric in the ground. Engineer David Geiger, who in 1968 had formed a partnership with Horst Berger, patented both a diamond-shaped pattern of steel cables over which a vinyl-coated Fiberglas fabric

Roof over the open-air theater in the abbey ruins in Bad Hersfeld, West Germany, 1968. This membrane roof of PVC-coated polyester can be centrally bunched at the main mast to provide an open-air theater or lowered in four minutes to cover the theater. This retractable protective covering can also be dismantled and stored at the end of the theater season, thereby prolonging its life.

Section of roofing of the main sports area in the Olympiapark, Munich, 1972. This prestressed cable-net construction of ridges and hollows (or high and low points in a state of equilibrium) is covered with acrylic glass sheets which are flexibly linked together and buffer-supported. Some 89,500 square yards are covered by this tension roof. The covered area for the stadium alone is approximately 41,250 square yards. The size and technical complexity of this structure make it one of Frei Otto's most formidable.

CONSTRUCTIONEER ®
EVERY OTHER MONDAY, NEWS-PHOTO COVERAGE OF NEW YORK, PENNSYLVANIA, NEW JERSEY, DELAWARE

Winter Operations Issue

"June In January" A Reality
Under The Buffalo Bubble

One of the prime uses of air-supported structures is on construction sites. This massive tent covers a site in which all foundation, underground piping, and electrical work is being done. Work can proceed uninterrupted through the winter. (Environmental Structures, Inc.)

When work is completed, the bubble is deflated, dismantled, lifted from the completed site, and returned to the manufacturer for cleaning and re-use. (Environmental Structures, Inc.)

Birdair has developed this 78-foot-wide by 420-foot-long prototype design to evaluate a lower cost method for "mothballing" inactive ships until needed for service. It provides a unique solution for environmental control by covering, sealing, and dehumidifying the enclosed space. (Birdair Structures, Inc.)

was stretched and an elliptical-shaped concrete compression ring in which the cables carrying the fabric were anchored. In this case the ring sat atop the earth berm, but in other structures it has been used atop columns or walls. From the computer analysis involved in the project, Geiger developed and patented techniques for determining the placement and loading of cable net restraints for the low-profile, air-supported fabric roof. These same principles and techniques now have made it possible to cover huge spans such as the 10.4-acre Pontiac, Michigan, Silverdome.

The success of the Osaka Pavilion caused a surge of interest in air structures for many applications. But the air-supported-structure industry still lacked a fabric that could satisfy building codes and be permanent enough to meet the needs of prospective investors and satisfy lending institutions. Again, it was another government need (just as the military's need had inspired development of pneumatic radomes in the 1940s and the Expo '70 Pavilion was a government commission) that prompted the most important advance in the field: an acceptable fabric. The National Aeronautics and Space Administration (NASA), looking for a new fabric for Apollo astronauts' space suits, commissioned Owens-Corning Fiberglas Corporation to come up with a durable and noncombustible, yet thin, light, and flexible fabric.

Owens-Corning had been experimenting with an ultrafine glass yarn called Beta yarn. Under contract to NASA, they wove the yarn into fabric, had it coated with Teflon TFE fluorocarbon resin manufactured by DuPont

This picture speaks for itself. The roof of the U.S. Pavilion at Expo '70 was delivered by truck to the construction site. To try this with any other kind of roof you need truck fleets. (Geiger Berger Associates, P.C.)

U.S. Pavilion, Expo '70 in Osaka, Japan. (Geiger Berger Associates, P.C.)

Company, and the astronauts were set for takeoff. Later, David Geiger, in his search for a suitable membrane to cover his newly developed support system, worked with Owens-Corning, DuPont, and Chemical Fabrics of Bennington, Vermont, to adapt this fabric to construction use. It was thickened, woven into stronger and more porous fabric, and coated with more Teflon TFE. Now the tent — which had always been covered with material subject to weather deterioration — could be considered a permanent item.

Teflon TFE–coated Beta Fiberglas has a potential service life of at least twenty years; is virtually impervious to the effects of weather and sunlight; won't stretch, shrink, mildew, or rot; is very strong, lightweight, and flame resistant (it can pass the "burning brands" fire test in which heated wood blocks are placed on it); and requires no cleaning because dirt cannot stick to its surface. Its cost is also 30 to 40 percent as much as conventional roofing.

The first application of this material was for the LaVerne College Student Center in LaVerne, California, in 1973. This tensioned fabric structure was designed by the Shaver Partnership and fabricated by Birdair. The multiconed fabric membrane is supported by a network of cables attached to steel columns that function like circus-tent poles. Geiger-Berger engineered the project and conducted computer analysis to determine the best placement of cables and columns, which are set at 15-degree angles. The use of fabric covering on this student center reduced building costs 30 percent below that of conventional construction.

With the technology gained at Osaka and the first usage of the new Fiberglas Teflon material at LaVerne College, the permanent tent building now is gradually becoming an economic and visual alternative to conventional steel, glass, and concrete buildings. Conventional buildings, in all their modernity, have not been able to take on the truly space-age look that comes so naturally to the modern tent architecture of today. Since the first permanent tent structure (LaVerne Student Center) was erected in 1973, the concept has taken hold and currently more than one hundred Fiberglas fabric structures are in design or study stages. These projects range from sports and recreation complexes to structures enclosing shopping centers, schools, apartments, and community facilities from Alaska to Saudi Arabia.

While David Geiger has made momentous contributions on the air-supported front, his partner Horst Berger made a most significant breakthrough in tension-structure engineering by discovering how to describe mathematically the shape of a tension structure — a problem that had hitherto eluded tension-structure designers. Berger developed a procedure to feed into a computer the predetermined locations of points on curves in space from an initial assumed shape. With this input established, the computer then corrects the geometry for one point at a time, allowing for stress loads, until all points are corrected and the accurate geometry of the entire structure is found. The computer output gives all cable forces, cable lengths, and fabric patterns. It's a design process in reverse, Berger says, that has the prestress forces as input and the shape as output.

The LaVerne College Student Center, LaVerne, California, was designed by The Shaver Partnership in 1968 and represents the first permanent, enclosed Fiberglas fabric roof structure in the United States and one of the first major attempts to reduce construction costs of large enclosed educational facilities. The flexible design permits rearrangement of the interior to accommodate athletic events, student activities, theatrical productions, and other recreational programs. (Photo courtesy of Birdair, who fabricated the structure.)

The tent roof of the LaVerne structure covers 1.4 acres. The Student Center's fabric roof was erected in three days, and the smaller Drama Lab roof (upper left in photo) took one day, with necessary tensioning of fabric on both following over the next few days. The Drama Lab encloses 10,671 square feet to the Student Center's 68,383. (Birdair Structures, Inc.)

To house a variety of Bicentennial celebrations in Philadelphia in 1976, Architects H2C2 and Engineer Horst Berger of Geiger Berger conceived a series of emblematic and festive tents that were placed around the city. The Independence Mall Pavilion houses a theater and the masts of the tension structure were tilted to ease forces on the valley cable anchorages. The fabricators (Birdair) received a pattern that specified both dimensions and fabric strengths. Because supporting cables came to a peak at different angles, the connector is asymmetrical to bring them to the same working point with equal forces. (Geiger Berger Associates, P.C.)

The Folklife Pavilion consists of ten rows of what are in effect half tents, together spanning sixty-eight feet. Supported by fifty-five-foot vertical masts, the structure comprises two rows of radial tents, with fabric cut away outside the masts. The fabric membrane is constructed essentially of parallel flat strips, stressed by cables only at the ridges (mast to mast), valleys (ground to ground), and the edges. (Geiger Berger Associates, P.C.)

U.S. Pavilion at Expo '74, Spokane, Washington. In the previous world's fair in Osaka, the U.S. Pavilion was an air-supported fabric structure. In Expo '74 the exhibition hall was fabric, but the building was a tension structure with a radial cable-net roof supported by a central column. (Geiger Berger Associates, P.C.)

Berger developed this procedure while working on radial tent roofs resting on square bases at Great Adventure Amusement Park in New Jersey. These buildings went up in 1974, and at the correct prestressing force, the tops of the tents came within one-eighth inch of the design elevation, proving the accuracy of the design. Fabric structures had been a sideline for Berger up until then; now he is considered one of the experts in the fabric-tension-structure field. His diverse, totally engineered designs are superb achievements.

The computer method of designing tension structures is a new and efficient approach to the problem. It is also strictly an engineering approach since the ultimate shape of the structure is dependent upon the computer results. The architectural approach brings the computer into play as a final check on results that are obtained by making a soap-film model. This is the method used by Frei Otto and many other lightweight structure architects, including Vela/Future Tents, Ltd., who furnished the following account.

First, a stretch model giving the basic architectural boundaries is built. This is a crude model and there is enormous flexibility at this stage of the design, and the architect can experiment with curvatures. Usually a minimum of two or three models are constructed. (This, by the way, is the way Horst Berger starts his projects, and he also relies heavily on his models.)

Next the soap-film model is made. The principle behind this is that any shape a soap bubble can assume is in a state of equilibrium (all forces

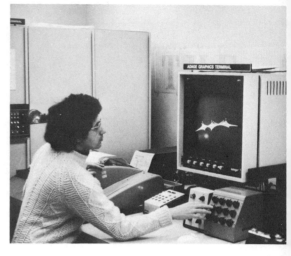

Drawing computer pictures at Columbia University. The twelve knobs at right can produce any configuration or geometric adjustment to obtain a corrected cable geometry on a designed structure. (Geiger Berger Associates, P.C.)

A computer drawing of multiple radial tent structures. The input is the engineer's predetermined location of points on curves in space from an initial assumed shape. The computer then charts and corrects the geometry on every stress point until all points check out correctly. (Geiger Berger Associates, P.C.)

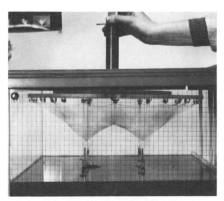

The computer method of designing tension structures is one approach to the problem. The other involves working with soap-film models and has been used by Frei Otto and many other lightweight structure architects, including Vela/Future Tents, Ltd., of New York City, who furnished the author with photographs and an explanation of the process.

When Vela/Future Tents was commissioned to design modular tent units for Anchor Industries, they first constructed several stretch models in order to start developing their design. At this stage a minimum of two or three models will be constructed.

Next a soap-film model is made. After the design has been refined, the critical sections of the model are photographed through the grid on the front of the soap box.

After the coordinates and points in space on the structure are confirmed, a cutting pattern for the fabric is made and an exact simulation of the tent is constructed.

Anchor Industries will supply these tents to rental agencies who in turn will lease them for parties, industrial fairs, etc. One unique feature of these tents is they are composed of modular units which can be sewn together in cruciform, square, or rectangular shapes. The latter two would produce courtyards surrounded by the tent.

being equalized), and a structure of that form can be built, and it will be in harmony with the laws of nature. A frame with threads is dipped into a soap and glycerin solution. Wheels located at the ends of the threads allow them to be lengthened or shortened so modifications in the design can be made. The framework is mounted upside down and lowered into a Plexiglas box containing the solution. When it is raised, a soap film should form on the threads. This is a minimal surface where all forces on the surface are equal. If a soap membrane won't form, then changes in the design must be made. The architect experiments with the natural forces until he is satisfied with the design.

Next a camera is set up in front of the machine and the critical sections are photographed through a grid on the front of the soap box. In this way an exact section through a major axis is recorded and mathematical formulas can establish coordinates and stress points. These figures are then checked out by computer and from this a cutting pattern for the fabric can be made. Now the final model is made, and this is an exact simulation of the tent to which only slight refinements in the design may be made. It is this model that can be subjected to wind-tunnel, snow-loading, or any other kind of stress test.

The architects at Vela/Future Tents feel that these models are absolutely necessary: lightweight tension structures are not easy to visualize and they say it is therefore necessary to work continually with the form in the shape it will be assuming, and that is the model. But whatever the approach, it is virtually impossible for a tension structure that conforms to the harmonious laws of nature to be unattractive.

The largest air-supported structure in the U.S. is the Silverdome, twenty-five miles south of Detroit in Pontiac, Michigan, and home of the Detroit Lions. The Silverdome is so named because of the silvery, translucent effect of the fabric roof. It is just the success story the industry needed, displaying all the advantages of a fabric structure: it goes up quickly (the Pontiac Silverdome was finished 100 days ahead of schedule), it is lightweight and therefore less expensive to support (the combined fabric dome weighs 200 tons, where a comparably sized conventional roof would weigh about 6000), it is translucent and thus offers significant savings in lighting (even the minimum level of natural light on overcast days is ample for any indoor activity. Also, the light is glareless and shadowless, providing optimum visibility for participants and spectators alike; it is ideal light for telecasting purposes; and it is a less expensive alternative to a conventional roof. (The Silverdome was completed within construction budget: $529 per seat. At current prices the per-seat cost for the Houston Astrodome would be more than twice that figure and for the New Orleans Superdome, nearly five times.)

Now under development are thermal-active fabrics that will limit solar heat gain in summer, but utilize it in winter. Some work is being done on ways to capture the solar heat between two fabric layers and direct it to air-conditioning equipment. Another alternative would be some sort of a shutter mechanism — perhaps retractable solar shades — that would admit 65 percent of the solar heat when desired: At this point no further heating would be required. One structure that has been planned and

Great Adventure Amusement Park, New Jersey. Work on this structure in 1975 led to one of the most significant breakthroughs in tension-structure engineering — how to mathematically describe the shapes of a tension structure. It was developed in determining the exact geometry and stress patterns of this radial tent resting on a square base structure. The computer program developed the shape and provided the cable lengths and the patterning dimension for the fabric. (Geiger Berger Associates, P.C.)

Architect Paul Rudolph designed this sports ▶ stadium with a tensioned roof for Dammamm, Saudi Arabia. (Paul Rudolph)

After serving NBC's *Today* show in New York during the Democratic presidential nominating conventions of 1976, this patented fabric structure designed by Geiger Berger Associates was packed up and sent to Kansas City where it was pitched atop a hotel and helped NBC through the Republican convention. The frame is constructed of twelve pipes of equal length, which equalize prestress forces. (Geiger Berger Associates, P.C.)

University of Riyadh Recreational Facility, Saudi Arabia. Because of the windswept location, subject to severe sandstorms, the building was designed to have a low silhouette, a cable-reinforced, air-supported roof, supported on earth berms faced with rock. Mechanical rooms, locker rooms, offices, and other facilities are located under the berm. These structures also serve to anchor and distribute the high cable loads under windy conditions. (Birdair Structures, Inc.)

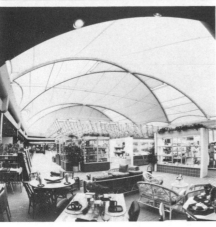

Bullock's department store of Menlo Park, Northern California, chose a fabric roof to cover a 96 × 162 foot opening in a metal deck roof, and in doing so became the first retail establishment covered with a permanent Teflon-coated Fiberglas fabric roof. Here workers winch skin onto framework made of laminated wood arches braced by steel tubes and cross-ties resting on steel columns in the building's frame. Quadripods were temporarily erected atop arches to assist in winching. Thin strips of fabric (hanging down) are attached to top of arches before the fabric goes on. (Geiger Berger Associates, P.C.)

Another tent, also designed by Vela/Future Tents, Ltd. This tent serves as a bedroom for partner Nicholas Goldsmidt's New York loft. Modern architecture has done away with fabric indoors (except for curtains) and here it serves as an excellent alternative to a dry wall room. This tent is ten feet high and covers a nine-foot-square area. A room this size would be claustrophobic, the tent is not. The curtain wall can be opened or closed and the roof is a prestressed membrane connected to the ceiling and cabled to the floor. The interior is lined with hand-dyed silk, giving it an exotic flare. The frame is aluminum, and it took only a few hours to erect. (Vela/Future Tents, Ltd.)

Pontiac Silverdome, home of the Detroit Lions, has the world's largest air-supported dome to date. The dome is restrained and shaped by a network of eighteen large steel cables. The three-inch diameter cables vary in length from 550 to 750 feet and weigh up to 15,000 pounds each. They were installed by a giant Sikorsky Skycrane helicopter instead of cranes and winches, which saved three weeks in construction time and 25 percent in costs. (Geiger Berger Associates, P.C.)

These upside-down tents are located atop an open plaza in front of a Duval County office building in Jacksonville, Florida. Rather than being stretched upward into tentlike peaks — the basic tension design — the canopy's fabric is pulled downward to form two inverted funnels. Masts in the center of each funnel support the fabric's edge by means of horizontal bars, alleviating the need for support from other buildings or ground anchors.

Architect William Morgan and Engineer Horst Berger designed the 46-foot-wide, 113-foot-long canopy. (Geiger Berger Associates, P.C.)

The fabric vaults on the two-story building can be seen glowing at night and have already begun to be compared to a piece of female lingerie. The Owens-Corning Fiberglas fabric coated with DuPont Teflon is a light beige color when it arrives from the fabricators; however, it quickly bleaches to a stark white. Dirt cannot stick to its surface, it won't stretch, shrink, mildew, or rot; it's strong, lightweight and flame resistant, and it costs 30 to 40 percent as much as conventional roofing. Bullock's also plans to save $21,000 a year in electricity costs alone as a result of this heat-reflective roof. The roof covers 18,000 square feet. (Owens-Corning Fiberglas Corp.)

This superbly designed tension structure will be erected at Sea World in Orlando, Florida, providing a soothing and sensible contrast to the nearby Disney World complex. The building is designed by Horst Berger. (Geiger Berger Associates, P.C.)

Tenting in paradise — Maho Bay, St. John, U.S. Virgin Islands. Maho Bay is a new camping resort dedicated to the belief that it is possible to live in comfort and harmony with a fragile environment without spoiling it. The tent houses measure sixteen feet by sixteen feet and are set on plank decks that cantilever over thickly wooded hillsides. Each contains a primary sleeping area, a living room that converts into a second bedroom, a screened cooking and dining area and an open porch for private sun-bathing. (Maho Bay Camps, Inc.)

This soaring 100-foot-high freeform tent covers a combination skating rink, tennis court, and exhibition space in St. Louis' Edgar M. Queeny Park. The peaked fabric roof is 223 feet long and 134 feet wide at its extremes. The masts are simply designed and made from three five-inch-diameter standard pipes arranged in a triangle and laced with short 1.5-inch-diameter sections. Architect is Jones Mayer Associates, Inc., St. Louis, which developed the design with Horst Berger. (Geiger Berger Associates, P.C.)

The world's largest fabric structure: the cost, $180 million; the size, 105 acres or 80 football or 53 soccer fields; the place, Jeddah International Airport, Jeddah, Saudi Arabia, some 30 miles from Mecca. (Owens-Corning Fiberglas Corporation)

Not at all out of the question is midtown New York covered by a membrane. Cars would be kept out and the underneath area would have the freshest air in Manhattan. The idea of controlling the environment of an entire community by enclosing it in a huge membrane is no longer science fiction. (Birdair Structures, Inc.)

would incorporate these retractable shades is the Government Services Administration fabric structure in Denver, a huge structure called Meg 2 that would provide office space for several thousand government workers. The fabric roof is transparent around the perimeter and above the tree-lined main boulevard that bisects the structure so the occupants get a view of the Colorado mountains as they work.

The abundance of oil money in the Middle East has enabled the Arabs to commission the largest fabric structure in the world at the Jeddah International Airport near Mecca. The structure will cover 105 acres (ten times the area under the Silverdome), the cost will be $180 million, and by 1980, when the first part opens, it will begin accommodating an estimated 720,000 Moslems making their annual pilgrimage to the Kaaba in Mecca by air. The airport structure will consist of two identical roof systems and 5.5 million square feet of Fiberglas coated with Teflon will be used to form 210 tentlike units — each 148 feet square — which will be anchored to 148-foot-high pylons and suspended 66 feet above the terminal floor at their four corners, sweeping up to 115 feet high at their peaks. Skidmore, Owings, and Merrill are the architects and have designed a structure quite in keeping with the spirit of the place — the tentlike units composing the air terminal roof blend harmoniously with the spreading tent cities set up around Mecca to accommodate the pilgrims. This is probably one of the greatest structures to be built in modern times . . . and it's a tent.

5 TENT ART

If the bough of eternity has grown from the root of your good fortune, and if life is a fitting garment upon your body — beware! lean not against this tent of the body which is a shade for you, for its four pegs are weak.

— The *Rubáiyát* of Omar Khayyám*

You can't take everything with you when you leave on the midlife journey . . . if I could give everyone a gift for the send-off on this journey, it would be a tent. A tent for tentativeness. The gift of portable roots.

— Gail Sheehy, *Passages*

A surprising number of artists consider their work to fall within the aesthetic framework of the tent. Particularly in this era of conceptual art, where the viewer's interaction with the artist's material is an essential part of the work, the tent form is a willing participant in the exchange of energy. The tent is shelter; it is framework and facade; it is both a primitive and a *living* shape.

If a single criterion qualifies the works that follow as tents, it is the artists' explanations of their own visions. What we see in the form must at times give way to what the artists have seen.

Of the twenty individuals represented, it is interesting that the majority — indeed, the first twelve whose works are discussed — are women. Even more significantly, almost all of the artists who relate their works *comfortably* to the tent form are women. Certainly fabric art has been labeled "feminine art": throughout every era the materials involved in tentmaking and its sheltering shapes have been basic to woman's relationship to her world.

Harriet Feigenbaum builds deceptively primitive structures out of branches, wire, and sometimes rocks and hay. Her works evoke a mul-

---

* *Khayyám* is Persian for "tentmaker."

tiplicity of times and places — Druidic emplacements, hut and haystack shapes, corncribs and baptistries, forests turned deserts. Hers are tent armatures: where there is a covering it is likely to be hay, in structures that to a great extent resemble yaks. Her vision is architectural. Her strong, clean shapes appeal to the intellect as much as to the emotions.

Battery Park City — A Mirage began as a spoof on the luxury housing that was to have been built over the past ten years on this Hudson River landfill site near Wall Street. It consisted of linked tripod "dwellings" on sand whose visual focus (enter now landscape architecture) was Ellis Island, the traditional entry point of the alien "invader" of America.

Ms. Feigenbaum's *Cycles* are a series of site-specific projects that juxtapose elements of diverse cultures and times — in this instance, methods of drying and curing hay which are likewise sheltering in form.

Nil Yalter, born in Turkey and living now in France, is a very thorough tentmaker. Her 1974 *Yurt* (or *Topak Ev,* Turkish for "circular house") embodies a diversity of tent images — the ancient shelter form, stark metal sculpture, a meditation space, a museum of individual works on animal hides, and textual matter. It is a particular duality of the yurt that intrigues Ms. Yalter, however: in those cultures, including Turkey's, where the yurt is still found, it is both a lifetime shelter and a lifetime prison for the woman who inhabits it. Exploding the traditional prudery of the yurt dweller, Ms. Yalter has here emblazoned the exterior of the enclosure with images of the vagina.

Feigenbaum, *Cycles,* trees, branches, hay, about 10 acres, Nassau County Museum of Fine Arts, New York, 1976.

Harriet Feigenbaum, *Battery Park City — A Mirage,* branches, wire, 100′ × 10′, Art on the Beach, 1978.

Barbara Zucker's *Dark Huts*, part of a 1973 exhibition at Sarah Lawrence College, are deliciously yurtlike, both in form and placement, though in miniature. Each of the fifty-odd structures was given an opening.

Katherine Sokolnikoff's tent subjects are "the shapes and structures that people in other cultures created and endowed with great significance." Her *Porcelain Garden Tent* is a rare miniature of the genre. Her human-scale *Tuareg Tent,* shown here on the Battery Park landfill we saw above (and later stolen from an exhibition at the University of Pennsylvania's Institute of Contemporary Art in Philadelphia) was conceived with various interchangeable fabric shields: a "summer" cover of horsehair and silk shown here, and for late fall in Philadelphia, a cotton organdy silk-screened by The Fabric Workshop to simulate the woven-palm mats of the Aïn tribe.

Miriam Sharon, an Israeli, has also worked with ancient tent forms. Her 1976 *Negev Sand Tent* project involved the recreation of a period Bedouin tent with help from both the Iben-Barry Bedouins and workers at the Kerem Shalom kibbutz. Ms. Sharon is interested, in all her work, in a kind of "meditation space," calling the viewer to consider more profoundly his environment, and in the case of the sand tent, to preserve it.

In 1977, Ms. Sharon brought her *Sand Tent Surfaces* to a factory in the coastal town of Naharia. These are four works resembling collapsed tents which were attached to (in most instances, hung loosely from) the interior walls of the work space. The soft textures and enveloping shapes offered repose and relief from the machine age.

In related "Desert People" projects, such as *Ashdoda,* Ms. Sharon has animated a group of assistants wearing tentlike costumes who seek to involve spontaneously the Ashdod harbor workers in sensitivity rituals. One seaman reported that for the first time in twenty years, he "really felt the rocks in front of his boat."

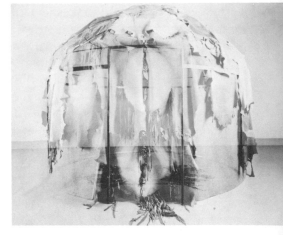

Nil Yalter, *Yurt*, metal, felt, hides, 8' × 8', 1974.

Barbara Zucker, *Dark Huts*, hydrocal, cheesecloth, pigment, 50 units, "In Spaces" exhibition, Sarah Lawrence College, 1973.

Sokolnikoff, *Tuareg Tent*, branches, horsehair, silk, Art on the Beach, New York, 1978.

Sharon, *Ashdoda,* Harbor "Desert People" Project, Ashdod Harbor, Israel, 1978. (Photo: Rachael Harpaz)

Katherine Sokolnikoff, *Porcelain Garden Tent*, 7" × 5" × 8", Collection of Dr. Arthur Ashman, 1978.

Sharon, *Sand Tent Surfaces,* Project in factory in Naharia, Israel, 1977.

Mary Beth Edelson, *Mother's House*, black hand-painted canvas, 9' × 7' × 13', N.A.M.E. Gallery, Chicago, 1978.

Edelson, *Inner Space*, Private ritual performance in front of tent construction, New York City, 1978.

Mary Beth Edelson's tents are primarily environments for meditation or ritual, and they are often womb related — dark, soft, offering shelter. *Mother's House,* shown here, accommodates one person at a time on a soft mattress and contains a photographic piece, *Aging in Diana's Grove,* portraying in a series of images (some superimposed) the slow aging of a woman. The tent itself defines the passage from the outside world to her mythic world, the setting for the exploration of self or for interaction with others, for mythic rites, and for what Ms. Edelson describes as "photographic rituals" of the human body in its shroud (another "tent" which evokes another passage).

Ms. Edelson's private ritual performance of *Inner Space,* here in a time exposure, took place in front of *Mother's House.*

Anne Healy has been exhibiting fabric works since 1970. Her tent-shaped installations date primarily from 1968–1973.

Death's Door (1972) is of yellow nylon cloth over aluminum rods and wood. It is, in tent terms, upright.

Hellebore (1973) is of black nylon and is, as tents go, upside-down.

Mildred Stanley lives and works in suburban Virginia. In 1969–1971 her work concentrated on fabrics that often assumed tent shapes — cheesecloth, paper, or nylon as seen here in her *Ceiling Piece* (1969). From 1971–1975, tent framing and hardware became increasingly important in

Stanley, *Ceiling Piece,* nylon fabric, 8' × 8' × 8', 1969.

Anne Healy, *Death's Door,* nylon, cloth, aluminum rods, wood, 10' × 10' × 10', 1972.

Healy, *Hellebore,* nylon cloth and rope, 10' × 11' × 7', 1973.

her work (see photograph on page 145), sometimes supplanting the tent fabric entirely.

In her *Dreamboat* installations, **Diana Carulli** uses transparent fabrics in a loose tent shape as a scrim on which to project visual images. Sometimes chosen with a single objective and sometimes at random, the images are calculated to induce or influence dreams while inside the shelter. In the photograph, a projection is visible in the upper left corner of the dreamboat, while the artist lies inside below.

Jody Pinto's *Tall Chair* (1977) is a smaller version of a thirty-five-foot-tall work exhibited at the Institute of Contemporary Art in Philadelphia in 1976. The spectator is invited *into* the work, there to experience in a new way his or her own person and environment: the participant is both protected and exposed.

For the same show Ms. Pinto designed a remarkable piece of "tent-wear," the *Dress/Hammock/Enclosure*, seen in the photograph in the closed position. It can be worn as a dress but expands into a hammock and then into a tentlike enclosure when the wearer wishes to rest or sleep. Ms. Pinto writes: "It was possible to strap yourself into a tree by letting out a series of straps within the garment's hood, hem, back, and arms, or, in the case of the other garment, by removing a quiver (worn over the shoulder and leaning against the wall in the photograph), which contains two thick branches and two lengths of rope. The branches slip into the hem and hood of the garment and the rope fastens to the branches of a nearby tree." The piece recalls animals who carry their own shelters about with them.

Hera was born Betty Calvert in New Orleans and worked under the name Betty Voelker until 1977, the year she began exploring tent forms. Her *Sweet Skirt* — which was part of a show, "Locations," in the Rose Art Museum at Brandeis University in 1977 — is a construction of three concentric circles of white taffeta, trimmed with hot pink ribbons and plastic flowers. It is much too large to be worn, but it may be entered. Inside are the less innocent paraphernalia of womanhood: birth-control pills, mirrors, doll parts, baby bottle nipples, and so on.

Death Singer, another tent work from the same Brandeis University exhibit, is a deep purple celebration of death and its images. It too is intended to be entered.

The tent works that follow emphasize framework instead of covering. Often they are the symbol rather than the shelter.

Mildred Stanley's *Yellow/Pink Piece* marks the evolution of her work from fabric to armature.

Merle Temkin's art is designed to be portable and collapsible. (She is a New York City artist and feels strongly the premium of space.) Her 1978 *Shelter for a Small Animal* evokes the shelter and, at the same time, the animal it might shelter.

The detail from *Sweet Man* (1978) shows fantasy in both shape and material — mylar over cardboard over wood. It is another work that hovers between animal and shelter.

Diana Carulli, *Dreamboat*, ripstop nylon over plastic tubing, 6' × 7' × 8', 1978.

Jody Pinto, *Tall Chair*, wood, cheesecloth, rope, 35' × 8', Institute of Contemporary Art, Philadelphia, 1976.

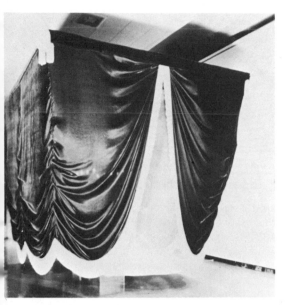

Hera, *Sweet Skirt*, nylon net taffeta, ribbons, silk flowers, mirrors, dolls, 10' × 10', "Locations" exhibition, Rose Art Museum, Brandeis University, 1977.

Hera, *Death Singer*, velvet, rayon, earth, plastic candles, flowers, flamelit bulbs, wood, 8' × 7' × 10', "Locations," exhibition, Rose Art Museum, Brandeis University, 1977.

Pinto, *Dress/Hammock/Enclosures*, Institute of Contemporary Art, Philadelphia, 1976.

Temkin, *Sweet Man* (detail), mylar over cardboard over wood, 4' × 6', 1978.

Merle Temkin, *Shelter for a Small Animal*, wood sticks, sisal rope, 3' × 3', 1978.

Mildred Stanley, *Yellow/Pink Piece* (detail), wood, rope, 12' × 16' × 8', 1975.

The metal framework for **Nil Yalter's** *Yurt* exists alone as a clean piece of sculpture, inviting meditation within its symbolic shelter.

Harriet Feigenbaum's *An Octagonal Domed Building* (1978) is an Italian baptistry turned tent armature. Its primitive materials — branches and wire — contrast with the complexity of its construction.

Robert Stackhouse, like Harriet Feigenbaum and Mildred Stanley (in her later works) creates what might be called tent frames — but as long passageways, such as *Running Animals/Reindeerway* (1976) and *Niagara Dance* (1977). In *Shiphall, a Passage Structure Borrowing Some Lines from the Oseberg Burial Ship* (1977), the saddle roofline is an aesthetic bridge between ancient maritime shapes and modern tent shapes produced by artists like Audrey Hemenway.

Audrey Hemenway describes the construction of her *Garden Web,* an open-work tent of wood and synthetic rope designed to keep animals out of a 25 × 40-foot garden: "It was a long, tedious job, rather like knitting a house." Both strength of line and strength of frame (which, like a bird or an early airplane, is a whole made up of fragile parts) drew her to the tent form.

Ecological Environment (1977) is a major work in terms of size alone, enclosing 1600 square feet under four irregular peaks and a saddle roof that "accepts" weather.

Harriet Feigenbaum, *An Octagonal Domed Building,* branches, wire, 14¼′ × 8′, O. K. Harris Gallery, 1978.

Nil Yalter, *Yurt* (framework), metal, 8′ × 8′, 1974.

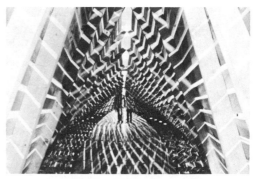

Robert Stackhouse, *Shiphall, a Passage Structure Borrowing Some Lines from the Oseberg Burial Ship* (interior), wood, 66' × 11' × 16', Walker Art Center, Minneapolis, 1977.

Stackhouse, *Shiphall* . . . (exterior).

Audrey Hemenway, *Garden Web*, wood and synthetic rope, 25' × 40' × 12', 1977–1978.

Hemenway, *Ecological Environment*, fiber glass, cable, 1600 sq. ft., 1974.

Cornelius Rogge, *Tent-Project*, Park Rijks-
museum Kröller-Müller, Otterlo, Holland,
1976.

Rogge, *Inside Out Tent*, canvas, iron frame,
strips, 51' × 51' × 80', Amstelpark, Amsterdam, 1978.

Cornelius Rooge, whose recent tent works in Holland are cleanly linear
and architectural in character, calls his tents "vulgar offers" catering to
the public taste. He neither expects his viewers to interpret his work nor
desires that they do so. Its meaning, he insists, will become clear in time.

Sam Cady, a New York artist who summers in the country, creates
illusionistic life-sized paintings of objects such as tents and rowboats on
shaped canvas or Masonite. The subjects appear realistically three-di-
mensional as can be seen by these two paintings from his tent series,
Tent Billowing in the Wind and *Tent, Late Morning (Sears Best)*. These
are freestanding works that look like giant cut-outs.

Leandro Katz writes of his paper, bamboo, string, and audio construction, *The Teepee*: "Writing a statement on my work is almost to reverse
the process involved in it, since the work originates precisely in the
region where language is formed: instead of entering the institution of
grammar and its norms, it chooses to remain outside such norms and to
establish a preliminary checkpoint where the conditions of what is said
are first examined by a series of critical references that precede articu-
lation — like repeating a word until one realizes its oddity."

Byron Burford's *Great Byron Burford Circus of Artistic Wonders* (of Iowa
City, Iowa) is a creative fusion of the visual and the performing arts, held
inside a classic canvas circus tent provided by a grant from the National
Endowment for the Arts. Though here the tent is traditional, the performances inside are far from it: Mr. Burford's tableau of circus images
and sounds, such as the figure of a tiger raising and lowering its paws
almost imperceptibly, repeats itself every eighteen minutes to the spectators inside the darkened tent. Live performances are often part of the
experience at his gala openings — sideshows, "visiting" circus bands,

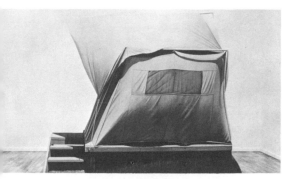

Sam Cady, *Tent Billowing in the Wind,* oil on canvas, 6'6" × 7'9".

Cady, *Tent, Late Morning (Sears Best),* oil on canvas, 6' × 18'.

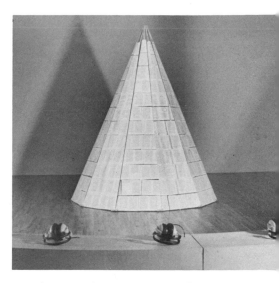

Leandro Katz, *The Teepee,* paper, bamboo, string, and audio construction, John Gibson Gallery, Inc., 1978.

Byron Burford, *The Great Byron Burford Circus of Artistic Wonders,* Iowa City, Iowa (exterior).

Burford, *Circus* (interior).

and zoo animals, almost anything that contributes to the evocation of the circus. Professor Burford (of the University of Iowa) has taken his show to the Venice Biennale and has received grants from the Ford and Guggenheim foundations. His work is a museum that visits museums.

Rafael Ferrer's tent constructions are related to his love of maps and faraway places; his real love, however, appears to be pigment. Like Nil Yalter's *Yurt*, his tent is simultaneously a collection of artifacts and images.

Mr. Ferrer's three major tentworks, *La Luna, Sudan,* and *Sahara* (or *La Vida Secreta*) date from 1976–1977. A Philadelphia canvas-maker produced the tent forms according to the artist's specifications. His first tent, *La Luna,* was ten feet square and windowless — capable of hiding the artist at a gallery opening (Mr. Ferrer's idea). His second, *Sudan,* was eight feet square with small bifurcated windows on each side and a toucan perched inside near the roof. *Sahara* (or *La Vida Secreta*) is a triangular tent with a nineteen-foot-long façade "like a Spanish colonial church, very high in front in order to exaggerate its importance," whose 2 × 4-foot entrance, in Mr. Ferrer's words, leads "nowhere." The colors are of almost unimaginable strength and sensitivity.

Christo, whose project to wrap the Whitney Museum is shown above, does not feel his works fall within the tent format. His materials and construction techniques — in such pieces as the 1970–1972 *Valley Curtain* in California (documented in the Maysles Brothers' film, *Running Fence*) and the 1969 *Wrapped Coast,* where untold numbers of weathered rocks were sheltered by a million square feet of canvas, are close cousins of the tent, even if his inspiration is not.

Rafael Ferrer, *Sudan,* mixed media, 81″ × 96″ × 96″, Nancy Hoffman Gallery, 1976. (Photo: Bevan Davies)

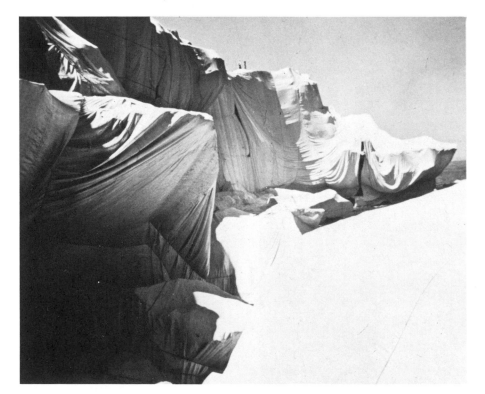

Christo, *Whitney Museum Wrapped,* lithograph and collage, Whitney Museum of American Art, New York, 1971.

Christo, *Wrapped Coast,* one million sq. ft., Little Bay, Australia, 1969.

6 STAGE AND SCREEN

Therefore let us devise some entertainment for them in their tents.

— William Shakespeare, *Love's Labor Lost*, IV.iii.373

In its relation to the tent, ballet is a special case among the performing arts. The tent in ballet is closest to being its own art form because of its possibilities for movement and its integration into the visual whole of the work. The photograph of Oscar Araiz's *Le Sacre du Printemps,* which opens this chapter, is perhaps the best example of the tent that is at once set, costume, and sculpture. It is the unifying element in the choreography, a co-participant with the dancers.

Alwin Nikolais, whose dancers are often clothed in unusual fabric constructions, has shown a particular affinity for the tent. (Mr. Nikolais is responsible for sets, lighting, and costumes, as well as choreography.) Two of his ballets are especially relevant: "Mirrors" (1958), from the series *Vaudeville of the Elements,* opens with an unshaped terra-cotta–colored cloth, which assumes a peaked tent shape as it moves upward, finally glowing with light. His ballet *Tent* (1968) employs a full company of dancers in motion under — and in shifting relation to — the suspended fabric of the set.

The tent in legitimate theater has its own history of magic. It could bring an audience inside an enclosure with the performers, as in *Jumbo;* it could isolate the performers, physically and/or emotionally, from the audience, as in *Victoria Regina,* for example, where we see the queen very much inside The Queen's Tent, and we hope we're not observed as intruders; or in the case of an untold number of opera sets, the tent's

Sheri Cook is the central figure in this grouping from Oscar Araiz's ballet, *Le Sacre du Printemps,* in a 1978 performance by the Royal Winnipeg Ballet. (Photo: Jack Mitchell)

The set from Alwin Nikolais' 1958 ballet, "Mirrors," from the series *Vaudeville of the Elements.* (Photo: David S. Berlin)

A scene from the Nikolais ballet *Tent,* first performed by the Nikolais Dance Theater in 1968 and still in the company repertoire. (Photo: Brynn Manley for Chimera Foundation for Dance)

softness was able to suggest vast perspectives that hard architectural designs could manage only with difficulty.

But America is the country of the movies, and the history of the movie epic is to a great extent the history of the tent in cinema: it has been near impossible to produce such a major work without vast quantities of tent cloth. Of course sandy biblical tales and Roman doings in the eastern Mediterranean both seemed to require huge budgets and a screening time of at least three hours. But the tent, along with sex and violence, was a fundamental element in almost every superfilm that predated *Star Wars*.

Not that there wasn't room in the movies for genteel European tents, Shakespearean tents, safari and Salome tents — and a selection of distinctly American tents such as one might find in any county seat in Ohio, for the circus, the revival, the garden party, and the campground.

But they began in the desert . . .

Surely the most riveting tent scene of the early cinema was Rudolph Valentino's in *The Sheik* (1921). As film censorship was even less developed than film-making, moviegoers were treated to Middle Eastern passions they had only dreamed of seeing on the vaudeville stage. Somehow Valentino emerged from this tent both "breathless" and "panting."

The 1917 production of *Cleopatra* (shot in California in the summer of 1916) duplicated enough of Egypt and Rome to be compared favorably with the spectacles of D. W. Griffith. Theda Bara played Cleopatra with much rolling of the eyes. Here Miss Bara, in the chariot, is driven down an avenue of tents to her final appointment with the asp.

This is Camp Cecil B. DeMille, built for the 1923 extravaganza, *The Ten Commandments*. It was the largest location camp built to that time, housing a production staff of 2500 in separate men's and women's quarters (note the "no-man's-land," as it was referred to, in between). For its day *The Ten Commandments* had a massive budget, some 1.5 million dollars: Mr. DeMille, nevertheless, called it "the cheapest picture ever made" because of the almost instant return on his capital — and all this despite scathing reviews of the film's melodramatic second half, set in modern times. (Photo: Museum of Modern Art)

In this harem scene from the 1925 *Ben-Hur* with Ramon Navarro, acres of cloth were draped from MGM's ceilings. "Probably the most comprehensive spectacular ever filmed," wrote the *New York Times* reviewer. Six years later, the film was re-released with recorded music and additional sound effects.

On the Broadway stage, Rodgers and Hart's *Jumbo*, which opened at the Hippodrome in 1935, used the tent to good effect. The stage was extended over the pit to create a vast circus arena, and a warm red canopy covered both performers and audience. Brooks Atkinson wrote that the circus was recreated "in both odor and appearance."

That same year at the Broadhurst Theater, Helen Hayes had one of her greatest triumphs in *Victoria Regina*. Here, as Queen Victoria, she surveys her favorite country-side at Balmoral from inside a garden tent, while waiting for Prime Minister Disraeli. (Photo: Museum of the City of New York)

Shakespeare's *Richard II* opened on Broadway at the St. James Theater in 1937 to ecstatic reviews and excesses of royal blue tentcloth. In the "accusation of treason" scene pictured here, Maurice Evans (as King Richard) is seated at right. Second on his right is Augustin Duncan, the play's old and near-blind director, in the role of John of Gaunt — in the tiger-striped sleeves. (Photo: Museum of the City of New York)

Ten years later, Loretta Young as the Princess Berengaria prepares to wreak havoc on Henry Wilcoxon (Richard the Lion-Hearted) in this unforgiving publicity shot for Paramount's *The Crusades* (1935). Critics praised Miss Young who, if her acting was less than inspired, still bore up well under the weight of the name Berengaria.

Left: In a classic depression-era spoof, *Ali Baba Goes to Town* (20th Century-Fox, 1937), Eddie Cantor appears as Aloysius Babson, an American who falls in love with an entire movie troupe on location in the desert, joins them as an extra and, after an overdose of painkiller, finds himself in Baghdad in the year 937 — his name, of course, shortened to Ali Baba. This is the pre-painkiller Mr. Cantor.

Right: In Baghdad he is blessed with a harem of 365 wives, led by Gypsy Rose Lee. One of the harem numbers is entitled "Swing Is Here to Sway."

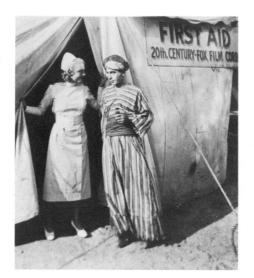

Among the African genre films was 20th Century-Fox's *Stanley and Livingstone* of 1939. Here we see Spencer Tracy as Henry Stanley, still on the trail of old Sir Cedric Hardwicke, who plays David Livingstone. The plot doesn't trouble itself overly with historical fact: you see, Tracy is in love with Nancy Kelly, who loves only Richard Greene. But the whole affair got good reviews for Tracy. (Photo: Museum of Modern Art, New York)

The *New York Times* reported a number of "harem dames in peek-a-boo slacks."

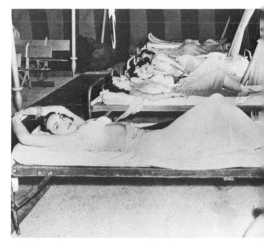

A rare shot of a harem at rest. (In this film the production stills are infinitely more interesting than the final footage.)

Arabian Nights, released by Universal Pictures in 1942, was produced by Walter Wanger, the then president of the Academy of Motion Picture Arts and Sciences, who should have known better. He made almost *no* effort to connect his movie to Sir Richard Burton's classic tales of the same name. Of course, Maria Montez does bring a '40s freshness to the role of Scheherazade.

The end of the Second World War signaled a return to the screen of some serious cinema. Laurence Olivier's 1945 production of *Henry V* begins as a stage play set in the old Globe Theatre of Shakespeare's time, then shifts in an astonishingly believable fashion to rural France in the scenes preceding the Battle of Agincourt. The Elizabethan stage sets at the Globe are as accurate as the French and English battle tents. (Photo: HBW Films)

Left: Now this gentleman and his dark steed would be fun in any tent. It *is* as close as we come to the flying horse of the original *Arabian Nights*.

Right: In the 1953 production of *Julius Caesar*, MGM brought together James Mason (shown here as Brutus), Sir John Gielgud, Marlon Brando, and Louis C. Calhoun under director Joseph L. Mankiewicz. But Mr. Mason never looks quite at ease around so many tents and so much armor.

In *King Solomon's Mines* (MGM, 1950), Deborah Kerr and Stewart Granger have tracked down Miss Kerr's explorer brother, Richard Carlson, under a tent one might expect to see on the beach at Deauville. (Photo: Museum of Modern Art, New York)

In a yet-to-be-explained scene from *King Richard and the Crusaders* (Warner Brothers, 1954), Laurence Harvey (Sir Kenneth) receives an arrow from Rex Harrison (Saladin)'s bow, stands up and — no arrow! It's an unexpected bit of humor that shows the elasticity, indeed the indestructibility, of Laurence Harvey and of Sir Walter Scott's *The Talisman,* on which the film was based. (Photo: Museum of Modern Art, New York)

Not so lucky the recipient of this Mongol sword thrust — from an unidentified Spanish production of *Genghis Khan.* (Photo: *Movie Star News*)

A latter-day desert epic, Columbia Picture's 1962 *Lawrence of Arabia,* with Peter O'Toole, shows the tent unfairly pitted against the airplane (albeit a World War I vintage craft). Actually, three hours and forty minutes is a lot of time for action film clichés. (Photo: Cinemabilia)

In the 1963 version of *Cleopatra,* director Joseph L. Mankiewicz and producer Walter Wanger were back, in Todd-A-O, for four hours and three minutes of "surpassing entertainment." Though costuming and make-up fell prey to a certain updating, the sets involving Cleopatra's barge — with draperies drawn for the feast and orgy in honor of Mark Antony — are given higher marks for historical accuracy.

The draped crib belonging to Cleopatra and Caesar's child has clean enough lines, but isn't that congoleum on the floor and a stereo cabinet against the far wall?

The tent reached deeper into Americana with the 1960 United Artists production of *Elmer Gantry,* starring Burt Lancaster. The revival circuit was portrayed at its most convincing — in a tighter form, most critics felt, than it had been in Sinclair Lewis's original 1927 novel.

In David Storey's play, *The Contractor*, first produced in America in 1971 and shown here in its 1973 production at Chelsea's Westside Theater, the action of the play is set around the erection and dismantling by five workmen of a garden tent for a home wedding. (As tent construction goes, this is quite a change from Broadway's *Carnival* of 1961, where an entire circus tent was set up on stage in the few minutes after curtain-rise.) *The Contractor*'s purposefully slow pacing and the symbolism of the tent's removal at the end leave the viewer with the feeling that, despite enormous turmoil, nothing much has really happened. (Photo: Amnon Ben Nomis)

The garden tent is very American, too. In *The Godfather* (Paramount, 1972), Marlon Brando, as Don Vito Corleone, dances with the daughter he has just given away in marriage to one of the slugs on the left. (Photo: Museum of Modern Art, New York)

Carry On Camping (Peter Rogers Productions, 1972) is marvelous relief. "A significant opportunity for sheer vulgarity buffs" (*N.Y. Times*), it is a late product of the English series that began with *Carry on, Nurse* and, some fear, will never end. It is the kind of movie where the actors keep their real first names on the screen. Shown here are the ladies of the Chayste Place Finishing School — fleeing innuendo, perhaps? (Photo: New York Public Library)

And, peace almost theirs, "Sid" James and "Joan" Sims deplore the miseries of "life in the open and sex in secret." (Photo: New York Public Library)

PART 3

TENTS FOR CAMPERS

7 A CONSUMERS' GUIDE

Sometimes as I am falling asleep in a dark, quiet room I have for a moment a great and treasurable illusion of the past. The wall of a tent leans up over my face, not visible but audible, a slanting plane of faint sound: the susurrous of blown snow. Nothing can be seen. The light-emission of the Chabe stove is cut off, and it exists only as a sphere of heat, a heart of warmth. The faint dampness and confining cling of my sleeping-bag; the sound of the snow; barely audible, Estraven's breathing as he sleeps; darkness. Nothing else. We are inside, the two of us, in shelter, at rest, at the center of all things. Outside, as always, lies the great darkness, the cold, death's solitude.

— Ursula K. LeGuin, *The Left Hand of Darkness*

Designers are having a field day with camping tents, producing an abundance of unique styles made from both natural and space-age fabrics in bold and daring colors. The tent has come a long way from the bulky, highly flammable "wet-wax"-coated model that required at least two persons to get it out of the car trunk, carry it to the campsite, and pitch it. Modern tents are lightweight, stronger, compact, more weatherproof, and a breeze to pitch and take down. They range from plain to fancy, all the way from basic pups to family tents complete with dining rooms, bedrooms, curtains, and wall pockets for storage. Some weigh as little as four pounds (including stakes and poles) and sleep one or two; others sleep ten or more with room to spare for play and storage. And the guy lines we used to trip over have been done away with on many new models, as have obtrusive center poles and the smells that used to emanate from the old models when they got hot (though no one really found them offensive).

The vast number of new designs and developments has resulted from the old reliable supply and demand principle: camping is now the fourth most popular sport in the U.S. today. Even before the onset of the Second World War there were some 20 million automobile campers following the highway trails in this country. In 1977, over 58 million campers — one American in every four — visited one of the more than 20,000 campgrounds on the continent, and well over half of them camped out in tents. The demand for new and better tents absolutely exists and manufacturers are competing to make their tents lighter, stronger, roomier, more weatherproof, and easier to pitch. No matter how, when, or where you intend to use a tent — whether it be for backpacking, mountain climbing, or leisurely vacationing; in winter or summer; in a public campground or alone by the seashore, in the woods, on a mountain, or atop or attached to your car — there's a tent for you at a price you can afford to pay. In short, there's something for everyone.

Doing a little homework before heading out to buy a tent can save both time and money, not to mention enhance your camping trips as a result of your having chosen the right tent. Establishing needs and priorities — number of people, where and how you'll be camping, and so on — is essential.

How many people should the tent accommodate? For comfort, at least twenty-one square feet of floor space per person, and about half that for small children, is required for maximum comfort and ease of movement. If you use cots, you should allow for more. If you pack a lot of gear, some storage space should be included in your estimate of necessary space. Also bear in mind that tents with rectangular floors use space more efficiently than those with square or circular floors. For example, a 7 × 9-foot (63 square feet) tent will provide more room between sleepers than an 8 × 8-foot (64 square feet) or one with an eight-foot diameter (50 square feet).

What shape is best? Tents with vertical sides afford more usable space than those with sloping sides. If you're tenting in rainy areas, you'll need enough room to stand up and move around while you and whomever you're camping with wait for the rain to let up. On the other hand, low-profile tents with sloping sides shed water and wind best, so sacrifices may have to be made if you plan on camping in windy or rainy areas.

Cabin-style tents with vertical sides are roomy and are recommended for large families and semipermanent camps. With modern outside frames they are easily erected and this makes them suitable for car camping — traveling by day and camping out at night.

Many families prefer to use a medium-sized tent (about 8 × 10 feet) for the adults and a smaller pup for the kids (5 × 7 feet). But it's best to have the adult tent slightly on the large side; kids can get scared during the night and come scurrying in with the adults. On such occasions, the pup can be used for storage.

Backpackers need lighter, smaller tents they can easily carry for long distances. Snow camping and high-altitude mountaineering demand strong, stable tents with built-in safety features. These tents must be able to withstand heavy winds and snow loads and often have two entrances in case one becomes blocked. Also special venting is provided in case you have to cook inside, and vestibules and special pockets are optional.

To sum it up, the tent must be chosen for the efficiency with which it can meet its intended use. There are designs, features, and materials to fit virtually every need, and the consumer is fortunate that the market has such an abundance of variations. What you want you can get.

DESIGNS TO CHOOSE FROM

Even though it may appear that with all the options and designs no two tents are alike, they still come in a number of basic styles.

Tarp Tent

Actually nothing more than a flat sheet of protective material, the tarp tent is an old standby and good for pleasant summer weather. It is water-resistant, lightweight, pliable, and usually requires no more than a rope, a tree, and some imagination to make it into any workable shape.

The tarp tent, however, does fall short because it lacks protection at ground level: its loose sides are not attached to a floor, making the occupant quite vulnerable to rain, wind, dust, and mosquitos. Prices range from three dollars for a small plastic tarp to thirty dollars for a good coated nylon style.

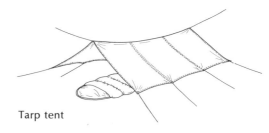

Tarp tent

Tube Tent

Though it can serve as adequate shelter on a balmy summer night, don't expect protection from any wind or rain, and watch the condensation resulting from body moisture condensing on the nonbreathable plastic walls. The tube tent is simply a plastic sleeve and resembles a large garbage bag open on both ends. It is suspended by running a line through the tent and tying it to two trees. Then the sides are expanded by placing heavy stones along them on the inside of the tent. These tents weigh a couple of pounds and cost about three or four dollars. You get what you pay for here, and that's very little, though it can be enough.

Tube tent

Modified Tube Tent

Called a "super tube" by some manufacturers, all the modified tube has in common with the tube is its open-ended design, and in the case of the modified tube the open ends are usually covered with mosquito netting. Not having any ends or solid flap panels makes this tent unsuitable for use in the rain, wind, or cold. And, like the tube, condensation can be a problem as this tent is constructed of urethane-coated fabric, which is also nonbreathable. The floor is made of a heavier grade of the same material. Aluminum poles support the tent and pegs anchor it. A pullout (see page 171) on each side provides adequate sleeping space inside.

Future improvements will probably make this tent a viable alternative.

pullout

Modified tube tent

Without end flaps and breathing fabric it is suitable for use only in moderate weather or extremely arid zones. These tents are also reasonably priced at about fifty dollars. The weight of tent, pegs, and poles is in the vicinity of three pounds.

One-Person Shelter

These superlight tents are among the latest innovations in tent design. Though highly effective, they are not popular because hiking is not a one-person activity. The tents are not adequate for alpine or deep winter use, and none of them comes equipped with a frost liner, even as an option, perhaps because manufacturers are in agreement that winter camping should not be done alone.

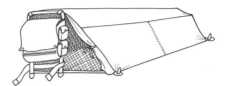

One-person shelter

Many of these designs use the backpack as an integral part of the shelter, so an obvious advantage is that the contents of the pack are handy. Actually the tent is little more than a fancy sleeping-bag cover. One-person tents have a sewn-in floor, mosquito netting, and a venting system, but no rainfly (a rooflike structure suspended above the tent, see below). They weigh from two to four pounds and prices usually start at sixty dollars.

Pup/Scout Tent

These small or medium-sized tents are generally supported by two vertical end poles and are held taut by guy lines staked into the ground. They're simple and sturdy and are used for one or two campers with a minimum amount of gear. A-frame tents are a variation on the pup tent, as are backpacking tents (see below). A-frames have support poles that follow the lines of the tent sides rather than center poles which allows easier access to the tent.

Pup/scout tent

Backpacking Tent

This is one of the best compromises of weight and design. Backpacking tents are almost always made of lightweight nylon and are intended to take, at most, just a few minutes to erect. Since nylon, unlike heavier cotton, can't be both waterproof and breathable, most nylon tents are made of breathable fabric and come equipped with a waterproof rainfly. Most are small, though some models sleep more than four. And, most of these can be separated into more than one pack, so no one carries the whole load.

Backpacking tent with fly

The standard backpacker's tent usually lacks a couple of features that can be handy on the trail — a vestibule, which is a short compartment at the front for gear stowage, boot removal, cooking, and brushing off snow; and a frost shield or liner, which would extend the practical use of the tent into all seasons. These features are available on snow and expedition tents.

Backpack models weigh anywhere from three to twelve pounds and range in cost from about fifty to two hundred dollars.

Lineless or A-Frame Tent

Self-supporting tents are extremely popular among campers. Most of these tents are modified pup and wall-design tents and come equipped with a rainfly. Aluminum alloy poles (they pack in sections) are inserted through sleeves at either end or partially inside the tent after the floor is spread out and staked down. The pairs of poles join at the top and are held to the floor below by grommets. Lines extending from the pole tops and tent sides are staked down to hold the tent securely. Properly tied down, the tent stands up very well in high winds.

Lineless or A-frame tent

The lineless tent — and there are many variations on the design — may be pitched on an area only slightly larger than the tent floor itself, and no bushes, trees, or ropes are required for guy line support. One obvious advantage is that on crowded camp trails there's no worry about anyone tripping over guy ropes since, of course, there are none.

These tents weigh and cost only slightly more than the standard back-packer's tent. All in all, this is an excellent choice. Most models run from $100 to $250; a good quality unit can be had for about $125. Weight runs five to twelve pounds.

Snow Tent

These tents have elaborate entrance, vestibule, vent, and anchoring systems. Though designed for winter operation, they serve in summer as well since many hikers cannot afford both the more costly winter tent and a lightweight tent for other seasons.

Most models have a snow tunnel entrance at one end with a standard flap arrangement at the vestibule end. This allows for easy entrance if gear is stowed or if cooking is taking place at the vestibule exit. Some of these tents have a zippered cook hole in the tent floor, which lets the occupant cook inside during harsh weather without messing the floor. Even so, it's best to cook inside only when absolutely necessary: nylon is not fully fireproof and begins to melt at fairly low temperatures and stoves, portable heaters, and even small candles use oxygen and generate massive amounts of carbon monoxide. So an efficient vent system is as imperative as keeping the flame away from the tent fabric.

Snow tent

In many cases the winter tent will require flukes or snow anchors instead of regular stakes. Also, this tent has wide flaps along the bottom of the side walls, which may be loaded with snow for added stability and warmth.

Weight and costs are substantially more than the standard backpacking tent. Plan on anywhere from eight to twelve pounds and at least $150 to $250. And bear in mind that with the potential perils of winter camping, the extra weight and cost are totally justified.

Expedition Tent

The expedition tent takes the snow tent design to its ultimate, incorporating the finest materials and workmanship to provide shelter in the most extreme conditions. Many models include an optional snow liner and extra-long fly that almost reaches the ground. For long-term camping at high altitudes in bitter cold, all models include a highly efficient vent system, the double-entry system, and a cooking hole or vestibule. And fabric research has produced Gore-Tex, which under ideal conditions is a breathing and waterproof material that renders the rainfly unnecessary (though manufacturers recommend carrying one along for added wind and cold protection).

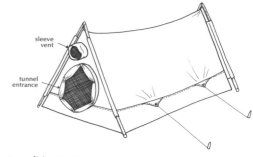

Expedition tent

Some of these tents come with an insulated floor composed of two layers of waterproof material between which is a waffled insulating grid. The result is tiny air pockets that help keep cold out, though some manufacturers have discontinued this feature since lightweight sleeping pads that are somewhat more efficient are now available.

The expedition tent, like the snow tent, can serve the hiker year round, but the expedition tent can sometimes be too warm inside in intense summer heat.

Weights range from about six to twelve pounds or more, like the snow tent, but prices are higher, up to $300.

Exoskeleton Tent

A variation on the lineless theme, the exoskeleton tent is completely self-supporting as well. This tent is hooked to several assembled sections of aluminum tubing that hold it firm, tight, and highly stable. The involved frame does require extra tubing, which adds weight, but you're spared stakes and ropes. Also, the entire tent can easily be lifted and repositioned.

Exoskeleton tent

These tents, as with most all-purpose tents, have a netted window at the rear and a separate mosquito net inside the weather flap. The overhang of the contoured rainfly allows the flaps to be left open in humid heat and still protect the interior from the rain. A disadvantage, however, is the difficulty of stabilizing these flaps in a high wind, especially with the rainfly attached (which aggravates the situation). Only a few come equipped with wind lines near the top.

Exoskeletons vary in size. A two-person model weighs from ten to twelve pounds and the four-person tent can hit twenty-five pounds, which disqualifies it for backpacking. The price of the smaller units varies widely — from $200 down — while the larger unit can cost $200 to $300 and up.

Dome Tent

The dome is another of the lineless models, but provisions have been made on it for securing a stabilized network if a strong wind whips up. From an engineering point of view (and Buckminster Fuller's) the dome is one of the most efficient shelter designs possible — it is quite stable in wind, can handle weight from snow or water accumulation, and makes best use of space in relation to exterior size. The more refined dome designs can be pitched in a couple of minutes with a half-dozen fiber

Dome tent

glass rods. Like the exoskeleton, this tent can be picked up and carried once it's erected. Most models include a rainfly as standard equipment since the upper portion has to be made of breathing fabric.

One early disadvantage of the dome was occasional difficulty in separating the fiber glass support rods that were joined by metal ferrules. This would happen after the tent had been weighted down by rain or snow, bending the rods somewhat and causing the connections to freeze. Manufacturers have now solved this problem and domes are enjoying the popularity they rightly deserve.

The rainfly on the dome is a bit heavy, and frost shields are not available, though rather good protection from rain and cold is offered by the rainfly alone. Models weigh from under six to over thirteen pounds complete and cost from about $100 to $275.

One modification of the dome has only four supports and a rectangular floor and is appropriately called a "wedge" by a company that manufactures it. It defeats the initial purpose of the dome, but makes a fine trail shelter nonetheless.

Tunnel Tent

The tunnel tent is a newcomer to the market, and has proven itself to be one of the most stable and comfortable tents made, performing perfectly against the very worst of conditions.

A rainfly is built into the tent and the shape is aerodynamic and capable of withstanding severe winter winds, heavy rains, or thousands of pounds of snow loading. And no amount of wind will make the rainfly flap. Though it takes a little more time to erect than some of the simpler tents, the extra comfort and safety obtained make it worth it. A disadvantage is the means of entry and exit, which is made difficult by the guy lines supporting the tent. Weighing in at just six pounds, there are two shells of fabric — an inner breathing shell and an outer waterproof shell, with an optional vestibule and hollow fiber glass supports with aluminum ferrules that are kept together by shock cords (see page 180) and don't stick together.

Tunnel tent

This tent has been enthusiastically accepted by serious mountaineers and so far is only manufactured by Early Winters & Recreational Equipment, Inc., though other companies make variations. The price with the vestibule can exceed $300. It may be too much money and tent for some, but in this case you get what you pay for.

Wall Tent

The wall tent has been around for centuries and can be as large or as small as specific needs demand. Basically an A-shaped configuration with high vertical walls, there is a great deal of living space inside. The tent is supported either with two wooden poles or the poles plus a horizontal ridgepole to keep the tent from sagging. Guy lines attach to the sides and hold them outward.

Wall tents can be rigged to keep the floor free of supports; however,

Wall tent

this is usually contrived by cutting down a dozen or so stout young trees and constructing an exterior frame with them. (See photo of an encampment in the Klondike that uses this method, page 46.) Environmental considerations have rightly discontinued this practice.

This tent tends to weigh a lot, especially with poles and pegs, but it is still one of the old reliables for the vehicular, horseback, or boat camper. With all that weight — and they can weigh over 300 pounds — at least you get a lot of room: The tent has a high weight to space ratio.

Cabin Tent

The cabin tent is a wall tent with high vertical sides usually supported by an exterior frame that can be a roof-truss style or a yoke-type.

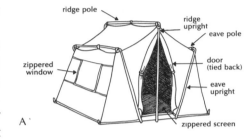

The roof-truss style is the predominant design. Three horizontal poles — a center ridgepole and two opposite eave poles — are connected independently to vertical poles leading to the ground. The three-section outside frame makes for a sound, stable structure that is easy to set up. Tension is adjusted by shortening or lengthening the poles. The only disadvantage is that the ridgepole is in the middle of the doorway, but the doorway is designed to be big enough for easy entrance and exit on each side of the pole.

The other cabin-shaped tents have a yoke-type frame, so called because the frame supports and shapes the tent with bowed poles connected by a central horizontal ridgepole (like a yoke). There are no eave poles on this tent; the U-shape yokes pass around to the sides of the tent and dig into the ground. The obvious advantage is that the door is not blocked with this arrangement. The potential disadvantage is maintaining tension if the ground is soft: fabric tension is adjusted by moving the uprights from one spot in the ground to another.

Cabin tents: A. roof-truss cabin tent; B. yoke-type cabin tent

These cabin tents provide a lot of interior room and uninterrupted floor space; they come in many sizes and sleep from four to ten. Some are equipped with attached or attachable screen rooms or awnings for sleeping out on balmy nights or relaxing in the shade. Families like the roominess and convenience of a cabin tent.

Prices range from $100 to about $275 and cabin tents weigh anywhere from twenty to sixty pounds.

Umbrella Tent

Medium-sized and square, umbrella tents have characteristic pyramid-shaped roofs with sides that gradually slope outward. The older models are of the inside frame variety, the new ones are supported by an exterior frame that makes a roomy enough interior for two to four people; the older center pole models limit both headroom and living space. The umbrella tent is a favorite of boat and car campers because of a desirable ratio of weight to room and comfort. This tent is carried in a canvas bag and fits quite easily into a boat or car trunk.

The average umbrella tent weighs no more than forty pounds, many weigh less, and it is not much of a problem to carry to a tent site, even

Umbrella tent

one that is a substantial distance from the unloading point. Smaller models can, with difficulty, accommodate up to four cots; prices range from $50 to $200.

Ice-Fishing Tent

The ice-fishing tent — usually similar to the design of an umbrella tent with an exterior framework — can be set up on the ice to shield the occupant from the icy winter winds that come lashing across large frozen expanses.

Ice-fishing tent

The few models available come equipped with features such as base sod cloths to keep out wind, jigging holes with flap covers built into the floor, rings inside for suspending equipment, and special vents. The tent anchors into the ice with metal spikes.

Some carrying bags for these tents have handles and rings so they can easily be attached to snow machines. Total weight is about eight pounds and they retail for about $50 or $60, though there is one handmade model available, complete with a wooden floor, that sells for as much as $150.

Pyramid Tent

The lighter weight pyramid tent works nicely for large hiking parties. One pyramid tent can sleep three or four people and weighs less than two backpacker's tents, which hold two people each. These tents have a vertical side that provides a large floor area in relation to the weight of the tent. Headroom is limited along the sides and there is a center pole, which can sometimes restrict use of space, but the tent allows for efficient heating, enough sleeping room, and a gathering place for all the hikers in your group. Also, the shape can take quite a load of snow without great loss of interior space. These tents have provided shelter for serious mountain climbers and have proven their worth repeatedly.

Pyramid tents: A. with wall; B. without wall

The larger pyramids aren't carried by most hikers because of their weight. The rainfly for these tents is also big and bulky. Otherwise they're efficient tents, especially for long stops at base camps.

A good pyramid-style backpack tent sells for anywhere from $100 to $200 and weighs in at approximately eleven pounds.

Another version of the pyramid tent doesn't have sides that are perpendicular to the ground. It is actually a square tipi and enjoys some popularity among car and boat campers. Headroom can be limited, but there's a large amount of floor space in relation to overall size. Pyramid tents have been used by full-time campers like sheepherders and prospectors and were a common sight on the gold fields of California and the Klondike. One of their advantages is the shape, which sheds rain and snow more readily than other tents. They can be supported by an improvised outside frame, tied to an overhead tree limb, and one manufacturer produces a four-cornered aluminum frame. Like the umbrella and hiker's pyramid, a center pole severely restricts room inside.

This tent does not have an efficient space to weight ratio and saw its greatest use earlier in this century, but it will undoubtedly continue to find applications.

Explorer Tent

The forward half of the explorer tent bears a resemblance to a wall tent and the rear half is a pyramid. Good headroom is available upon entering, but not for long as the shape begins dropping quickly toward the back.

Another disadvantage is that the back slope collects rain or snow and can bear down on the occupant in his or her cot. Interior support systems can also be a problem: center poles can restrict use of interior space. For these reasons the explorer tent is not one of the more popular tents.

The explorer tent is slightly lighter than the umbrella, though the weight difference is negligible when considering how much more space you get with the umbrella tent.

Explorer tent

Baker Tent

The baker tent is a modified lean-to with a front wall that can be raised to provide open-air cooking and lounging space or closed to protect the inside area against wind and rain. The tent was originally designed to facilitate heating by allowing a reflecting fire inside. But open fires in tents are dangerous and so this feature is not an advantage.

A baker tent is fairly heavy for the space you get inside and almost impossible to fit with a rainfly. The open design prevents condensation from forming inside, so baker tents are made of fully waterproofed canvas drill. These tents do make good supply tents or additional sleeping quarters in mild weather, and they may also be connected right to your car.

Baker tents are still manufactured and can fit the needs of some campers. L. L. Bean's catalogue price for their nylon baker tent is $101, screened porch is $24, and a vertical protecting side curtain is another $13.

Baker tent

Screen or Net Tent

These warm-weather specials have either mosquito netting for sides or flaps that roll up to expose large panels of netting. On a still, dry summer night they can be perfection.

They come in various designs, though they are for the most part A-frame or cabin tent designs. The smaller ones weigh very little and can certainly provide the occupant with the feeling of sleeping under the stars, but there is neither protection from the elements nor privacy in any kind of group camping situation, unless your tent has flaps that car zip up to cover the netting.

On the smaller models made of netting without canvas flaps, neither the weight nor cost is much less than that of a more traditional canvas tent. And if the extra flaps are provided to cover the netting, allow for even more weight and expense. The screen or net tent is called a fair-

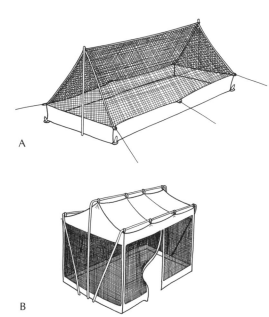

Screen or net tents: A. one-person; B. family

weather tent and it's just that. One weighs about six pounds and can cost up to $100.

The screen cabin tent is usually used as a dining tent and can add an element of luxury to your camping trip. They make excellent backyard dining and party quarters as well. But again, the same drawbacks with net sides exist. The models with polyethylene roofs imported from eastern Asia (mainly Taiwan) retail for from $45 to $55 whereas the canvas roof models go for between $80 and $130. The cheaper model is quite a popular item these days.

Cottage Tent

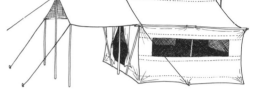

Cottage tent

These are among the largest and most luxurious tents available. Some models are extravaganzas with as many as two or three bedrooms, a kitchen, sun porch, clothes closet, and provision for a rubberized bathtub. This model also sports an aluminized fabric roof that reflects heat or cold away from the lucky occupants. The roof also has holes lined with asbestos for cooking and heating stove pipes. This model takes man and machine (mobile crane) to erect, but less luxurious, more easily manageable, and totally adequate cabin tents are available for the person who really wants a home away from home. Cottage tents are heavy and expensive, but they are an excellent choice for the very long term camp. Once you get one to the site and get it erected, it's a waste if you don't stay awhile. Some guides and outfitters erect them at their base of operations and leave them up all season. The average cottage tent costs about $250.

FABRIC

A tent must be comfortable and dry. This means the material must have two qualities that are difficult to combine in a lightweight fabric — breathability and water-repellency. Breathability refers to the fabric's ability to let air circulate through it: you do not want to keep the exhaled moisture of the tent's occupants in because stuffiness and condensation on the tent's walls results. The human body can exhale a pint of moisture during a night, and if the moisture cannot escape, you'll wake up in it.

The other side of the tent is exposed to rain — and it can rain more than a pint — so your tent fabric must be able to protect you from without as well. Cotton fabric is the only material that breathes and is waterproof, but it is heavy and not suited for lightweight backpacking tents. Cotton also is subject to mildew and rot if not dried and stored properly. If touched from the inside of the tent during a rainstorm, it will begin to leak as a result of capillary action. Also, cotton fibers can swell and shorten when wet so tent stakes must be loose enough to avoid the wet tent's pulling the stakes from the ground or tearing seams. Also, cotton weaves tend to weigh more after treatment with fire retardants than nylons do. But the advantages of cotton still make it king in the tent business.

Featherweight nylon is ideal in the weight department, but it falls flat in breathability and water-repellency. As a solution for the backpacker who needs the lightest tent possible, manufacturers make the roofs of their nylon tents out of porous nylon so body-produced heat and moisture can pass out, and they suspend a waterproof fly a few inches above the roof to shed water. This system works okay; however, in wet weather, the double roof's ability to eliminate water from within can become overloaded, making it quite uncomfortable inside.

At present there are two synthetic fabrics designed especially to incorporate breathability and water repellency.

1. Gore-Tex, a super-lightweight, Teflon-like plastic film, has pores that are 20,000 times smaller than a water droplet (so it sheds water) and more than 700 times larger than water vapor molecules (so moisture can pass through the fabric). It is so thin that it must be bonded to another fabric or sandwiched between two fabrics, usually ripstop nylon and rayon. Gore-Tex works best when body heat warms the air and creates a slightly higher vapor pressure inside the tent. It is this pressure which pushes water vapor through the Gore-Tex and out the tent. If vents are open, no pressure can build up inside and the moisture stays in and condenses on the cooler surfaces of the fabric, just as it does on uncoated nylon. And in cold weather, when the occupants are bundled up in their sleeping bags, since the heat stays in the bags and does not heat the air, a Gore-Tex canopy can frost up. But it remains a formidable achievement, and under the right conditons, it does work.

2. A fabric that is expected to be a breakthrough in the family-tent field has been developed by a major fabric-producing company. In addition to combining water repellency and breathability, it is one-third lighter than canvas and will not rot or mildew. The fabric is made of polyprophlene and is composed of three layers — the two outer layers are made of strong, durable material and the center layer is a feltlike mat consisting of very fine filaments. These layers are melded into a sandwich that has excellent flexibility, even at low temperatures, and will never stretch or shrink. These qualities have contributed to the creation of even more exciting and functional tent designs as fabric behavior has always been a limitation. (In fact, Bill Moss [see pages 190–192], has used this fabric in new designs for himself and for the manufacturer.) The material is also flame retardant (additives increase its inherent flame retardant qualities along with making it more durable), and it breathes and repels water better than canvas. A water particle cannot find its way through the labyrinth of very fine fibers but air can pass through freely. This fabric acts on the principle of a maze in repelling water and breathing, whereas Gore-Tex can be compared to a selective sieve.

So, besides the two newer fabrics mentioned above, campers have had a choice of the heavier cotton tent, the nylon fly tent, or a variety of tents made from either nylon or polyester with cotton to incorporate the breathability advantages of cotton with the lightweight features of the synthetic fabric. The two materials can be woven together in a blend or specific fabrics are used on specific sections of the tent. Some tents have cotton tops and synthetic walls. (This is not a bad idea if the tent is to be used in cold, windy areas, since relatively impermeable walls can prove

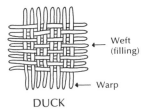

← Weft (filling)

← Warp

DUCK

DRILL

Weave of fabric

a better buffer against cold winds than porous cotton.) Other tents have breathable walls and waterproof roofs. The floors are usually made of heavy-duty vinyl-covered nylon. This stands up to the abuse a floor gets. Plastic has also been used as a floor material, but it can become dry and brittle and crack after prolonged use, so avoid it.

It's all a matter of weight and compactness. A lightweight fabric must be used in order to make a tent easy to carry for the hiker and compactable for him or her to stuff into a small bag, although weight and compactness are not necessarily prime considerations for the camper who will take the tent to the campsite by car, boat, or on horseback. Again, it is your demands that determine the type of fabric you will want.

The following (with the exception of the two new fabrics mentioned above) are the fabrics that have been most commonly used by tent makers:

Duck

This is the strongest and heaviest of cotton tent fabrics. The name is derived from a trademark of a duck stenciled on heavy sailcloth imported from Europe about 1840. Duck is tightly woven so that each warp yarn passes over or under the weft or filling yarn. This construction is similar to that of loop potholders made by children. Duck is manufactured in weights from seven to fifteen ounces per square yard. Army bivouac and truck tarps are made from twelve- to fifteen-ounce duck, while seven- to eight-ounce weights are suitable for camping tents, though some of the larger wall and cottage tents are made from ten-ounce duck. The density of this fabric is an advantage in that it provides privacy for those inside the tent. If only duck were lighter, it would be perfect for all tents.

Twill and Drill

Twill is woven in such a way that each warp yarn passes over two or more weft yarns, under the next two, and so on, producing a staggered weave that creates a noticeable diagonal pattern in the weave of the cloth. Denim blue jean fabric is a twill and has a very high thread count per square inch. Drill is a twill cloth that is more loosely woven into a three-leaf twill. Khaki is drill cloth, and drill is the lowest quality of tent fabric.

Cotton Poplin

This is a ribbed, tightly woven sturdy fabric made by using weft yarns that are heavier and coarser than warp yarns. Poplin comes in weights from four to eleven ounces per square yard. Five-and-a-half- to eight-ounce weight poplin is used on some of the better family tents.

Ripstop Nylon

Nylon is the staple of backpackers and other tent-weight-conscious campers, and ripstop is the form of nylon most commonly used. It has a gridwork of heavy threads woven in at intervals — usually quarter-inch — to increase fabric strength.

Nylon Taffeta

This lustrous-finish lightweight nylon is the same on both sides and has good abrasion resistance. Taffeta may weigh less than two ounces per square yard and is sometimes coated with polyurethane to make it waterproof.

Vinyl-Coated Nylon

Used for tent floors, this heavyweight plastic-coated nylon is stronger and more resistant to abrasion than coated taffeta. However, its vinyl coating has been known to soften or peel if exposed to harsh solvents, such as insecticides or kerosene.

Polyethylene-Coated Polyethylene

Just that. It's water and mildew proof and is commonly used for tarpaulins and tent floors. It is a tough woven fabric with a polyethylene coating on both sides.

FIRE-RETARDANT AND WATERPROOF TREATMENTS

In 1972, the Camping Division of the Canvas Products Association International developed the CPAI-84 flammability standard. This states that a fabric be fire-retardant but not fireproof. On fabric that has been treated with flame retardant, when subject for twelve seconds to a flame, the fabric smolders but will not ignite, and when the flame is removed, the fire will die. This legislation came about largely because of the public's strong reaction to children being burned in play tents made of highly flammable wax-finished cotton. (Cotton is wet-waxed in order to waterproof it.) In fact, most of the early tent fires, including the tragic Ringling Brothers, Barnum & Bailey Big Top fire of 1944 in which 168 persons were killed, resulted from the highly flammable properties of wet-wax canvas.

Cotton tents waterproofed with a light dry finish won't flash-flame, though they will burn slowly. And with a flame-retardant treatment, they will smolder when exposed to flame. However, when treated they are more expensive, stiffer, darker in color, and some 20 percent heavier than similarly untreated fabric. So, still, there are definite disadvantages to flame-retardant treatment of cotton tents.

Moreover, the National Park Service and the United States Forest Service have not found a single case of anyone being burned in a backpacking-type tent (which is made from nylon and never wet-waxed). Many backpackers, along with *Backpacking* magazine, object to flame-retardants being used because they are possibly carcinogenic. Some tent fabrics are treated with Tris, the same carcinogenic chemical used on children's sleepwear, which caused a recent stir, and the possible hazards of the modified thiourea compounds also in use are as yet undetermined. Backpackers also object to flame retardant fabrics because they think flame-retardant treatment is perhaps unnecessary: the nylon and Gore-Tex materials used on backpacking tents do not flash-flame like cotton does, they burn with a small localized flame, smolder, and melt. But, at the present time, California, Louisiana, Massachusetts, Minnesota, and Michigan require that camping tents sold in their states meet CPAI-84 standards. These regulations have given Gore-Tex a rough time — in the CPAI tests; it doesn't extinguish quickly enough after the flame source is removed and therefore cannot be sold in the five states mentioned above. Many manufacturers don't want to deal with a fabric they can't market nationwide.

No matter how tightly nylon fabric is woven, it is never waterproof because the threads will not expand when wet to fill the holes between the threads. Also, the threads do not absorb the waterproofing chemicals used on cotton, so nylon has to be coated with a polymer, polyurethane, or vinyl finish which can peel off the tent with time and use. When this vinyl coating is applied to both sides of a tent it will stick because it bonds right through the nylon, but it substantially increases the weight of the tent. But waterproofing is a necessity with nylon and if it is treated only on one side and peels off with wear and tear, it can be recoated.

Cotton, on the other hand, being a natural fiber, swells when wet and therefore is theoretically waterproof. But if touched during a rainstorm from the inside, it will leak by capillary action, and loosely woven drills and twills are by no means waterproof fabrics. Tightly woven poplin and duck can be waterproofed with a light dry finish, but the more loosely-woven fabrics require the heavy "wet-wax" finish, and this finish is quite susceptible to mildew as well as being the fire hazard mentioned above.

CONSTRUCTION

The best way to evaluate the workmanship, construction, and basic design of any tent is to set it up right there in the retail outlet. Though they may not like it, salespersons should be willing to allow this, especially if it may mean a sale. And it's the only way you as a consumer will really know what you're getting — as opposed to taking an unfamiliar tent home with you and then not being satisfied with it. Perhaps if there is a display model available, you can take it down and then set it up again. If it's not possible or practical to set up the tent in the store, make sure it is returnable.

Below are listed the component parts and systems of the tent with tips on what to look for and avoid in each area.

Framing

Tents are either internally or externally framed. Before you buy a tent, inspect the poles. They should be free of burrs so they won't bind when being joined or snag the tent fabric. More manufacturers are coming out with shock-corded poles. Shock cord is an elastic rope made of bands of rubber sheathed in nylon. By running a length of shock cord through the hollow tubes that are to be joined in order to set up the tent, the sections snap easily into position and there's no fumbling for the right poles since they're already attached. Also, the possibility of losing a pole section is eliminated. Shock-corded poles are a definite advantage and are usually found on the better backpacking tents. However, so far only one or two tent manufacturers have shock-corded the poles of their larger family tents. Shock cords are also used quite efficiently as guy ropes. (See next section, Anchoring.)

A few tents come with aluminum pole segments that telescope inside each other. This makes them quite compact, but they are subject to bending and jamming if proper care and handling are not exercised.

Poles are usually made of aluminum alloy. The most common are 6061, 6063, and 7001. Some of these alloys are tempered and you can identify them by the letter *T* in the code number, such as 6063-T6.

Joints made of brass-on-aluminum or plastic-on-aluminum are far better than pure aluminum because they are less likely to freeze, and they wear better. Nevertheless, joints can jam. To prevent this it is always best to keep pole joints lubricated with oil or silicone spray. If poles do get stuck, heat them where they are jammed. Just keep in mind that your stove or fire can melt the aluminum, so rotate the pole to distribute heat evenly. Then a tap should dislodge it.

Poles used on the new dome and tunnel tents must be very flexible and very strong. The most popular material for flexible tent poles is a fiber glass rod some 5/16 inch in diameter, which is attached to a metal sleeve or ferrule, forming a joint into which another rod is inserted. This pole-support system has the disadvantage of being heavier than rigid aluminum and can splinter or jam under heavy stress. When purchasing a tent with fiber glass poles, check to make sure there are no cracks in the poles or splinters at the ends. If there are, it indicates a weak pole.

Two other alternatives exist for the support of dome and tunnel tents. One is flexible aluminum alloy, the other is hollow fiber glass. Aluminum alloy has less spring than fiber glass and makes for a more rigid tent. The hollow poles also can be shock-corded. Hollow fiber glass is the lightest of all, and the machine-alloy connectors nearly eliminate joint failures.

On tents with outside frames, the bottom tips of most aluminum tent poles are supported by a grommet or similar device to secure the poles to the corners of the tent floor. This keeps the poles from sinking into the ground, thereby maintaining the form of the tent. Another way is to have an aluminum ring with a sliding pin that slips into the base of the pole sewn into each corner of the tent. Eureka! Tent, Inc., in Binghamton, New York, came up with this and it is successful in that the normal stress and strain of a pole in a side pocket is absorbed by the ring and pin. One other method of anchoring poles to tent sides is to have them slip into fabric pockets at the pole base. But pockets can sometimes be too snug or too short, and they are subject to abrasion where the pole bottoms touch the ground.

Tents without a means of securing the poles at the base are likely to be floppy in windy weather.

FRAME CONNECTIONS

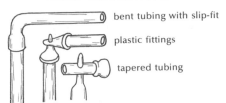

bent tubing with slip-fit

plastic fittings

tapered tubing

FRAME LENGTH ADJUSTMENT LOCKS

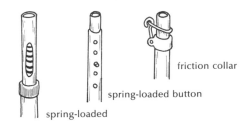

friction collar

spring-loaded button

spring-loaded

STAKE LOOPS

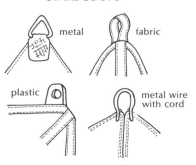

metal

fabric

plastic

metal wire with cord

UPRIGHT ENDS

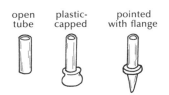

open tube

plastic-capped

pointed with flange

Tent construction details

Anchoring

The number of stakes and guy lines used in pitching a tent depends entirely on the tent design and the camping conditions. When staking conditions are poor, tent performance suffers because stakes cannot hold firmly in sand, snow, and soft or muddy soil. When the stakes pull out, conventional tents collapse. In conditions such as these, self-supporting tents perform best, but they also have to be securely anchored or, if there's nobody inside to hold them down, they will literally blow away.

Different ground surfaces dictate the use of different stakes. Tent stakes come in a variety of styles, and all have their limitations. Light aluminum or steel skewers, which work well only in firm soil or packed snow, are furnished with most tents. A spiral-threaded long nail put out by Camp Trails Company in Arizona is one of the best stakes of this type. The wider stakes made of aluminum and plastic are designed for softer ground. Most manufacturers supply only one type of stake with their tents; an exception is Stephenson's of Woodland Hills, California, who supplies none and leaves that decision up to the buyer, who knows best where he or she is going to be camping. Veteran campers have always carried a variety of extra stakes to fit the various terrains they'll be camping on.

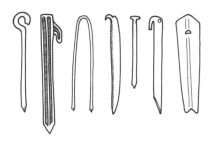

Tent stakes: (left to right) aluminum skewer with "O" closure at end; plastic stake; aluminum "U" peg; aluminum channeled stake (semicircular shaft of aluminum sheet with rolled lip at top for line); long nail; angle snow peg

When purchasing a tent, if metal stakes are supplied, check to make sure they are well finished. Poles and pegs should have no burrs to snag the tent material when it is packed. Hammering also can burr a metal stake, so check your stakes before packing them up.

The stake loops are another important factor in tent strength. These are the attachments that are most subject to stress, both from hammering the stakes in and holding the tent in place. Check the size of the tent's stake loops. Some manufacturers produce tents with loops through which only very thin stakes will fit. Fabric loops should be large enough to accept intermediate metal rings or a variety of stakes. Check to make sure the loops are securely sewn to the tent fabric. Metal rings between the loops and the stakes are a good idea — they are quite strong and help prevent rough stake edges from abrading and weakening the loop fabric. Rings are also preferred whenever stakes are driven deeply into the ground, burying the loops. Grit can become embedded in the fabric loop and the loop will eventually weaken.

There are also various ways to anchor a tent when staking will not work. Several manufacturers sell wide blades or deadman anchors (also

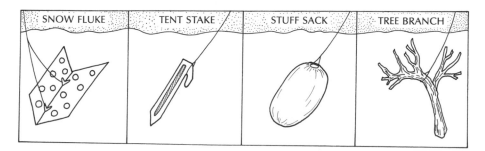

| SNOW FLUKE | TENT STAKE | STUFF SACK | TREE BRANCH |

Anchoring alternatives in snow

called snow flukes), which are designed to be buried under snow or sand. Buried tent stakes, stuffed sacks, or tree branches will also suffice.

Snow flaps (see page 169) are also an advantage in pitching a tent because rocks, logs, sand, or snow can be piled on the flaps to anchor the tent in sites where staking would not provide adequate holding power.

Guy lines are made from Manila rope, nylon rope, or elasticized shock cords. The shock cords are more expensive but are well worth the cost because they cushion the stresses caused by wind and allow for the natural stretching and shrinking of cotton fabric.

Tent Seams

The best and strongest tent seams are both double-stitched and flat-felled. A flat-felled seam is one in which the fabric edges are wrapped around each other into interlocking J's and sewn into double seams so that there are no open raw edges and the stitching binds together four layers of material. These seams, when properly sealed, will not leak and will withstand high winds. The next strongest seam is the lapped seam, and the weakest of all is the plain seam. All three types are strongest when they are double-stitched, which is considered a minimum essential construction requirement for all types of tent seams.

Seams with fewer than four and one half or five stitches to the inch will be weak (this flaw is common in less expensive tents). Better models have from seven to twelve stitches per inch, but more than twelve will weaken the fabric. It is recommended that high altitude tents, which must be especially wind-resistant, have at least eight stitches per inch and be double-stitched in flat-fell seams. The number of stitches per inch is related to the material used for the tent. Heavy cotton swells and can only take about six stitches per inch but nylon and other light materials may require seven or more.

Note the quality of sewing as well as the number of stitches per inch. Variations in the tightness of the thread, badly puckered and crooked seams, large needle holes, and dangling loose ends, where the stitching stops before the end of the seam, weaken the tent construction and contribute to leakage. All seams should end with either backstitching, which is a type of sewing in which the stitch is run back on itself, or be tied off to lock the seam and prevent it from opening or unraveling.

Thread materials have varying strengths and weaknesses. Cotton thread by itself lacks sufficient strength to withstand heavy winds and is used in very inexpensive tents. However, wet cotton swells to plug the needle holes and stops leakage through them. Nylon is strongest but also stretches and is deteriorated by the ultraviolet radiation of sunlight and may melt during high-speed sewing. Dacron almost equals the holding power of nylon, resists the elements, and can be used with smaller needles (thereby creating smaller seam holes), but is less elastic. The most popular tent thread is a combination blend of a polyester core covered with a cotton exterior. This core is strong and rot resistant and

PLAIN SEAM — WEAKEST

single stitched   double stitched

LAPPED SEAM — STRONGER

single stitched   double stitched

FLAT FELLED SEAM — STRONGEST

single stitched   double stitched

Tent seams

is protected by the outside cotton which expands to fill the needle holes and also bonds well to seam sealants.

Even the best made tents may leak through the stitching holes. Seam sealants may be purchased, and sometimes they are supplied free with the tent by some manufacturers. When it is correctly applied to both sides of the seam the sealant not only weatherproofs but also protects the thread from deterioration by the elements and bonds and strengthens the stitch holes. Take along a tiny container of sealant on camping trips to plug small leaks.

Stress Points

Examine closely all stress areas such as stake and guy line loops, D-ring and grommet attachments, and zipper seams to make sure that these seam ends are reinforced with extra stitching. In better tents these points will be reinforced with additional fabric sewn into and along the tent seams.

Different tent styles have varying stress areas. A-frame models put primary wind loading stress on peaks, poles, guys, and stakes and secondary pressures on the side wall guys and stakes. Center pole types, which put lower angle strain on the sides and corner guys and the peak and pole have fewer stake problems. Tunnels and domes supported by flexible fiber glass rods pull primarily on the pole joints and less on the sides. External frame tents require extra fabric reinforcement on their pole sleeve ends where their canopy joins the frame and also sometimes on side wall guy points.

You can minimize stress on these areas by using additional guy lines and by siting your tent so that the lower, most vulnerable half is protected from the wind. Winter and high altitude campers can also build snow barriers or dig their tent platform down into the snow. On a windy site you can increase your tent stability by opening any windward apertures and closing the leeward ones to make your fabric inflate or balloon to lessen any deformation and movement.

Floors

In almost every environment visited by the camper, from the alpine ridge to the desert, the tent floor is a positive element of safety and comfort. It keeps dampness, insects, dirt, and debris out.

Floors are best made from heavy-duty vinyl-coated nylon, polyurethane-coated nylon taffeta, or polyethylene-coated woven polyethylene. Many manufacturers recommend that ground sheets of nylon or plastic be placed underneath the tent floor to keep out moisture as well as to protect the floor from sharp objects on the ground. Others recommend an inside sheet to protect the floor from abrasion of shoes and cot rails. Placing the sheet inside will also trap water that leaks into the tent through its floor and corner seams.

Most tents feature tub floors with edges that extend part way up the sides. When it's raining out, equipment within that is touching the coated sides of the tub floor will not start a leak and, therefore, stay dry. Excessively high coated sidewalls are not necessary and only increase condensation.

You should also check to see where the floor seams are placed. There inevitably will be seams near the ground, but the fewer the better. They can leak.

Entries

Family tents   Family tents usually have one door, and, considering the type of use a family tent gets, one door is sufficient. Occasionally there will be full doors front and back. Stag brand tents by Hirsh Weis of Portland, Oregon, also have a split seam in back with a zipper opening marked as an emergency door. Most doors on family tents split down the middle and consist of a screen and a storm flap cover. It's far better for both of these to be zippered so they can be opened from both outside and inside. And zippers should slide easily and close without leaving a gap for insects to enter. Some tents have tie tapes to secure storm flaps, but this is not such a good arrangement.

Ideally the door should be protected by an overhang that lets you enter through the screen during a rainstorm without letting rain enter the tent. Some tents have awnings that provide substantial extra shelter in front of the door. Protection over the door is a definite advantage, if not a necessity.

An awning can provide an extra room to the family tent when it is equipped with walls and mosquito netting is draped from it. This is an option to consider if you need the extra space.

Backpacking tents   Most backpacking tents, especially those used at high altitudes, have two entries — one zippered and one tunnel. Zippered entrances open wide and are quick and easy to use for entering and venting the tent. They also produce a taut wind-resistant surface when closed. Their drawback is the fact that zippers can jam. Not only can they ice up when exposed to water and wet snow, they cannot stop fine blown snow from penetrating the tent. Because the zippered entry can become incapacitated, a tunnel entrance is also built into the backbacking tent. The tunnel is simply a sleeve closed by a drawstring, and because of its function as an escape exit, the tunnel is located at the opposite end of the tent from the door. Also, the tunnel can be joined to the tunnel of another tent to provide passage from one tent to another. The disadvantage to tunnels is that they can be difficult to tie, gather tightly, or use for venting, and entry or exit usually has to be made on all fours.

The vestibule is another form of entrance. It is an extension of the fly or canopy beyond the tent door. Vestibules vary in size and can be optional or built-in. They can be a useful place for cooking or storing packs and other gear, and they provide a means to keep the rain away from an open tent door.

For summer hiking, the vestibule is not a necessity. It adds weight and expense to the tent. In summer a simple solution is to carry a lightweight tarp to cover gear or to set up as a windbreak for outdoor camping.

Windows and Vents

Family tents   Ventilation in most family tents is provided by two or more screened windows and the door. For rainy or cold weather it's best to have storm flaps that can be closed or partly closed, preferably by zippers, from the inside. Sometimes window storm flaps are secured only by tie tapes on the outside. They are only slightly less rainproof than zippered closures, but the disadvantage of having to secure them from the outside in a rainstorm is obvious.

Some family tents have triangular windows that open from the top point, enabling the camper to make a small or large opening with ease. This works well.

Vents — especially those on nonbreathable nylon tents — should have protective awnings or covers so they can be left at least partially open in rainy weather and body moisture can escape from the tent.

Backpacking tents   Backpacking tents have vents, not windows. And proper venting in the backpacking tent is absolutely imperative; people have suffocated in sealed tents and carbon monoxide poisoning is one of the primary causes of death in winter camping. When cooking inside your tent, make absolutely certain the tent is properly ventilated as carbon monoxide can kill with no warning: you simply fall asleep and never awaken.

A gasoline stove should also never be filled inside a tent. Gasoline vapor is highly combustible and can explode. So be careful with a stove in a tent. Spilled gasoline can also disintegrate the urethane finish on the tent floor.

The accepted procedure for providing good ventilation in backpacking tents is to have ridge vents at front and back which provide cross ventilation. These vents are placed as near the ridgeline as possible. In that position they exhaust warm air and are close enough under the tent fly to be protected; therefore, the vent can be left open in foul weather.

Instead of having two ridge vents, many tents have one at the rear and let the door itself act as the front vent. If a door zips down the center and across the bottom (like an inverted *T*), it won't work as well as if the doors zip up the sides, with the two zippers meeting at the apex. This type of door forms quite an efficient ridgeline vent right under the fly.

An exhaust vent is important for any tent in which cooking will be taking place. Usually located at the highest point in the tent, some exhaust vents look like small tunnel entrances. The purpose of these vents is to draw air out, so bear in mind another source of fresh air must be available to enable air to flow.

Sometimes this other vent is a chimney vent which is located at the bottom of the tent and, when open, supposedly creates a chimney effect draw: cooler air enters through the chimney vent and forces moist, warm air out through a top vent or door. This type of vent is handy and works well on a still day or night when the draft created will force stagnant warm air out, but in foul weather rain and snow enter the vent and it cannot be used.

Cook Holes

In backpacking winter and expedition tents, where the occupants literally can get snowed in, a zippered cook hole lets them cook inside.

In many cases cooking is done on the ground of a floorless vestibule. But when the vestibule is attached to the tent and shares the tent floor, it should have a cook hole: if not for cooking, then for placing wet boots and soiled apparel.

Some people, instead of using a cook hole, carry sheets of Masonite or asbestos on which they place their stove, and this makes for a sturdy enough arrangement.

The main disadvantage to cook holes is their being vulnerable to damage from being trod upon with heavy boots. They also may leak water.

The original cook hole was called a "relief hole" and was designated as an indoor latrine. It is also handy for sweeping debris out of the tent.

Zippers

Family tents   One way of judging the quality of a tent is by checking the zippers. Good tents have larger ones (numbers five or six); inferior tents have small zippers that will break after the first season's use and maybe even trap you in your tent in the process. Coil zippers are self-correcting (to a point) and are smoother than the toothed ones, though the toothed ones are still the strongest and are less apt to fail. Both are used, so let your needs determine which you select — pick the toothed if you camp along sandy beaches or mud flats because the coil zippers are clogged easily by sand and dirt. Brass zippers are excellent except around corners, and they are stronger and more durable than the nylon ones. Avoid aluminum zippers — they jam and break easily.

A little care will prolong the life of metal zippers. Clean them occasionally with a toothbrush and lubricate the teeth by rubbing a candle over them. Another point to check is the placement of zippers. The same rules apply to family tents as backpacking tents and are covered in the following section.

Backpacking tents   Zippers must be conveniently placed for efficient operation of any tent, and especially the backpacking tent. Mosquito netting zippers should follow the same pattern and direction as the door zippers. Then, when you unzip, the door zipper is right there.

The worst zipper pattern is the inverted *T*. This is a sure sign of an inexpensive tent. Its greatest disadvantage is that the door peak cannot be opened for ventilation, and in order to leave the mosquito netting open it has to be gathered or tied aside.

Most backpacking tents have a semicircular quonset style or arch door opening that can be easily opened with a single sweep of the hand. Another type of door is the triangular one with zippers along each side. This style provides easy ventilation because the top can be left unzipped, forming a small triangular ridge vent. Triangular doors are larger than arched doors, but the latter are a bit easier to use.

No-See-Um-Proof Netting

No-see-ums, or punkies, are tiny flying insects that are common to the lake states and Canada. They are fierce biters and tiny enough to pass through standard mosquito netting. Tents with no-see-um-proof netting are preferred by most hunters and fishermen, and logically so. Its disadvantages are that it tears easily and its fine mesh is rather difficult to see through. It is also more expensive and is found only on the best tents.

Modesty Curtains or Dutch Doors

The modesty curtain is a short piece of fabric between three and four feet long which is attached to the inside of a family tent door to screen the interior from outside view. Since this does not extend all the way to the tent roof, it permits ventilation on hot days while providing privacy in a crowded campground.

A similar type of arrangement is the Dutch door, which is the modesty curtain sewn onto the mosquito netting so it becomes a permanent part of the flap. The fabric panel often is not removable and can block the passage of air, but only to a negligible degree.

Clothing Loops

D-rings or brass hooks at the ridge of better tents create storage facilities for clothing and tools. Although battery-powered lanterns can be safely supported by these loops, gasoline and kerosene ones cannot. These mantle lanterns generate enough heat to burn through the material of even flame-retardant tents. While butane and propane lanterns are safer than the gasoline models because they do not flare, these also must be kept away from the walls. In addition, both liquid and bottled gas lamps deplete the oxygen and fill the tent interior with poisonous carbon monoxide. Do not hang any heaters from these loops and only use catalytic models inside your tent.

COLOR

Choose the color of your tent fabric not only with your climatic and environmental conditions in mind but also with caution. While bright hues are attractive and cheery in overcast cool weather, some poorly made models are the brightest and some of the best tents come only in duller colors. In addition, strong reds and oranges can aggravate tension in some people and make a tent interior feel even warmer on a hot day. However, if your camping areas are cool, cloudy, or heavily shaded by trees, dark fabrics will make you feel colder and may fail to admit enough light for you to find your belongings. The same dark color may be relaxing in areas with constant hot and dazzling sunlight. Also consider whether you want your tent to blend in with the natural colors of your surroundings or whether you prefer a high-visibility structure that is easy to locate from a distance. For example, light blue cannot only be depressing in cold weather but can also be difficult to locate in a snowy landscape during the late afternoon. On the other hand, pearl gray and light blue are ideal for heat reflection in hot weather and transmit light to the interior very well. Tents made of two or more colors, such as ones with a light roof and dark walls or even stripes, are a happy solution for some campers. Others are irritated by the resulting multicolored light and color effects.

TENT CARE

Camping tents that are adequately cared for may last fiteen years or more. The average tent spends most of its time in storage as the average camper uses it only twenty-one days a year. Maintenance and proper packing and storage are essential to insure the tent's long life and usability.

Do not pack a wet tent unless unavoidable. However, if you must, unpack and dry the tent (preferably in the sun) the first chance you get. Some tents can be machine dried, but manufacturers agree that air drying is better. A wet cotton tent may be stored temporarily for a day or two, and the nylon tent, of course, will not mildew — but dampness breeds rot in natural fibers and even synthetic fiber tents often have cotton zipper tapes and stitching. Metal zippers and grommets may also corrode if a tent is not thoroughly dry when packed.

Before packing, clean out the tent with a whiskbroom and soft sponge to remove any crumbs or assorted debris (pebbles, pine needles, twigs, and so on). Canvas and nylon are more apt to puncture than tear, so sweep the tent thoroughly. Organic matter that is not removed will ferment. Try to wipe up bird droppings and sap spots before they dry and harden. If this is not possible, scrub them off with a mild soap and water solution and a soft brush. Don't use harsh detergents or solvents as they may damage the tent's waterproof and/or flame-retardant coatings. Vacuum the inside of the tent if you can, or turn the tent inside out and shake it. After loosely rolling up the tent, sweep off any dirt sticking to the outside.

Avoid folding the tent (especially along the same lines each time) or stuffing it into too snug a container (which will cause creases to form), as this may weaken the fabric along those folds. Tents may be kept in waterproof sacks while camping or traveling, but for longer-term storage use a porous sack capable of holding the loosely rolled tent without cramming. Avoid leaving the tent in a waterproof covering for long periods of time — especially stored in the trunk of a car where the heat, dark, and probable dampness are ideal conditions for breeding bacteria and mildew.

Metal pegs, joints, or poles may corrode and stain the tent fabric or cause creases if they are not packed separately. If you must pack everything together, cover the sharp-pointed ends with fabric or cardboard to prevent punctures. Metal parts exposed to salt sea air corrode rapidly; check and clean before packing.

Store the tent in a dry, well-ventilated area. Concrete floors are to be avoided as they can produce enough moisture to cause mildew. Air your tent as often as you can. This helps to disperse moisture from condensation and to prevent mildew.

Mildew occurs as spotty discolorations with a distinctly musty odor. It will destroy any natural fabric or thread on which it forms if it is not removed. If mildewing occurs, wash out with a mild soap and dry (in the sun, if possible) and then apply a mildew-retarding solution, which can be purchased from a hardware or camping supply store.

New tents should be checked for waterproofing before being used. Cotton tents should be pitched and hosed down completely. This will cause the material to shrink somewhat, making the weave tighter and more waterproof, and weather the canvas so it is less likely to mildew. Rub beeswax or paraffin into the stitching on canvas seams and work it in with your fingers. In a pinch, even Chap Stick will work. Better yet, buy and apply a commercial canvas-waterproofing treatment. Some manufacturers furnish these sealants with their tents.

Nylon tents may be waterproofed with silicone sprays and plastic sealants. Test first for leaks, but be sure the tent is dry before applying waterproofing and allow plenty of drying time for the sealant to set.

Small holes may be repaired with waterproof adhesive tape applied from the outside, preferably after the tent is dry, and small leaks may be stopped by the application of wax inside and out.

To prevent stress damage to grommets and guy lines from high winds, attach loops of shock cord to all guys and awning lines. Shock cord can be purchased at camping supply stores as can extra grommets and tools with which to apply them.

While camping, try to carry such items as tape, safety pins, needle and thread, and pieces of tent fabric for emergency repairs. Although most tents are flame resistant, all are easily damaged by fire. Nylon will melt, and even a small spark or cigarette burn can cause a hole to smolder through cotton canvas. Never cook inside a tent unless it was specifically designed for that purpose — in which case follow the manufacturer's directions carefully. The citric acid in orange juice or lemonade can damage nylon, so be wary of spills. Gasoline will ruin rubber and cause urethane coating to peel off so keep it away from your tent floor. Clear your tent site of small obstructions before setting up — floors can be damaged by such simple nuisances as sharp stones and sticks. Don't use aerosol products such as insect repellents or hair spray in or even nearby a tent. These products may contain chemicals that destroy the tent's waterproofing and flame resistant coatings.

"Did you ever see a cubical bubble?" Interview with Buckminster Fuller, The North Face. The North Face is not afraid to try new designs and they have come up with some remarkable ones. With the introduction of the Oval Intention in the fall of 1975 they were the first tent manufacturer to employ R. Buckminster Fuller's patented geodesic principles into the backpackable tent market. In recognition of Fuller's invention of the geodesic dome (and now over 100,000 exist in over fifty countries), The North Face dedicated their 1978 spring–summer catalog to him, and, when he paid a visit, they declared it "Bucky Day" and presented him with the six-meter, six-frequency geodesic dome you see him stepping out of. (Courtesy of The North Face)

Penthouse Manufacturing, Inc., in Carlinville, Illinois, makes this car-top tent.

Tents can be washed, and sometimes even in the washing machine. But check the instructions (and be sure to remove the guy lines before you do it). And if you've got a larger family tent that won't fit into the machine or you're hesitant about machine washing your backpacking tent, then you must resort to using a sponge and water in the shower, the bathtub, or the backyard. Dry-cleaning fluid will help remove pitch and resin, though this and some detergents can clog the pores of Gore-Tex. To clean Gore-Tex use cold water and a very mild, pure, low-sudsing soap (such as Ivory Flakes). Hot water and strong detergents can also cause the Gore-Tex laminate to peel off. To dry the tent, the general consensus is that the sun does the best job.

Just give your tent a little consideration; after all, it is not indestructible. And a little care goes a long way.

TENTMAKERS, MANUFACTURERS, AND THEIR TENTS

Two innovative tentmakers are Bill Moss in Maine and "Tent Tom" Glenn in Nepal. Moss's tents are futuristic while Glenn's are keeping an age-old craft alive and well. The manufacturers, on the other hand, are innovators in their own right. You can now purchase either the old reliable tent styles with most of the flaws ironed out or try some of the newer dome, tunnel, or hybrid types.

Most of the tentmakers and manufacturers included here will supply you with catalogs and current price lists free of charge. It only costs the price of a postcard, so you definitely owe it to yourself to investigate the market. It's constantly changing — manufacturers are phasing out old models, introducing new ones, developing new materials and hardware — you name it, they're working on it.

Listed in the charts at the end of this chapter you will find data supplied directly by various manufacturers. The charts give pertinent information on all the tents available from each one, but this is by no means the last word, or even a complete listing of manufacturers. At a glance you can see which companies specialize in the type of tent that interests you, and then there is specific information, plus selected photographs, to enhance your knowledge of their line. The following section is geared to provide you, the tent buyer, with information it might otherwise take weeks to accumulate and to enable you to talk "tents" at any sporting goods store. With this material to get you started you will be more likely to end up with the right tent for your needs.

Bill Moss — Master Artist-Tentmaker

"I am an artist. A tent to me is a piece of sculpture you can get into."
— Bill Moss

Bill Moss is an artist-craftsman who has restored the ancient art of tentmaking to its royal standards of excellence in designing for the future. His works have been shown at the Museum of Modern Art in New

Moss-designed tents in Abu Dhabi on the Persian Gulf. These tents are capable of withstanding 100 mph winds and maintaining temperature below 85° inside on 120° days.

York and he is the inventor of the paper dome cottages coated with plastic, emergency tent shelters which when dropped by helicopters open and inflate like parachutes before they hit the earth, and over thirty patented tent and tentlike structures. One of his achievements that is taking hold is the Optimum 200 — a leakproof summer house that packs into a two-foot square box and weighs a total of fifty-five pounds, has no-cost air conditioning to keep the interior twenty-five degrees cooler than the outdoors, and is a meticulously crafted space-age sculpture shaped like a three-leaf clover with swooping fluid curves.

Unlike many works of art these tents are made to withstand heavy utilitarian use and punishment by the elements. Jacques Cousteau's oceanography expedition used Moss's tents on Easter Island. The Smithsonian Institution commissioned Moss to design its canvas pavilion for the 1976 Bicentennial Folk Festival in Washington, D.C. Moss created the interior of the Ford Pavilion at Expo '74 in Spokane, Washington, and the respected L. L. Bean outdoor equipment company hired him to create a two-man camping tent. The Arabs, supreme tent-masters of the ages, have bought large hunting tents as well as thousands of smaller shelters used for temporary housing of Arab emirate families, construction sites, schools, and hospitals.

Mr. Moss began as a painter and studied art. He later worked in the U.S. Navy as an underwater demolition diver and even taught painting to the officers. For the next ten years he illustrated outdoor scenes for *Ford Times,* and his assignments sometimes found him camping out in "heavy, smelly, leaky tents." Meanwhile, he had begun making his own sculptured fabric paintings, which finally departed from the wall to become walk-into environments. At last, his 1957 design of a pop tent for the Ford Company fused his art and visions together. He decided to commit himself to the perfection of his tents.

For several years Moss licensed his designs to other manufacturers, insisting on design control through membership on their boards of directors. By 1975 he established his own tent company — Moss Tent Works, Inc., in Camden, Maine — to assure the total artistic freedom and precise quality of workmanship necessary for the proper production of his creations. His wife Marilyn, a weaving expert experienced in managing a leather goods shop, became the general manager, and his father-in-law, a retired General Motors research director, became the first company president.

Moss's revolutionary tension-structure designs tackled a problem that most architects had avoided because of conservative clients and the difficulty of design. Moss solved the two main drawbacks of the pup tent: its lack of space near the top of its inverted *V* shape and its concentration of stresses where the fabric meets the tent poles. Other typical solutions aggravated the existing situation by merely enlarging the whole size of the tent and reinforcing the same stress point. In contrast, Moss eliminated these issues entirely by using a flexible fiber glass rod through a sleeve to make a covered arch instead of an A-frame. Not only did this multiply the interior space but it also distributed the tent pressures over the entire surface. The cut of the stretched fabric produces tension to

Top: The O'Dome, an experimental vacation home fabricated of plastic-coated paper. Bottom: Star Gazer, a freestanding urethane-coated tent.

The Siesta Sunshade with detachable floor (for laundering or separate use).

hold the fiber glass poles in their pockets. These poles in turn transfer those stresses back out again onto the cloth to make the covering material a structural support itself instead of an independent skin. This makes it possible for some tents to be freestanding and require only enough anchorage to the earth to prevent their shifting in the wind. This concept is now widespread and has been integrated into the design lines of many manufacturers.

Another striking feature of Moss's tents is the winglike hyperbolic paraboloid shape (illustrated, for instance, by the Optimum 200), one which is also used by other contemporary architects. This form not only is the single solution for creating constant tension across the entire surface of a material but it also spills the wind by bending away from the direction of the pressure. To design a tent with strains evenly distributed over the widest areas, Moss sketches his works in paper to find the weak points and also makes cloth models combining arcs, parabolas, and eye shapes. (Called by architects *vesica piscis,* which refers to the intersection of circles. Church doors are often designed this way.) Because of all these design factors both the fabric and all construction craftwork must be of excellent quality — as indeed they are, at Moss Tent Works, Inc.

Tent Tom — Upholding Ancient Tradition in Nepal

California-born Tom Glenn has been living in Katmandu, Nepal, since 1971. Known locally in Nepal as "Tent Tom," he began, in 1972, to organize a factory to produce beautiful handwoven tents and canopies, fabrics and rugs. Glenn's tents are inspired by traditional Nepalese and Tibetan designs sometimes enhanced by innovations of his own. He has spent several years researching weaving and dyeing techniques and exploring Himalayan design. These tents were customarily used by royalty and the upper classes for outings in the Himalayan mountain regions. The appliquéd designs are symbolic and could identify the tent owner at a glance.

All tents include ropes made by hand from goat's hair and bamboo stakes, and are usually made from cotton drill weave and tapestry fabrics (other available materials include nylon, fire-proofed canvas, and PVC-coated fabric). The tents are vividly decorated with bias tape appliqué, an ancient craft form flexible enough to show off both traditional and original designs. "Tent Tom" also supplies accessory pillows that are appliquéd in the same design as the tent. And if you want a Tibetan-type hand-knotted wool carpet to cover the floor, that too can be ordered with the tent: rugs are Glenn's other specialty.

The whole enterprise is a blend of East and West. Tom has combined traditional Eastern craftsmanship with elements of contemporary design and function. These tents are not curiosity pieces but splendid works of art that are extremely functional.

Various models and designs are available on import order, and tents can be custom-made as well. Tom's mother, Mrs. Pat Heald, handles United States distribution of her son's tents and rugs. For more information, write her at Design Center Northwest, 5701 Sixth Avenue South, Suite 219, Seattle, Washington 98108.

"Tent Tom" Glenn fastening a guy rope on one of his appliquéd Himalayan tents.

Another of Glenn's tents, based on ancient Himalayan designs and handmade at his factory in Katmandu, Nepal.

Manufacturer
ANCHOR INDUSTRIES P.O. Box 3477 1100 Burch Dr. Evansville, Indiana 47733

Model	Type	Materials	Weight lbs. oz.	Dimensions Height (inches) Max/Min	Length × Width (inches)	Capacity Rating (# persons)	Number of Entries	Colors	Special Features
Woodsman Wall Tent (5 models)	wall	poly.-cotton						assorted	
smallest (W-97)			55	72/36	108 × 84	3	2		
largest (W-1416)			95	90/42	168 × 192	8	2		
Woodsman Supreme (5 models)	wall	poly.-cotton						assorted	
smallest (WS-97)			70	72/36	108 × 84	3	2		
largest (WS-1416)			130	90/42	168 × 192	11	2		
Grizzly (GR-8610)	exoframe	poly.-cotton	35	84/66	102 × 120	4	1	blue or 2-tone green	
Huntsman (HT57)	pup	poly.-cotton, nyl.	16 8	42	60 × 84	2	1	light blue or light green	
Mountain tent (MT7686)	pup	poly.-cotton, nyl.	24 8	72	90 × 102	3	1		2 side vents
Backpacker (BP58)	backpack	rip. nyl.	7 8	52	60 × 94	3	1	yellow roof with orange or blue	
Canoe (CA7686)	backpack	rip. nyl.	9 8	72	90 × 102	3	1	yellow roof with orange or blue	2 wnds.
Universal	wall	duck nyl. & dac. duck						khaki, white, or gray	custom sizes and wnds. avail.
International Pyramidal tent	pyramid	duck, nyl.			most popular are 168 × 168 192 × 192			khaki, white, or gray	custom sizes and wnds. avail.
Tee-Pee (3 models)	tipi	army duck					1	white	
smallest TP12FR			65	150	144 diameter				
largest TP18FR			90	177	216 diameter				
Permanent camp (7 models)	wall	cotton						assorted	permanent platform complete
smallest (PC-98)			80	84/36	108 × 96	3	2		
largest (PC-1620)			180	120/60	192 × 240	15	2		
Assembly tents	assembly*							assorted	

* Available in custom orders

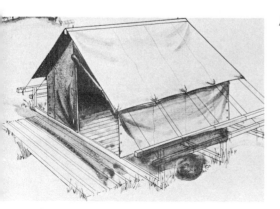

Anchor Industries Permanent Camp

Anchor Industries Huntsman

Manufacturer
A16 WILDERNESS CAMPING OUTFITTERS   4620 Alvarado Canyon Rd.   San Diego, California 92120

Model	Type	Materials	Weight lbs. oz.	Dimensions Height (inches) Max/Min	Length × Width (inches)	Capacity Rating (# persons)	Number of Entries	Colors	Special Features
Half Dome (4-person)	dome	rip. nyl.	6	48	83 × 94	4	1	blue or green	1 wnd., dble. wall
(2-person)			5 4	50	52 × 94	2	1		
Trail Tarp	tarp	rip. nyl.	1 10½	NA	120½ × 120½			golden brown	

Manufacturer
ALASKA TENT & TARP, INC.   529 Front St.   Fairbanks, Alaska 99701

Model	Type	Materials	Weight lbs. oz.	Dimensions Height (inches) Max/Min	Length × Width (inches)	Capacity Rating (# persons)	Number of Entries	Colors	Special Features
Wall Tent (15 models)	wall	canvas						off-white	overlapping door flaps, rope reinforced eaves & corners, FR models avail., mosquito netting opt., arctic tent
smallest (T10983)			15	72/36	72 × 96	4+	2		
largest (T11320)			37	90/48	114 × 144	6+	2		
Dog Sled Tent (T10801)	A-frame	canvas	21	66	90 × 90	2+	1		dbl. wall construction, top vent, tent folds to 1'×8' bundle to fit in dog sled

Alaska wall tent

A16 Half Dome

Rain fly on A16 Half Dome

Manufacturer
ATHALON PRODUCTS, HIGH LONESOME   3333 E. 52nd Ave.   Denver, Colorado 80216

Model	Type	Materials	Weight lbs. oz.	Dimensions Height (inches) Max/Min	Dimensions Length × Width (inches)	Capacity Rating (# persons)	Number of Entries	Colors	Special Features
High Lonesome (2 models)	cabin	cotton duck nyl. vny.						white	3 wnds.
smallest				80/48	96 × 120	2	1		
largest				84/48	120 × 144	4	1		
Woodsman (4 models)	wall	cotton duck						white	1 wnd., full
smallest		nyl. vny.		80/48	96 × 120	2	2		screen door
largest				112/60	168 × 192	8	2		
Guide (8 models)	wall	cotton duck						white	asbestos shield,
smallest		nyl. vny.		80/48	96 × 120	2	1		sod cloth, wnd.
largest				110/60	192 × 240	12	1		ridge-pole openings
Outfitter (4 models)	wall	cotton duck						white	sod cloth
smallest		nyl. vny.		80/48	96 × 120	2	1		
largest				99/60	144 × 168	6	1		
Herder (5 models)	pyramid w/wall	cotton duck nyl. vny.						white	
smallest				75/30	84 × 84	2	1		
largest				105/48	120 × 120	4	1		
Colorado range (3 models)	pyramid	cotton duck nyl. vny.						white	no center pole
smallest				87	72 × 96	2	1		
largest				90	114 × 114	4	1		
Whelen Lean-to	lean-to	nyl. or cotton		83	84 × 72	2		orange or white	avail. in 2 fabrics

Athalon High Lonesome The Guide

Manufacturer
L. L. BEAN, INC. Freeport, Maine 04033

Model	Type	Materials	Weight lbs. oz.	Dimensions Height (inches) Max/Min	Dimensions Length × Width (inches)	Capacity Rating (# persons)	Number of Entries	Colors	Special Features
Allagash tent	A-frame	rip./nyl., taf./nyl.						green or gold	dbl. walls, 1 wnd.
small (55480)			6	42	84 × 60	2	1		
large (55490			10	72	108 × 84	4	1		
Pine Tree Lodge (3 models, #10, 12, 13)	cabin	nyl./poplin						pearl gray	FR avail., 3 wnds.
smallest (#10)			35	90/60	96 × 120		1		
largest (#13)			51	96/60	120 × 156		1		
Nylon Baker tent (5546R)	baker	nyl./poplin	11 12	72/20	90 × 90		1	green	floor, 1 wnd., net door, opt., 6'×20' screened porch
Nylon Umbrella tent (3 models)	umbrella	nyl./poplin						green/gold	3 wnds.
smallest (5612R#8)			18 3	78	84 × 96	3	1		
largest (5611R#12)			27 12	92	139 × 139	6	1		

Manufacturer
BISHOP'S ULTIMATE OUTDOOR EQUIPMENT 310 Millwood Rd. Bethesda, Maryland 20034

Model	Type	Materials	Weight lbs. oz.	Dimensions Height (inches) Max/Min	Dimensions Length × Width (inches)	Capacity Rating (# persons)	Number of Entries	Colors	Special Features
Ultimate (2-person)	external frame box	rip. nyl.	10	40/36	84 × 60	2+	2	burnt orange/ white	2 pocks., shock cords
(4-person)			16 6	60/54	108 × 84	4+	2		4 pocks.
(6-person)			30 13	77/68	144 × 96	6+	2		6 pocks.
Pachlite II	A-frame	rip. nyl.	(w/ridge- pole) 9 6	46/45	84 × 60	2+	2	burnt orange/pale blue/white	2 pocks., ridgepole
Net tent	I-pole wedge	rip. nyl.	5	40/36	84 × 48	2	1	burnt orange/ white	2 pocks., WP door and fly

L. L. Bean Baker tent

Bishop's Expedition Tent

Manufacturer
CANNONDALE CORPORATION   35 Pulaski St.   Stamford, Connecticut 06902

Model	Type	Materials	Weight lbs. oz.	Dimensions Height (inches) Max/Min	Length × Width (inches)	Capacity Rating (# persons)	Number of Entries	Colors	Special Features
Wabash (C-891)	backpack	rip. nyl.	8 12	57/36	87 × 48 87 × 72	2	1	gold/rust/blue	1 wnd., 1 vest.
Lackawanna (C-892)	backpack	rip. nyl.	9 8	46/46	87 × 58	2	2	gold/rust/blue	2 vests.
Aroostook (C-893)	backpack	rip. nyl.	11 6	72/72	87 × 72	3–4	2	gold/rust/blue	2 vests.
Susquehanna (C-895)	backpack	rip. nyl.	7 6	46/46	87 × 58	2	1	gold/rust/blue	1 wnd., 1 vest.

Cannondale Susquehanna and the Bugger bicycle trailer

Cannondale Wabash

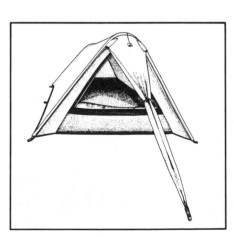

Manufacturer
THE COLEMAN CO., INC. 250 N. St. Francis St. Wichita, Kansas 67201

Model	Type	Materials	Weight lbs. oz.	Dimensions Height (inches) Max/Min	Length × Width (inches)	Capacity Rating (# persons)	Number of Entries	Colors	Special Features
Peak 1™ (#838)	backpack	nyl.	5 10	44/40	97 × 60	2	1	yellow/ brown	1 wnd., weather fly, cargo pock., under wnd., stuff sack, opt. shock cord kit
(#856)			7 10	59/54	97 × 84	4	1		
Coleman® Models:									
Family Classic (#8481B840)	cabin- exoframe	poly., vny.	36	84/72	132 × 120	5	1 dbl.	white/tan	2 wnds.
Mid-sized Classic (#8481B830)	cabin exoframe	poly., vny.	35	78/69	120 × 96	4	1 dbl.	white/tan	2 wnds.
Compact Classic (#8481-810)	cabin exoframe	poly., vny.	19	60/56	96 × 81	3	1 dbl.	white/tan	1 wnd.
Backpack Classic (#8551A814)	Backpack	nyl.	6 6	42/37	93 × 60	2	1 zip side	white/tan	vent w/weather fly
Delux Oasis (#8471A22)	cabin exoframe	poly-cotton, vny.	52	90/60	156 × 108	6	1 dbl.	white/green	3 wnds.
Family Oasis (#8471A832)	cabin exoframe	poly-cotton, vny.	48	90/60	144 × 96	5	1 dbl.	white/green	3 wnds.
Delux American Heritage (#8491-865)	Cabin exoframe	poly., vny.	37	84/54	156 × 120	6	1 dbl. dutch	white/green	3 wnds.
Family American Heritage (#8491B825)	Cabin exoframe	poly., vny.	34	78/54	134 × 98	5	1 dbl. dutch	white/green	3 wnds.
Compact American Heritage (#8491B815	Cabin exoframe	poly., vny.	30	78/54	116 × 86	4	1 dbl. dutch	white/green	2 wnds.
Villa del Mar (#8426-874)	Cabin exoframe	poly., vny.	48	96	144 × 108	5	2 flaps	tan/gold	2 wnds.
Vacationer (#8491A845)	Cabin exoframe	nyl., vny.	29	78	134 × 98	5	1 dbl. dutch	white/red	3 wnds.
Mountain (#8428-800)	pop- exoframe	poly., vny.	15	42	84 × 60	2	1 dbl. dutch	green	3 wnds.

Villa del Mar® with Van Conversion Kit

Coleman Villa del Mar®

Coleman Vacationer

Manufacturer
DENVER TENT COMPANY   4004 Grape St.   Denver, Colorado 80216

Model	Type	Materials	Weight lbs. oz.	Height (inches) Max/Min	Length × Width (inches)	Capacity Rating (# persons)	Number of Entries	Colors	Special Features
King (139KS)	cabin	poly.-cotton	55	90/60	156 × 108	8	1 double door		3 wnds., FR
Royal (4 models) smallest (97R) largest (915R)	cabin	poly.-cotton	31 55	85/40 85/40	108 × 84 108 × 180	3 8+	1 double door		1 wnd.
Crown (109C)	cabin	poly.-cotton	47	90/60	120 × 108	5	1 double door		1 wnd.
Denver (675BP)	backpack	rip./taf./nyl.	6 8	48/12	72 × 90	2	1 flap		1 wnd., NP w/fly

Coleman Peak 1™ two- and four-man

Denver Tent Company Denver Backpack

Manufacturer
EARLY WINTERS, LTD.   110 Prefontaine Pl. S.   Seattle, Washington 98104

Model	Type	Materials	Weight lbs. oz.	Dimensions Height (inches) Max/Min	Dimensions Length × Width (inches)	Capacity Rating (# persons)	Number of Entries	Colors	Special Features
Starship® (#0105)	dome	Gore-Tex® laminate*	6.6	48	108 × 72	2–3	1	gold or green	1 wnd., 4 shock-corded alum. poles, 4 pocks.
Light Dimension® (#0102)	tunnel	Gore-Tex® laminate*	3.8	39/19	97 × 56	2	1	gold or green	back vent, 2 shock-corded fg. poles, 2 netting pocks.
Winterlight® (#0103)	tunnel	Gore-Tex® laminate*	4.5	39/25	102 × 56	2	2	gold or green	3 shock-corded fg. poles, 2 pocks.
Earth Station™ (#0104)	dome	Gore-Tex® laminate*	9.7	54	92 side-side 102 corner–corner	4	1	gold or green	2 big wnds., 6 shock-corded alum. poles (equal lengths), 4 pocks., free-standing
Sleep Inn®	sleeping bag cover & bivvy sack	Gore-Tex® laminate*	1.1	NA	90 × 32	1	NA	gold or green	mosquito netting
Omnipotent® (#0101) w/vest.	tunnel	integrated dbl. wall**	6.3	38/29	93 × 54 139 × 54	2	2	blue	dbl. wall, opt. vest. zips to front door, Gore-Tex® doors, 4 shock-corded FG poles

* Gore-Tex® laminate: nylon taffeta-Gore-Tex® membrane-polyester nexus.
** Outer Wall: 2.2 oz. polymer coated nylon; Inner Wall: 1.5 oz nylon.

Early Winters Earth Station

Early Winters Omnipotent

About as small as a tent can get, Early Winters Sleep Inn

Manufacturer
EUREKA! TENT, INC.   625 Conklin Rd., P.O. Box 966   Binghamton, New York 13902

Model	Type	Materials	Weight lbs. oz.	Dimensions Height (inches) Max/Min	Length × Width (inches)	Capacity Rating (# persons)	Number of Entries	Colors	Special Features
Catskill (3 models) smallest largest	backpack A-frame	rip./nyl. taf.	6 10 6	42 72	60 × 84 84 × 102	2 4	1 1	green/yellow	no-see-um netting
Mojave	A-frame	taf./nyl.	4 15	42	60 × 84			green	no-see-um netting
Timberline: small large	ext. frame, backpack	rip./nyl.	1 1 5	42 58	63 × 86 86 × 104	2 4	1 1	copper/ sandstone green/yellow	no-see-um netting, 1 wnd., opt. vest., shock-corded frame
Timberline Base Camp	ext. frame, backpack	rip., poly.	17 10	75	102 × 123		1	dark green willow green	opt. vest.
Alpine: small large	ext. frame exo-frame	rip.	9 10 15 12	44 65	60 × 93 84 × 106	2 3	1 1	copper/blue green/yellow	
Saranac	backpack	rip., taf./.nyl.	6 5	42	60 × 120	2	1	green/yellow	attached vest., no-see-um netting
Yukon	dome	rip.	7 9	48	60 × 90	2	1 A-Door	willow green/yellow	1 roof vent
Aleutian/(hexagon)	dome	rip.	9 12	52	86 × 96	2	2 A-Doors	willow green/yellow	1 roof vent
Back Country	pyramid, backpack	rip.	5 12	64	96 × 42	1	1 A-Door	copper/ sandstone green/yellow	
Mt. Marcy	mod. wall, backpack	taf./nyl.	4 4	42	60 × 96	2	1	green	3 wnds.
Nu Lite	backpack	taf.	3 12	42	60 × 88	2	1	assorted	
Space Tent: small	ext. frame umbrella	poplin	54	96/72	120 × 120		1	tan	3 wnds.
large	umbrella		65	96/72	141 × 141		1		

Eureka! Tent Riverside Lodge, in use at
Strawberry Fields by the Sea, a camping and
cottage resort on Robin's Bay, Jamaica

Eureka! Timberline without rain fly

Model	Type	Materials	Weight lbs. oz.	Height (inches) Max/Min	Length × Width (inches)	Capacity Rating (# persons)	Number of Entries	Colors	Special Features
Riverside Lodge (4 models)	cabin	poplin						pearl gray	3 wnds.
smallest			46	90/60	120 × 96		1		
largest			60	96/60	192 × 120		1		
Lakeside	cabin	poplin, vny./nyl.	80	108/60, 72	192 × 120		1	pearl gray	7 wnds., 2 rooms
Terrace Tent	cabin	poplin, vny./nyl.	56	96/60, 72	120 × 120		1	pearl gray	3 wnds., awning
Chateau (3 models)	cabin							tan	2 wnds.
smallest 7			27	72/42	86 × 90		1		
largest 12			38	84/52	135 × 96		1		
Travel-aire	ext. frame umbrella	poplin, vny./nyl.	23	80/60	104 × 104		1	tan	1 wnd.
Drawtite® (3 models)	exo	poplin						tan	1 vent, 1 wnd.
smallest, Alpine			14	(Fr.) (Rear) 48/30	60 × 93	2	1		
largest, Storm King			44	(Fr.) (Rear) 78/50	108 × 147	5	1		
Vagabond 9	umbrella	poplin, vny.	28	80/60	104 × 104			tan	2 wnds.
Screen House	screen	poplin					2, zip	tan	
small 1210			32	92/68	120 × 144				
large 1410			35	92/68	120 × 168				
Trail-Lite	backpack	taf./nyl.	7 4	72	84 × 104	4	1	green	
Portage Special	wall	taf.	7 2	72/24	84 × 87	3	1	green	3 wnds.
Portage Special II	backpack	taf.	7 14	72/24	84 × 108	4	1	green	3 wnds.
Mountain Tent	backpack	poplin, vny./nyl.	9	42	60 × 96	2	1	tan	
Mountain Major	backpack	poplin, vny./nyl.	13 12	60	72 × 108	3	1	tan	
Mountain Cruiser	backpack	poplin, vny./nyl.	18 4	72	90 × 96	4	1	tan	
Caddis	modified tube	rip./nyl.	7	(end) 43/35	43 × 96		2	caramel/ sandstone	
Expedition Timberline: small	ext. frame backpack	rip./nyl.	8 14	42	63 × 86	2	1		opt. vest.
large			12 6	58	86 × 104	4	1		
Summit	A-frame	rip./nyl.	7 11	57	60 × 102	2	1		
Expedition Summit	A-frame	rip./nyl.	8 11	57	60 × 102	2	1	caramel/ sandstone	snow tunnel entrance
Great Western (3 models)	hybrid umbrella	rip./poly.						willow green/yellow	3 wnds.
smallest			18 3	78/66	84 × 84		1		
largest			27 4	92/76	139 × 139		1		
Teton: small	cabin	rip./nyl., poly.	25 3	84/60	120 × 96		1	sandstone/ tan	3 wnds.
large			28 5	84/60	144 × 108		1		
Chenango Flu		nyl./poly.	11	90/72	144 × 144			assorted	
Ice-Fishing	umbrella	poplin/ vny.		73/63	85 × 85		1		1 wnd., 1 vent
Indian Teepee		poly./cotton		168	Dia. 180				

Manufacturer
GERRY CO.   5450 North Valley Highway   Denver, Colorado 80216

Model	Type	Materials	Weight lbs. oz.	Dimensions Height (inches) Max/Min	Dimensions Length × Width (inches)	Capacity Rating (# persons)	Number of Entries	Colors	Special Features
Mountain Ark (T140)	A-frame	nyl.	6 12	46	88 × 57	2	1	brown/ orange with khaki fly	
Windjammer (T142)	tripodal exo	nyl.	7 9	48	84 × 96	2–3	1	brown/gold with khaki fly	skylight
Year Round II (T106)	backpack	nyl.	6 14	43/36	92 × 55	2	1	blue/gold or brown/gold/ khaki	1 wnd.
Camponaire II (T113)	modified pyramid	nyl.	9 8	65/42	84 × 78	3	1	blue/gold or brown/gold/ khaki	
Fortnight II (T114)	modified pyramid	nyl.	10 14	72/48	84 × 96	4	1	blue/gold or brown/gold/ khaki	
Meadow (T303)	backpack	nyl.	5 6	48/44 48/32	84 × 54	2	1	green/khaki	
Mosquito (T301)	backpack	nyl.	5 5	44/32	84 × 48 84 × 54	2	1	green	

Manufacturer
HIRSCH-WEISS   White Stag   5203 S.E. Johnson Creek Blvd.   Portland, Oregon 97222

Model	Type	Materials	Weight lbs. oz.	Dimensions Height (inches) Max/Min	Dimensions Length × Width (inches)	Capacity Rating (# persons)	Number of Entries	Colors	Special Features
Skyliner (2 models) large (#20053) extra large (#20054)	cabin	poly.-cotton	45 52	93/60 96/60	140 × 107 168 × 118	5 7	1 dutch door	silver/blue	5 wnds., adj. spring-loaded frame, roped in floor w/wire stake loops

Gerry Fortnight II

Gerry Windjammer

Model	Type	Materials	Weight lbs. oz.	Dimensions Height (inches) Max/Min	Length × Width (inches)	Capacity Rating (# persons)	Number of Entries	Colors	Special Features
Van Tent (#20055)	van	polyester poly.-cotton	27	87/76	93 × 83	2–3	2 dutch doors	silver/ pumpkin	3 wnds., magnetic tape
Van/Pickup tent #21048	van	poly.- cotton, & nyl.	21	87/76	103 × 84	3	1 dutch door	silver/ pumpkin	1 wnd., zip, opening for vehicle
Oakwood (3 models) small (#20056)	cabin	poly.-cotton	33	81/56	114 × 91	4	1 dutch door	silver/green	3 wnds., spring-loaded frame, roped in floor w/wire stake loops
extra large (#20058)			45	94/60	173 × 104	6			4 wnds
Parkdale (2 models) small (#20059) large (#20060)	cabin	poly.-cotton	26 34	78/54 84/54	115 × 91 138 × 104	4 5	1 dutch door	blue or green or pumpkin	3 wnds., adj. frame
Ranger (2 models) small (#21049) large (#21050)	cabin	poly.- cotton, polyester	20 25	78/54 84/54	116 × 89 138 × 104	4 5	1 dutch door	pumpkin/ green	3 wnds., adj. frame
Cape Cod (2 models) small (#21051) large (#21052)	cabin	poly.- cotton, polyester	16 21	75/57 84/60	116 × 91 137 × 104	4 4	1 dutch door	pumpkin/ brown	3 wnds., adj. frame
Breezy Hatchback (2 models) small (#21053)	cabin	poly.- cotton, polyester	19	75/51	114 × 90	4	1, zip.	pumpkin/ green	3 wnds., adj. frame
large (#21054)			24	78/54	137 × 100	5			4 wnds., adj. frame
Sky Country (2 models) small (#24058) large (#24059)	backpack w/fly	rip.-nyl. & nyl.	6 9 9 12	45 60	66 × 90 90 × 108	2 4	1 1	brown	1 rear vent, free standing shock-corded frame
High Country (2 models) small (#24060) large (#24061)	backpack w/fly	rip./nyl.	7 11 10 15	45 62	66 × 90 90 × 108	2 4	1 1	blue	front-rear vents, vest., shock-corded frame

Hirsch-Weis White Stag Camping Skyliner

Hirsch-Weis White Stag Sky Country

Hirsch-Weis White Stag Alpine II

HIRSCH-WEISS (cont.)

Model	Type	Materials	Weight lbs. oz.	Dimensions Height (inches) Max/Min	Length × Width (inches)	Capacity Rating (# persons)	Number of Entries	Colors	Special Features
Igloo (#24065)	backpack w/fly	rip. nyl./taf. nyl.	6 11	50	62 × 94	2	1	green	rear vent, fg. frame
Alpine (3 models) smallest (#24062) largest (#24064)	backpack w/fly	rip. nyl./taf. nyl.	6 10 5	42 72	60 × 90 84 × 102	2 4	1 1	green	rear vent, shock-corded dbl. A-frame
Trail Companion (3 models) smallest (#24066) largest (#24068)	backpack w/fly	rip. nyl./taf. nyl.	4 10 8 13	42 72	60 × 84 84 × 96	2 4	1 1	brown	1 wnd., alum. poles
High Lake (2 models) small (#24045) large (#24046)	backpack	rip.-nyl./ rip.-poly.	5 6 12	42 60	60 × 84 84 × 84	2 4	1 1	green	1 wnd.
Packer (#24069)	backpack	rip.-nyl./ rip.-poly.	4	36	54 × 84	2	1	blue	1 wnd.

Manufacturer
HOLUBAR MOUNTAINEERING, LTD.   P.O. Box 7   Boulder, Colorado 80302

Model	Type	Materials	Weight lbs. oz.	Dimensions Height (inches) Max/Min	Length × Width (inches)	Capacity Rating (# persons)	Number of Entries	Colors	Special Features
Chateau	backpack	rip./nyl.	10 4	66/28	125 × 86	3	1	blue	2 wnds. vents, avail. as kit
4-Person	backpack	rip./nyl.	10 11	72/36 (at doors)	96 × 96	4	2	gold	2 wnds.
Expedition	expedi- tion	rip./nyl.	10 1	47/47	114 × 60	2 (w/gear)	2	gold/brown	
Tarp tent	tarp				132 × 108	5		brown	
Royalight II	backpack	rip./nyl.	6 14	54/30	90 × 60	2		blue	rear vent window

Holubar Chateau

Manufacturer
JANSPORT   Paine Field Industrial Park   Everett, Washington 98204

Model	Type	Materials	Weight lbs. oz.	Dimensions Height (inches) Max/Min	Length × Width (inches)	Capacity Rating (# persons)	Number of Entries	Colors	Special Features
Trail Dome (2-3)	dome	dac./nyl.	7 6	50	87 × 100	2/3	1	blue/gray or green tumbleweed	1 vent, 1 top vent
Large Trail Dome (4-6)	dome	poly./nyl.	13	69	115 × 132	4/6	1	blue/gray or green tumbleweed	1 wnd., 1 top vent
Original Trail Wedge (4460)	wedge	rip.	5 6	52	53 × 90	2	1		1 wnd.
Mountain Dome (4468)	dome	nyl. dac./ rip.	8 8	50	87 × 100	2/3	2	blue/orange/ gray or green/ yellow/ tumbleweed	2 vents, 1 tunnel
Isodome 1	dome	dac./rip, nyl./taf.	15 14	54	125¾ × 103	4 to 6	1	blue/orange/ gray or green/ yellow/ tumbleweed	3 wnds., top vent
2			10 1	48	96 × 80	3-4	1	yellow/gray/ russet	vent in door fly, top vent
3			8 6	48	90 × 67	2-3	1	yellow/gray/ russet	vent in door fly, top vent

Jansport Isodome

Manufacturer
KIRKHAM'S OUTDOOR PRODUCTS AAA Tent and Awning Co. 3125 S. State St. Salt Lake City, Utah 84119

Model	Type	Materials	Weight lbs. oz.	Dimensions Height (inches) Max/Min	Dimensions Length × Width (inches)	Capacity Rating (# persons)	Number of Entries	Colors	Special Features
Expandable (#7199)	modular	duck & nylon	42 8	85/65	108 × 108	4	2	pearl gray/off-white	modular system Springbar™
Springbar Vacationer (#8140)	hybrid cabin	nylon	40	88	168 × 120	7 to 8	1	pearl gray	freestanding Springbar™
Springbar Traveler (2 models)	cabin	duck & nylon						pearl gray/white	Springbar™, 1 window
small (#8180)			44 12	85/75	120 × 96	4	1		
large (#9110)			48 12	85/75	132 × 120	5	1		
2-Man Campsite (#939-E)	2-man cabin	cotton & nylon	12 12	41/38	93 × 60	2	1	pearl gray	Springbar™
Cabana (#8315)	cabin	cotton	14 12	78/60	84 × 48	1	1	tan	Springbar™ used for dressing or portable john
3-Man Campsite (#952)	cabin	cotton & nylon	24 12	74/64	96 × 78	3	1	pearl gray	Springbar™
Supr-Lyt (3 models) smallest (#850)	backpack	rip. nyl. & taf. nyl.	5	36	84 × 84	2	1	blue, green	Springbar™ for low humidity regions
Wall (10 standard sizes available)	wall	cotton duck or wax-treated fire-retardant fabric						white or dark olive green	*no* Springbar™
smallest			36	84/48	120 × 96	6	1		
largest			93	120/60	240 × 192	15	1		
Backpacking	backpack (dbl. wall)	rip. nyl., taf. nyl.							twin skylights, no guying needed on fly
model #40			7	41	96 × 48	2	1	tan/rust	
model #50			8 4	41	93 × 60	2-3	2	tan/orange	
model #60			10 8	53	90 × 90	3-4	2	tan/blue	

Kirkham's Outdoor Products Springbar
Modular

Kirkham's Outdoor Products Springbar
Model 955

Manufacturer
LAACKE & JOYS CO. 1432 N. Water St. Milwaukee, Wisconsin 53202

Model	Type	Materials	Weight lbs. oz.	Dimensions Height (inches) Max/Min	Length × Width (inches)	Capacity Rating (# persons)	Number of Entries	Colors	Special Features
Wanderlust (#302)	backpack	rip. nyl.	9 3	64/36–49	72 × 96	3	1	gold	1 wnd., acces. pocks.
Expedition (#401)	backpack	rip. nyl.	7 5	48	60 × 86	2	1	orange/blue	1 wnd., access. pocks., A-frame poles— interchangeable
Pack Lite II (#201)	backpack	rip. nyl.	6 1	50/30	60 × 84	2	1	gold	1 wnd., interchangeable poles
Camper (#901)	umbrella	army duck	53 8	90/74	118 × 118	5	1 dutch	pearl gray	3 wnds., rear wnd. has vny. pane
Camper FR (#922)	umbrella	army duck	56	90/74	118 × 118	5	1 dutch	pearl gray	3 wnds., FR
Campmaster (#951)	umbrella	army duck	64	90/74	118 × 150	6	1 dutch	pearl gray	3 wnds., rear ext., vny. pane, mildew resistant
Junior Umbrella (#761)	umbrella	army duck	21	80	87 × 87	2	1 screen	pearl gray	1 wnd.
Explorer (#851)	explorer	can. poplin	15 8	72	96 × 84	3	1 screen	tan	1 screened vent
Nomad (#105)	cabin	can. poplin, vny.	32 8	84/60	108 × 90	3	1 screen	pearl gray	3 wnds.
Vagabond (#103)	cabin	can. poplin	44 8	90/60	120 × 96	3	1 screen	tan	4 wnds.
Cruisemaster (#862)	explorer	can. poplin	12	84/72	84 × 72	2	1	pearl gray	1 wnd., extend & stake out door for storage
Kitchen Camper (#921)	screen cabin	can. poplin, nyl. net, vny.	30	90/68	132 × 132	6	2 screen	pearl gray	opt. wind curtain
Wrangler (#1011)	cabin	can. poplin	54	90/63	144 × 120	6	1 screen & storm	yellow	4 wnds., front & rear vny. panes

Laacke & Joys Wildwood® Forest View

Laacke & Joys Wildwood® Kitchen Camper

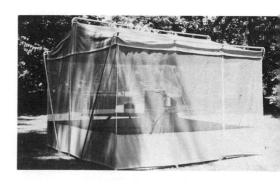

LAACKE & JOYS CO. (cont.)

Model	Type	Materials	Weight lbs. oz.	Dimensions Height (inches) Max/Min	Dimensions Length × Width (inches)	Capacity Rating (# persons)	Number of Entries	Colors	Special Features
Wrangler FR (#1022)	cabin	can. poplin	61	90/63	144 × 120	6	1 screen & storm	yellow	4 winds., FR
Forest View (#881)	umbrella	army duck	72	96/77	168 × 120	6	1 dutch	pearl gray	6 wnds., 2 rear vny. panes
Wayfarer (#601)	modified wall	can. poplin, vny.	16	72	102 × 84	3	1	pearl gray	1 screen vent, FR

Manufacturer
MOSS TENT WORKS, INC.   Camden, Maine 04843

Model	Type	Materials	Weight lbs. oz.	Dimensions Height (inches) Max/Min	Dimensions Length × Width (inches)	Capacity Rating (# persons)	Number of Entries	Colors	Special Features
Optimum 200	hybrid	cotton/nyl.	64	84		9	1	white	2 wnds., vacation home
Trillium	dome		13	(door) 65/42		6	3	tan/off-white fly	
Sundance	hybrid		7 2	(fr.)(rear) 53/34	95 × 43 95 × 66	2	1	yellow	freestanding, self-erecting, fly is part of tent
Parawing: small large	tarp	nyl.			144 × 144 228 × 228				hyperbolic paraboloid shape
Eave II	tunnel	nyl./rip, taf.	6 2	(fr.)(rear) 40/29	90 × 70	2	1	beige/yellow	fly vest., 1 wnd.
Eave III	tunnel	nyl./rip, taf.	7	(fr.)(rear) 46/37	90 × 79	3	1	beige/yellow	fly vest., 1 wnd.
Solus	backpack	rip./taf.	4	45	96 × 42 96 × 66	1	1		
Siesta Sunshade	3/4 dome	cotton		54	67 × 67				
Star Gazer	free-standing	urethane coated taf./rip. nyl.	6	52	86 × 70	2	1	lt. tan/ dk. tan	screened top wnd.

Moss Tent Works Optimum 200 (interior)

Moss Optimum 200 (exterior)

Moss Trillium

Manufacturer
THE NORTH FACE   1234 Fifth St.   Berkeley, California 94710

Model	Type	Materials	Weight lbs. oz.	Dimensions Height (inches) Max/Min	Length × Width (inches)	Capacity Rating (# persons)	Number of Entries	Colors	Special Features*
Morning Glory	pyramid	nylon	13 8	72/42	168 × 96	4	1	navy/gold or taupe	shock-corded poles, zip cook hole
VE 23	dome	nylon	7 12	46	98 × 84	2	1	sand/green	shock-corded poles, zip cook hole, 2 net wnds.
VE 24	dome	nylon	8 13	49	98 × 81	2	1	gold/sand	shock-corded poles, zip cook hole, 2 net wnds.
Tuolumne	backpack	nylon	5 8	50/36	84 × 50	2	1	navy/gold or taupe/blue	shock-corded poles, zip cook hole, 2 net wnds.
Sierra	backpack	nylon	6 15	48	89 × 56	2	1	navy/gold taupe/gold	shock-corded poles, zip cook hole, 2 net wnds.

Moss Solus

The North Face Morning Glory

Moss Eave

THE NORTH FACE (cont.)

Model	Type	Materials	Weight lbs. oz.	Dimensions Height (inches) Max/Min	Dimensions Length × Width (inches)	Capacity Rating (# persons)	Number of Entries	Colors	Special Features*
Mountain	expedition	nylon	7 5	48	94 × 56	2	2	navy/gold taupe/green	shock-corded poles, zip cook hole, 2 net wnds.
Oval Intention	dome	nylon	9 14	51/42	114 × 79	3–4	1	gold/navy, gold/taupe	shock-corded poles, zip cook hole, 2 net wnds.
North Star	geodesic dome	nylon	15	55	109 × 102	4	3	sand/gold	cook hole

* All tents come with fly sheet, VE 24 and North Star have full-coverage fly sheets.

North Face North Star

North Face VE 23

North Face Oval Intention

Manufacturer
OUTDOOR VENTURE CORPORATION   Box 337   Stearns, Kentucky 42647

Model	Type	Materials	Weight lbs. oz.	Height (inches) Max/Min	Length × Width (inches)	Capacity Rating (# persons)	Number of Entries	Colors	Special Features
Backpackers (5 models)	pup								
smallest (#90-121)		poly-ethylene	5	38	72 × 60	2	1	blue	
largest (#90-145)		nyl. taf.	30	56	84 × 84	3	1	orange	
Ice tent (#90-400)	ice	poly.	8	64	60 × 60	2	1	tan	freestanding frame, interior hose sod cloth
Van tent (#90-600)	van	poly.-cotton	38	90/70	108 × 108		1 dutch door	tan/white	2 side wnds.
Hikers tents (2 models)		nyl.				2 to 3	1	blue/white	1 wnd.
90-419	cabin		7 8	73/57	49 × 49				
90-510	umbrella		18	73/48	49 × 49				
House Canopy	canopy	poly. & fiber glass	37	88/71	144 × 144			yellow & blue	
Screen tents (3 models)	cabin	poly-ethylene						blue/yellow	
smallest (#90-277)			17	96/72	138 × 138		1		
largest (#90-274)			35	88/72	144 × 144		1		

Outdoor Venture Corporation The Enterprise

Outdoor Venture Ice Fishing

Outdoor Venture Van Tent

Manufacturer
PAUL PETZOLDT WILDERNESS EQUIPMENT   P.O. Box 489   Lander, Wyoming, 82520

Model	Type	Materials	Weight lbs. oz.	Dimensions Height (inches) Max/Min	Length × Width (inches)	Capacity Rating (# persons)	Number of Entries	Colors	Special Features
Super Wand	backpack	nyl.	12	48–43/14	102 × 60	2+	2	tan/green	cook hole, tunnel, nyl. & screen door
Baja	backpack	nyl.	9 2	48–45/14	102 × 60	2+	1	green	
Rain Fly	backpack	nyl.	2		132 × 108	2		green	

Wilderness Baja Tent

Paul Petzoldt Wilderness Equipment Rain Fly

Manufacturer
REI CO-OP   Recreational Equipment, Inc. P.O. Box C-88125   Seattle, Washington 98188

Model	Type	Materials	Weight lbs. oz.	Dimensions Height (inches) Max/Min	Dimensions Length × Width (inches)	Capacity Rating (# persons)	Number of Entries	Colors	Special Features
Ascent	A-frame	nyl. & cotton	6 2	41/12	4½ × 8	2	1 arch	brown/sand/ blue	dbl. wall, no ext. fly
Ridge	A-frame	nyl. & cotton	1 11	46/11	96 × 37–54	2	1 zip. arch	brown/green	
Dome	dome	nyl. & cotton	6 15	52/10	84 side–sd 96 cor–cor	2–3	1 zip. arch	green/yellow /sand	
Cirque	backpack	nyl. & cotton	5 12	54/12	96 (long) 64 (across mid) 42 (each end)	2	1 zip. arch	yellow/ brown	
Solarium	tunnel	nyl. & cotton	7 12	43/10	30 (vest.) 107 × 64	3	2 zip.	yellow/sand	vest. included
Great Pyramid	expedi-tion ext. frame	nyl. & cotton	11 5	78/23	96 × 80	4+	2 (tunnel & arch)	yellow/sand	
McKinley II	expedi-tion	nyl. & cotton	11 11	88/32	96 × 78	4	2 (tunnel & zip-pered U)	yellow/sand	
Crestline Expedit'n	expedi-tion	nyl. & cotton	8 4	46/11	28" vest. 88 × 60	2–3	2 (tunnel & arch)	red/sand	vest. included

Recreational Equipment, Inc., Great Pyramid

REI with snowflaps

Manufacturer
RIVENDELL MOUNTAIN WORKS　P.O. Box 199　Victor, Idaho 83455

Model	Type	Materials	Weight lbs. oz.	Height (inches) Max/Min	Length × Width (inches)	Capacity Rating (# persons)	Number of Entries	Colors	Special Features
Bombshelter	expedi-tion	nyl.	5　12	35	97 × 46	2	1 tunnel/ flap	gold/rust/tan	2 vents, 2 pocks., ridgepole
Gore-Tex® Bombshelter	expedi-tion	Gore-Tex®/nyl.	5	35	97 × 46	2	1 tunnel/ flap	gold/rust	2 vents, opt. cook hole, frost liner, & snow flaps

Rivendell Mountain Works Bombshelter

Manufacturer
SEATTLE TENT AND FABRIC   900 N. 137 St. P.O. Box 33576   Seattle, Washington 98133

Model	Type	Materials	Weight lbs. oz.	Dimensions Height (inches) Max/Min	Dimensions Length × Width (inches)	Capacity Rating (# persons)	Number of Entries	Colors	Special Features
5 models:	wall	duck						neutral, gray	also in 2 other
smallest			18	72/36	84 × 108		1		fabric weights
largest			49	114/48	168 × 192		1		
Scout Jamboree	wall	duck	12	68/24	108 × 84	2	1	green	1 wnd.
Umbrella Tent	umbrella	duck & nyl.	30	85/68	108 × 108	2–3	1	green	1 wnd.
			38	85/68	108 × 144				2 wnds.
Cabin Camper	wall	duck & nyl.	44	84/48	108 × 144	6	1	green	
Cabin Camper Delux	wall	poly.-cotton & nyl.	50	84/48	108 × 144	6	1	green	3 wnds.
Himalaya tent	backpack-explorer	poly.-cotton & nyl.	7 9	73	89 × 101	3	1	light green/yellow	
Zen tent	backpack-explorer	dac.-nyl. & nyl.	6	53/17	72 × 43	2	1	light green/yellow	
Tee Pee (12 models)	tipi								
smallest		10.38 oz.	20		120 (dia.)	4	1	white/khaki/	
largest		army duck	70		240 (dia.)	15	1	pearl gray	
smallest		10 oz. white	19		120 (dia.)	4	1	white	
largest		duck	64		240 (dia.)	15	1		

Seattle Tent & Fabric Himalaya

Manufacturer
SIERRA DESIGNS 247 Fourth Street Oakland, California 94607

Model	Type	Materials	Weight lbs. oz.	Dimensions Height (inches) Max/Min	Length × Width (inches)	Capacity Rating (# persons)	Number of Entries	Colors	Special Features
Starflight	explorer	nyl.	4 11	54/12	96 × 64	1	1	blue/yellow	
Wilderness	expedition	nyl.	6 10	45/36	88.5 × 55	2	1	blue, green or orange	cook hole
Glacier	expedition	nyl.	7 11	45/45	118 × 53	3	2	green or blue	cook hole
3-Man	pyramid	nyl.	8	72/13	93 (corner to corner)	3	1	orange or blue	1 wnd.
Pleasure Dome	expedition pyramid	nyl.	11	79/13	96 (corner to corner)	3	1	green/blue	2 wnds., cook hole
Aireflex	backpack	nyl.	6	48	86 × 53	2	1	blue/yellow	2 wnds.
Octadome (5ft.×7ft.)	dome	nyl.	8 3	68	78 (side–side) 84 (corner–corner)	4	1		4 wnds., dbl. wall
Octadome (6ft.×8ft.)	dome	nyl.	10 1	78	89 (side–side) 97 (corner–corner)	3	1		4 wnds., dbl. wall

Sierra 3-Man

Sierra Designs Octadome, with Yosimite Half Dome

Sierra Starflight

Manufacturer
TRAILWISE 2407 Fourth Street Berkeley, California 94710

Model	Type	Materials	Weight lbs. oz.	Dimensions Height (inches) Max/Min	Length × Width (inches)	Capacity Rating (# persons)	Number of Entries	Colors	Special Features
Fitzroy III	A-frame	rip./nyl., rip./taf., poly-urethane	8 5	51/49	102 × 60	2	2	blue or green, gold or navy	no-see-um-proof net, shock-corded poles, snow tun., fly, WR
Great Arc Tent	geodesic dome	taf., poly-urethane	6 8	44/24	102 × 64	2			no-see-um-proof net, WR

Trailwise Fitzroy III

Manufacturer
THE WENZEL COMPANY 1280 Research Boulevard   St. Louis, Missouri 63132

Model	Type	Materials	Weight lbs. oz.	Height (inches) Max/Min	Length × Width (inches)	Capacity Rating (# persons)	Number of Entries	Colors	Special Features
Eagle (3 models)	cabin	poly./cotton						green/white	
smallest (22107)			18	74/48	84 × 84	2	1		1 wnd.
largest (22109)			23	74/56	144 × 108	5	1		2 wnds.
Flamezel (3 models)	cabin	poly./cotton						brown/beige	2 wnds.
smallest (24002)			26	78/56	120 × 96	4	1		
largest (24004)			40	82/56	168 × 120	6	1		
Vantage (3 models)	cabin	poly./cotton						white/gold	
smallest (22120)			26	80/57	120 × 96	4	1		2 wnds.
largest (22122)			42	84/58	168 × 120	6	1		3 wnds.
Thunderbird (3 models)	cabin	poly./cotton						gold/bronze	
smallest (22111)			28	82/58	120 × 96	4	1		2 wnds.
largest (22113)			42	84/58	168 × 120	6	1		3 wnds.
Vantage Continental (21113)	cabin	poly./cotton	48	78/58	180 × 106	6	1	green/yellow	6 wnds., 2 awnings
Thunderbird Cottage (21116)	cottage	poly./cotton	38	81/70	144 × 108	5	1	gold/bronze	3 wnds.
Flamezel Screen (21175)	cabin/ screen	poly./cotton	46	91/66 & 60	108 × 180	6		white/blue	3 wnds.
Flamezel Umbrella (#211105)	umbrella	poly./cotton	20	75/58	96 × 96	3	1	blue/white	1 wnd.

The Wenzel Company Tall Trail

Wenzel Vantage® Continental

Model	Type	Materials	Weight lbs. oz.	Dimensions Height (inches) Max/Min	Length × Width (inches)	Capacity Rating (# persons)	Number of Entries	Colors	Special Features
Flamezel Mountain (#21101)	scout	poly./cotton	7	38	60 × 84	2	1 (zip front)	blue	storm door
Flamezel Pup (#21100)	play	poly./cotton	5	38	58 × 81	2	1	blue	front open, no door
Skyliner (#21125)	backpack	nyl.	5	38	60 × 84	2	1	blue	1 wnd.
Wilderness (#24001)	backpack	nyl.	6	60/18	84 × 84	3	1 (zip front)	brown/ mustard	1 wnd.
Shenandoah (#21127)	backpack	nyl.	5	42	60 × 84	2	1 (zip front)	orange	1 wnd.
Tall Trail (Teepee) (#21126)	tipi	nyl.	6	88	84 × 84	3	2 (storm screen)	green	2 wnds.
Vantage Screen House (#21114)	screen	poly./cotton	38	90/70	144 × 144	7	2 (zip)	blue/white	
Flamezel Screen House (#22114)	screen	poly./cotton	35	90/70	144 × 144	7	2 (zip)	blue/white	
(#22115)		polyethylene nyl.	20	96/72	138 × 138	6	1 (zip screen)	blue	
Flamezel Dining Canopy (#22116)	canopy	poly-ethylene	12	96/72	138 × 138	6		blue	

Wenzel Vantage® Cabin Tent

Wenzel Flamezel® Screen Tent

8 SOURCES

The white tents showed their canvas walls,
Where brief sojourners, in the cool, soft air,
Forgot their inland heats, hard toil, and year-long care.

— from "The Tent on the Beach" by John Greenleaf Whittier

This is the where-to-get-it section with listings of tent renters, manufacturers, tipi-makers, recreational vehicles (trailers with collapsible tent tops), tent kit suppliers, yurt designers, and books and magazines on tents and tenting. The tent field is booming, and therefore changing, so by no means should you expect this list to be all-inclusive, though you *can* expect it to be quite useful.

TENT RENTERS

The following is a list of firms that rent Fair, Party, and Commercial (FPC) tents. They are arranged alphabetically by state and city.

Alabama

Worth Tent Rental Co.
Rt. 4
Elba 36323
(FPC)

Arizona

Phoenix Tent & Awning Co., Inc.
2533 N. 16th St.
Phoenix 85006
(FPC)

California

HDO/West
625 Hazel St.
Glendale 91201
(FPC)

Lodi Tent & Awning Co.
701 N. Sacramento St.
Lodi 95240
(FPC)

Canvas Specialty
7344 E. Bandini Blvd.
Los Angeles 90040
(PC)

Goodwin-Cole Co.
1315 Alhambra Blvd.
Sacramento 95816
(PC)

Stuart-Sauter Co.
100 Utah Ave.
San Francisco 94103
(FPC)

Colorado

Denver Tent Co.
4004 Grape St.
Denver 80216
(PC)

Connecticut

Cunningham & Upson, Inc.
46-44 Hotchkiss St.
New Haven 06511
(FPC)

Bailey & Staub, Inc.
Box 67
New London 06320
(FPC)

E. G. Loomis & Son, Inc.
213 Boston Post Rd.
Orange 06477
(FPC)

Deicke Tent & Equipment Co.
785 High Ridge Rd.
Stamford 06905
(FPC)

Stamford Tent & Equipment Co.
860 High Ridge Rd.
Stamford 64801
(FPC)

Strong Tent & Awning Corp.
21 Maple Ave.
Windsor 06095

Florida

Florida Tent Rental, Inc.
3573 E. 10th Ct.
Hialeah 33013
(FPC)

Georgia

Andrew Tent Co., Inc.
P. O. Box 4400
Albany 31706
(FPC)

Bailie's Canvas Specialties
2344 Walden Dr.
Augusta 30904
(FPC)

Illinois

ESL Tent Co.
26 S. 20th St.
Belleville 62221
(FPC)

Danville Tent & Awning Co.
1706 Warrington Ave.
P.O. Box 63
Danville 61832
(FPC)

Galesburg Canvas Products
187 W. Losey St.
Galesburg 61401
(PC)

HDO Productions, Inc.
1520 Berkley Rd.
Highland Park 60035
(FPC)

Parasol Tent Rental, Inc.
P.O. Box 557
Highland Park 60035
(PC)

Peoria Tent & Awning Co.
513 N. Franklin St.
Peoria 61651
(FPC)

Armbruster Manufacturing Co.
8600 Old Route 66 S.
Springfield 62707
(FPC)

Indiana

Bauer's Tent Rental
R.R. 5 Box 108-A
Evansville 47711
(FPC)

Fort Wayne Tent Rental Co.
P.O. Box 7547
Fort Wayne 46807
(FPC)

Wolf Camp & Sailing Center
2405T W. Jefferson Blvd.
Fort Wayne 46804
(FC)

Lafayette Tent & Awning Co., Inc.
125 S. Fifth St.
Lafayette 47901
(FPC)

Terre Haute Tent & Awning Co.
315 N. 9th St.
Terre Haute 47807
(FPC)

Iowa

Cedar Rapids Tent & Awning Co.
533 First St., S.W.
Cedar Rapids 52404
(FPC)

Ottumwa Tent & Awning Co.
635 W. 2nd St.
Ottumwa 52501
(FPC)

Waterloo Tent & Awning
1029 Commercial St.
Waterloo 50702
(FPC)

Kansas

Wichita Ponca Canvas Products, Inc.
611 E. Central Ave.
Wichita 67201
(PC)

Louisiana

Foster Co., Inc.
746 Tchoupitoulas St.
New Orleans 70190
(P)

Maine

Air-O-Structures, Inc.
P.O. Box 296
Auburn 04210
(FPC)

Maryland

HDO/East
11010 Parklawn Dr.
Rockville 20852
(FPC)

Massachusetts

Alfred G. Peterson & Sons, Inc.
491 W. Main St.
Avon 02322
(P)

Peterson/Cape Cod Awning, Inc.
290 Falmouth Rd.
Hyannis 02601
(PC)

Smith Rents Tents
1520 East St.
Pittsfield 01201
(FPC)

Jesse G. Willis, Inc.
580 Pleasant St.
Watertown 02172
(PC)

Michigan

Fox Tent & Awning Co.
617 S. Ashley
Ann Arbor 48106
(FPC)

Benton Harbor Awning & Tent Co.
2275 M-139
Benton Harbor 49022
(PC)

Minnesota

Expressive Tent Rental, Inc.
P.O. Box 634
Minneapolis 55440
(PC)

Missouri

Coglizer Tent & Awning Co.
106 Joplin St.
Joplin 64801
(FPC)

Nebraska

Rogers Tent & Awning Co., Inc.
240 E. 1st St.
Fremont 68025
(FPC)

Lincoln Tent & Awning
3900 Cornhusker Hwy.
Lincoln 68504
(FP)

New Jersey

Deming Tent Co.
470 West Side Ave.
Jersey City 07304
(P)

Green Tent Co.
54 N. Main St.
Wharton 07885
(P)

New York

Smith Awning & Tent Co.
56-58 Grant Ave.
Auburn 13021
(FPC)

Brownie Tent Rentals
McBride Ave.
Clinton 13323
(FPC)

Nassau Tent & Awning Corp.
Farmingdale 11735
(P)

P. J. McBride, Inc.
12 Evans Ave.
Farmingdale 11735
(FPC)

Darby Tent Co., Inc.
77-22 164th St.
Flushing 11366
(FPC)

Geneva Awning & Tent Works
96 Lewis St.
Geneva 14456
(FPC)

S. L. Doery & Son Corp.
299 Rockaway Tpk.
Long Island 11559
(P)

The A & B Tent Co.
Peekskill 10566
(P)

Ohio

The South Akron Awning Co.
763 Kenmore Blvd.
Akron 44314
(FPC)

O'Neil Awning & Tent, Inc.
895 Walnut St.
Canal Winchester 43110
(FPC)

A Aable Rents Co.
1512 Green Rd.
Cleveland 44121
(FPC)

Shaffer Tent & Awning Co.
P.O. Box 247
Coshocton 43812
(FPC)

Glawe Manufacturing Co.
2269 N. Fairfield Rd.
Dayton 45431
(FPC)

Delphos Tent & Awning Co.
1454 N. Main St.
Delphos 45833
(FPC)

Toledo Tent Co.
300 Fassett St.
Toledo 43605
(FPC)

Oklahoma

Southwest Canvas Manufacturing Co.
2901 S.E. 15th St.
Oklahoma City 73109
(FPC)

Oregon

SEE Companies
12200 Jantzen Dr.
Portland 97303
(FPC)

See Fabric & Decorating, Inc.
2215 Claxter Rd., N.E.
Salem 97303
(FPC)

Pennsylvania

Al's Awning Shop
1721 W. 26th St.
Erie 16508
(FP)

A. Mamaux & Son
120 Blvd. of the Allies
Pittsburgh 15222
(FPC)

York Tent & Awning Co., Inc.
9 E. 7th Ave.
York 17404
(FPC)

Tennessee

Chattanooga Tent & Awning Co.
1110 Oak St.
Chattanooga 37404
(FPC)

Mahaffey Tent Co., Inc.
3826 Old Getwell Rd.
Memphis 38118
(FPC)

Memphis Delta Tent & Awning Co.
P.O. Box 287
Memphis 38101
(FPC)

Crown Tent & Awning Co.
717 3rd Ave. N.
Nashville 37201
(FPC)

Nashville Tent & Awning Co.
615 20th Ave., N.
Nashville 37203
(FPC)

Texas

CBF Industries, Inc.
P.O. Box 20204
10404 Harry Hines Blvd.
Dallas 75220
(FPC)

Alexander Tent Co.
119 Gray St.
Houston 77002
(FPC)

Aquila & Priscilla Tent Makers
Rt. 1 Box 355
Waco 76710
(FC)

Virginia

Norfolk Tent Co., Inc.
2401 Monticello Ave.
Norfolk 23517
(FPC)

Sunnyside Awning & Tent Co.
P.O. Box 2602
Roanoke 24010
(FPC)

Washington

Camp Lewis Tent & Awning Co.
1111 First Ave.
Seattle 98101
(FPC)

Mike Prebesac
2601 Elliott Ave., Rm. 4311
Seattle 78121
(FPC)

Wisconsin

Tom's Tent Rentals
3405 Geneva Ln.
LaCrosse 54601
(FPC)

John Gallagher Company
305 S. Bedford St.
Madison 53703
(FPC)

Dow Canvas Products, Inc.
2705 Calument Ave.
Manitowoc 54220
(FPC)

IGL-Wisc. Awning & Tent, Inc.
8768 W. Fond Du Lac Ave.
Milwaukee 53225
(FPC)

Oshkosh Tent & Awning Co., Inc.
135 High Ave.
Oshkosh 54902
(FPC)

Wyoming

Kistler Tent & Awning Co.
Box 671
Casper 82602
(FPC)

CAMPING TENT MANUFACTURERS

Alaska

Alaska Tent & Tarp, Inc.
529 Front St.
Fairbanks 99701

Arizona

Gila River Indian Enterprises, Inc.
2000 Vavages
Coolidge 85228

Camp Trails Company
4111 W. Clarendon Ave.
Phoenix 85019

Arkansas

Little Rock Tent & Awning Co.
1213 Broadway
Little Rock 72202

California

North Face
Tent Dept.
1234 Fifth St.
Berkeley 94710

Sierra Designs
Fourth & Addison Sts.
Berkeley 94710

Ski Hut
Tent Div.
1615 University Ave.
Berkeley 94710

Stephenson's
23206 Hatteras St.
Woodland Hills 91364

Trailwise
2407 Fourth St.
Berkeley 94710

Pacific Tent/Ascente
P.O. Box 2028
Fresno 93718

Outdoor Products
530 South Main
Los Angeles 90013

Riverside Tent & Awning Co.
3226 Franklin Ave.
Riverside 92507

Adventure 16 (A16) Wilderness
Camping Outfitters
4620 Alvarado Canyon Rd.
San Diego 92120

Sullivan Co., Inc.
245 S. Van Ness Ave.
San Francisco 94103

Colorado

Holubar Mountaineering Ltd.
Box 7
Boulder 80302

Athalon Products/High Lonesome
3333 E. 52nd Ave.
Denver 80216

Denver Tent Co.
4004 Grape St.
Denver 80216

Frostline, Inc.
P.O. Box 2190
Boulder 80302

Gerry Division
Outdoor Sports, Inc.
5450 North Valley Highway
Denver 80216

UTE Mountain Corp.
P.O. Box 3602
Englewood 80110

Pueblo Tent & Awning Co., Inc.
P.O. Box 34
Pueblo 81055

Connecticut

Cannondale Corp.
35 Pulaski St.
Stamford 06902

Georgia

Georgia Tent & Awning Co.
228 Margaret St. S.E.
Atlanta 30315

Idaho

Rivendell Mountain Works
P.O. Box 199
Victor 83455

Illinois

Penthouse Manufacturing, Inc.
Dept. PP
126 Broad St.
Carlinville 62626

Chicago Tent
1900 W. 18th Pl.
Chicago 60608

O'Henry Tent & Awning Co.
4862 N. Clark St.
Chicago 60640

Indiana

Anchor Industries Inc.
1100 Burch Dr.
P.O. Box 3477
Evansville 47733

American Tent & Awning Co.
632 S. East St.
Indianapolis 46225

Midwest Tent & Awning Co.
P.O. Box 64
Indianapolis 46206

Lafayette Tent & Awning Co.
125 S. Fifth St.
Lafayette 47901

Terre Haute Tent & Awning Co.
315 N. 9th St.
Terre Haute 47807

Iowa

Burlington Tent & Awning Co.
Burlington 54601

Centerville Tent & Awning Co.
1019 S. 18th St.
Centerville 52544

Burch Manufacturing Co., Inc.
618 First Ave., N.
Fort Dodge 50501

Mason City Tent & Awning Co.
408 S. Federal
Mason City 50401

Kansas

Hutchinson Tent & Awning
821 S. Main
Hutchinson 67501

Topeka Tent & Awning Co.
320 E. 2nd St.
Topeka 66603

Coleman Co., Inc.
250 N. St. Francis St.
Wichita 67201

Wichita Ponca Canvas Products, Inc.
Box 2177
611 E. Central
Wichita 67201

Kentucky

Debrovy, Hyman & Sons
415 E. Market St.
Louisville 40202

Outdoor Venture Corp.
Box 337
Stearns 42647

Louisiana

Monroe Tent & Awning Co.
West Monroe 71291

Maine

Air-O-Structures, Inc.
129 N. River Rd.
Auburn 04210

Moss Tent Works, Inc.
Camden 04843

L. L. Bean
Freeport 04033

Maryland

Loane Brothers, Inc.
310 N. Eutaw St.
Baltimore 21201

Bishop's Ultimate Outdoor Equipment
6804 Millwood Rd.
Bethesda 20034

C. R. Daniels, Inc.
3453 Ellicott Center Dr.
Ellicott City 21043

Massachusetts

Eastern Mountain Sports, Inc.
1041 Commonwealth Ave.
Boston 02215

Michigan

Fox Tent & Awning Co.
617 S. Ashley
Ann Arbor 48104

Battle Creek Tent & Awning Co.
128 E. Michigan Ave.
Battle Creek 49014

Acme Tent & Awnings Co.
18326 John R St.
Detroit 48203

Minnesota

Duluth Tent & Awning Co., Inc.
1610 W. Superior St.
Duluth 55806

Mankato Tent & Awning Co.
1021 Range St.
Mankato 56001

Holgaard's Inc.
3550 S. Hwy. 100
Minneapolis 55416

Missouri

Baker-Lockwood Awning & Tent Co.
12918 2nd St., B
Grandview 64030

Kansas City Tent & Awning Co.
1616 E. 31st St.
Kansas City 64109

Jefferson Tent & Awning Co.
2930 Gravois Ave.
St. Louis 63118

Wenzel Company
1280 Research Blvd.
St. Louis 63132

New Hampshire

Don Fisher Custom Canvas &
Upholstery
Homestead Bldg., Rte. 3
Meredith 03253

New York

Eureka! Tent, Inc.
625 Conklin Rd.
P.O. Box 966
Binghamton 13902

Buffalo Awning & Tent Manufacturing
Co.
384 Broadway
Buffalo 14204

Service Canvas Co., Inc.
147 Swan St.
Buffalo 14203

Jamaica Tent Co., Inc.
94 E. Industry Court
Deer Park 11729

Thomas Black & Sons
930 Ford St.
Ogdensburg 13669

North Carolina

D. W. Norvell Tent Manufacturing Co.
2210 High Point Rd.
Greensboro 27403

Kearns Tent & Awning Co., Inc.
P.O. Box 1748
2227 S. Main St.
High Point 27261

Carolina Awning & Tent
Manufacturing Co.
Rocky Mount 27801

Ohio

South Akron Awning Co.
763 Kenmore Blvd.
Akron 44314

R. J. Patton & Co.
1908 Dunlap St.
Cincinnati 45214

Queen City Awning & Tent Co.
318 E. 8th St.
Cincinnati 45202

Shaffer Tent & Awning Co.
Rte. 3
P.O. Box 247
Coshocton 43812

Roloson Tent & Awning Co.
302 S. Union
Lima 45801

National Canavas Products Corp.
901 Buckingham St.
Toledo 43607

Oklahoma

W. L. Dumas Manufacturing Co.
210 S. Main
Commerce 74339

Oregon

Star Route
Box 41
Cloverdale 97112

Hirsh Weis
White Stag
5203 S.E. Johnson Creek Blvd.
Portland 97206

Pennsylvania

Ehmke Manufacturing Co., Inc.
5200 N. Belfield Ave.
Philadelphia 19144

Webb Manufacturing Co., Inc.
1243 Carpenter St.
Philadelphia 19147

Tennessee

Camel Tent & Awning Co.
111 Jackson Ave., E.
Knoxville 37915

Crown Tent & Awning Co.
717 3rd Ave., N.
Nashville 37201

Nashville Tent & Awning Co., Inc.
615 20th Ave., N.
Nashville 37203

Texas

CBF Industries, Inc.
10414 Harry Hines Blvd.
Dallas 75220

Dallas Tent & Awning
2907 Gaston Ave.
Dallas 75226

El Paso Tent & Awning Co.
7322 N. Loop
El Paso 79907

W. K. Hill Awning & Tent Co.
1111 W. Drew
Box 66086
Houston 77006

San Antonio Tent & Awning Co.
P.O. Box 20426
4311 Dividenti
San Antonio 78220

Utah

Kirkham's Outdoor Products
AAA Tent & Awning Co.
24 W. Fifth Ave. S.
Salt Lake City 84101

Vermont

Metzger Brothers, Inc.
Rutland 05701

Virginia

Hogshire Tent & Awning
Manufacturing Co., Inc.
2401 Hampton Blvd.
Norfolk 23517

Washington

JanSport
Paine Field Industrial Park
Everett 98204

Camp Lewis Tent & Awning Co.
1111 First Ave.
Seattle 98101

Early Winters, Ltd.
110 Prefontaine Place, S.
Seattle 98104

Eddie Bauer Expedition Outfitter
P.O. Box 3700
Seattle 98124

Puget Sound Tent & Awning Co.
2107 Third Ave.
Seattle 98101

REI CO-CP
Recreational Equipment, Inc.
P.O. Box C-88125
Seattle 98188

Seattle Tent & Fabric Products Co.
P.O. Box 33576
900 N. 137th
Seattle 98133

Spokane Tent & Awning Co.
1916 E. Sprague Ave.
Spokane 99202

K-2 Corporation
Vashon 98070

Mountain Products Corp.
123 S. Wenatchee Ave.
Wenatchee 98801

Yakima Tent & Awning Co., Ltd.
P.O. Box 391
Yakima 98907

Wisconsin

Laacke & Joys Co., Wildwood®
1432 N. Water St.
Milwaukee 53202

The Godske Company
1234–36 Thirteenth St.
Racine 53403

Wausau Tent & Awning Co., Inc.
315 S. 4th St.
Wausau 54401

Wyoming

Paul Petzoldt Wilderness Equipment
P.O. Box 489
Lander 82520

RECREATIONAL VEHICLES

California

Happy Traveler Coaches, Inc.
3291 Russell
Riverside 92501

Indiana

AMF/Skamper Div.
P.O. Box 338
State Rd. 15   Bristol 46507

Midas International
55667 CR 155
Elkhart 46514

Recreational vehicle. (Courtesy of Starcraft Company)

Sioux tipi, by Goodwin-Cole Tentmakers

Ski Tow, Mfg.
29194 Phillips St.
Elkhart 46514

Starcraft Co.
2703 College Ave.
Goshen 46526

Steury Corp.
310 Steury Ave.
Goshen 46526

Travel Equipment Corp.
64686 U.S. 33 E.
P.O. Box 512
Goshen 46526

Coachmen Industries, Inc.
P.O. Box 30
Middlebury 46540

Jayco, Inc.
State Rd. 13 S.
P.O. Box 460
Middlebury 46540

Rockwood, Inc.
201 Elm St.
P.O. Box 85
Millersburg 46543

Vega Corp.
P.O. Box 26
Syracuse 46567

Venture Campers
W. Ohio St.
Topeka 46571

Ayr-Way Campers
Div. Rural Rte. 1, Hwy. 6
Wawaka 46794

Iowa

Superior Ideal, Inc.
1107 S. 7th
Oskaloosa 52577

Massachusetts

Jewell Manufacturing Co., Inc.
Dascomb Rd.
Tewksbury 01876

Michigan

Viking Recreational Vehicles, Inc.
580 W. Burr Oak St. M-86
P.O. Box 488
Centerville 49032

Krown Mfg.
1165 Reynolds Rd.
Charlotte 48813

Vanguard Industries
1047 M-86 W.
Colon 49040

J. C. Goss Co.
6330 E. Jefferson Ave.
Detroit 48209

Vesely Company
2101 N. Lapeer Rd.
Lapeer 48446

Minnesota

Bethany
6820 Auto Club Rd.
Minneapolis 55438

North Carolina

Cox Trailers, Inc.
P.O. Box 339
Grifton 28530

How-Lo Campers, Inc.
403 E. 28th
Kannapolis 28081

Pennsylvania

Coleman
Camping Trailer Div.
P.O. Box 111
Somerset 15501

Wisconsin

Curtiss Campers, Inc.
Rte. 1
Loyal 54446

TENT KITS

Mountain Adventure Kit Company
(formerly PolarGuard Kit Company)
11230 See Drive
Whittler, California 90606
(2-person tents)

Frostline
P.O. Box 2190
Boulder, Colorado 80302
(2-person, 3-person, and poncho or tube tents)

Holubar Mountaineering Ltd.
Box 7
Boulder, Colorado 80302
(2-person and 3-person tents)

Altra
5541 Central Ave.
Boulder, Colorado 80301
(2-person tents)

Emskits
Eastern Mountain Sports, Inc.
1041 Commonwealth Ave.
Boston, Massachusetts 02215
(2-person tents)

Sun Down Sleeping Company
979 Willamette St.
Eugene, Oregon 97217
(2-person tents)

Note: The book *Trailside Shelters* by Skye Davis (Harrisburg, Pa.: Stackpole Books, 1977) is a handy and complete reference book on tents and includes a chapter entitled "Making Your Own Portable Shelter."

TIPI MAKERS

Arizona

Phoenix Tent & Awning Co.
2533 N. 16th St.
Phoenix 85006

California

Tipi Makers
339 15th St. Shoppe 150
Oakland 94612

Goodwin-Cole Co.
1315 Alhambra Blvd.
Sacramento 95816

Simpson & Fisher
240 Steuart
San Francisco 95816

Indiana

Anchor Industries
P.O. Box 3477
1100 Burch Dr.
Evansville 47733

Missouri

The Wenzel Company
1280 Research Blvd.
St. Louis 63132

New York

Eureka! Tent, Inc.
625 Conklin Rd.
P.O. Box 966
Binghamton 13903

Pennsylvania

Webb Manufacturing Co., Inc.
1243 Carpenter St.
Philadelphia 19147

Vermont

Evergreen Tipi Makers
East Hardwick 05836

Washington

Seattle Tent & Fabric Products Co.
900 N. 137th
Seattle 98133

Note: A thorough book on tipis is *The Indian Tipi* (Norman, Oklahoma: University of Oklahoma Press, 1957) by Reginald and Gladys Laubin. Ballantine Books in New York has recently published this in paperback.

YURTS IN AMERICA

Yurts can be used as portable camping structures or as permanent homes, but if you want one, you'll probably have to build it yourself. No manufacturer in the U.S. makes completed yurts. American interest in hand-built, homemade yurts developed from the recent trend to explore low-cost shelter alternatives. A few dollars will buy a set of plans. Materials may run from two to three hundred dollars, or considerably less depending on how many of the supplies are salvaged from junk yards, demolition sites, and the like — or whether, for example, you chop your own poles.

William Coperthwaite, who first introduced and championed the home-built yurt in America, says he was motivated to design a structure that unskilled adults and children could build themselves, "participating in a major way in the creation of their own shelter." Coperthwaite's yurts take only two or three days to construct, thus allowing "more people to feel a sense of accomplishment before reaching their threshold of discouragement," as well as providing just about the fastest permanent shelter possible.

He describes his organization, The Yurt Foundation, as an information pool that provides technical knowledge to those exploring lifestyles closer to nature.

The Cascade Shelter, and Chuck and Laurel Cox, both sell designs for portable yurts; and Cascade Shelter, a co-op, also offers a variety of kits and will sell individual or custom yurt parts as well. Cascade Shelter has come up with its own design (developed for the Hoedad co-op who live and plant trees in the Oregon mountains) — not, they say, the traditional yurt — but practical, lightweight, strong, and easily struck.

Chuck and Laurel Cox, former students of Coperthwaite's, published plans for a portable sixteen-foot and/or twenty-foot insulated yurt. They've lived in their yurt for five years, including a year in Alaska, and have moved it at least three times.

Finally, Len Charney has written an inexpensive soft-cover book called *Build a Yurt*. It's 134 pages long and includes plans, line drawings, pho-

Interior of yurt designed by Chuck and Laurel Cox

Exterior view of yurts

Tightening cable on concentric yurt designed by Bill Coperthwaite, founder of the Yurt Foundation

Roof of concentric yurt

tographs, and step-by-step instructions written in cheerful, easily understood prose. He also refers back to Bill Coperthwaite (as do Cascade Shelter and the Coxes) as the best source of yurt information and suggests writing to The Yurt Foundation if you run into any problems. Here are the addresses:

Permanent yurts:

The Yurt Foundation
Bucks Harbor, Maine 04618
Plans: Standard yurt, 17 feet: $5.00
    Concentric yurt, 32 feet (supplement to standard yurt plan): $5.00
    Little yurt, 12 feet: $5.00

Build A Yurt by Len Charney
(New York: Collier Books, 1974)
$3.95

Portable yurts:

Chuck and Laurel Cox
Cox Farm
Crane Crossing Road
Plaistow, New Hampshire 03865
Plans for a 16-foot and 20-foot yurt: $4.00

"How to Build a Portable Yurt"
  by Cascade Shelter
  4500 Aster St.
  Springfield, Oregon 97477
  $8.00

BOOKS AND MAGAZINES

Several very helpful books for the tent enthusiast are the *Backpacking Equipment Buyer's Guide* by William Kemsley and the editors of *Backpacker Magazine* (New York: Collier Books, 1977), which gives a complete rundown on all available backpacking and camping equipment, and Skye Davis' *Trailside Shelters*. Another book that can serve as a guide to living outdoors is *Soft House* by Steve Futterman (New York: Harper & Row, 1976). The Canvas Products Association International, 350 Endicott Building, St. Paul, Minnesota 55101, tel: (612) 222-2508, has a camping brochure entitled, "Camping, It's a Natural," which is free upon request. It's a fine introduction to camping.

Camping Journal, Backpacker, Consumer Research, and *Consumer Reports* magazines publish sporadic reviews and ratings of tents. Any of these are worth consulting before you purchase a tent.

And *1979 Woodall's Campground Directory, No. American Edition* (published by Woodall Publishing Co., 500 Hyacinth Pl., Highland Park, Illinois 60035 and distributed by Simon & Schuster in New York) lists and rates 17,000 campgrounds.

BIBLIOGRAPHY   INDEX

BIBLIOGRAPHY

Andrist, Ralph K., editor in charge. *The American Heritage History of the Confident Years*. New York: American Heritage Publishing Company, 1969.

Appelbaum, Stanley, ed. *The New York Stage: Famous Productions in Photographs*. New York: Dover Publications, Inc., 1976.

Arthaud, Claude. *Enchanted Visions: Fantastic Houses and Their Treasures*. New York: G. P. Putnam's Sons, 1972.

Bartlett, John. *Familiar Quotations,* 14th Edition. Edited by Emily Morison Beck. Boston: Little, Brown & Co., 1968.

Bates, Daniel G. "Nomads and Farmers: the Yoruks of Southeast Turkey." *University of Michigan Journal* no. 52, Ann Arbor, Michigan, 1973.

Berger, Horst. "The Engineering Discipline of Tent Structures." *Architectural Record,* February 1975, pp. 81–88.

Bernier's Travels: Journey to Kachemire. Written at Lahor, 1665. Amsterdam, Holland: P. Marret, 1724.

The Holy Bible. Revised Standard Version. New York: Thomas Nelson and Sons, 1952.

Bird, Walter W., and Kinnius, Ronald A. "The History of the Air Structures in the USA." Pamphlet distribution by Birdair Structures, Inc., Buffalo, N.Y., 1976.

Brand, Stewart, ed. *The Last Whole Earth Catalog*. Menlo Park, Calif.: Whole Earth Truck Store, 1971.

Brent, Peter. *T. E. Lawrence*. New York: G. P. Putnam's Sons, 1975.

Briggs, Lloyd Cabot. "Living Races of the Sahara Desert." *Harvard University, Peabody Museum of Archaeology and Ethnology Paper,* vol. 28, no. 2. Cambridge, Mass.: Peabody Museum, 1958.

Charney, Len. *Building a Yurt: The Low-Cost Mongolian Round House*. New York: Collier Books, 1974.

Clarke, Thurston. *The Last Caravan*. New York: G. P. Putnam's Sons, 1978.

"Family Tents." *Consumer Report*. July 1977, pp. 424–429.

Coon, Carleton Stevens. "Tribes of the Rif." *Harvard, African Studies*, vol. IX. Cambridge, Mass.: Peabody Museum, 1931.

Cronyn, George W., ed. *American Indian Poetry: An Anthology of Songs and Chants*. New York: Liveright, 1962.

Davis, Skye. *Trailside Shelters*. Harrisburg, Pa.: Stackpole Books, 1977.

de Combray, Richard. *Caravansary*. Garden City, N.Y.: Doubleday & Co., Inc., 1978.

Drew, Philip. *Frei Otto: Form and Structure*. Boulder, Colo.: Westview Press, 1976.

Ekvall, Robert B. *Fields on the Hoof. Nexus of Tibetan-Nomadic Pastoralism*. New York: Holt, Rinehart & Winston, 1968.

Ekvall, Robert B. *Tents Against the Sky: A Novel of Tibet*. New York: Farrar Straus and Young, 1955.

Ewers, John C. *Murals in the Round. Painted Tipis of the Kiowa and Kiowa-Apache Indians*. Washington, D.C.: Smithsonian Institution Press, 1978.

Faegre, Torvald. *Tents: Architecture of the Nomads*. Garden City, N.Y.: Anchor Press/Doubleday, 1979.

Field, Claud. *Dictionary of Oriental Quotations (Arabic and Persian)*. New York: MacMillan Co., 1911, repub. by Detroit: Gale Research Co., 1969.

Futterman, Steve. *Softhouse*. New York: Harper & Row, 1976.

Glaeser, Ludwig. *The Work of Frei Otto*. New York: The Museum of Modern Art, 1972.

Haggerty, James J. *Spinoff 1978, An Annual Report*. National Aeronautics and Space Administration, Office of Space and Terrestrial Applications, Technology Utilization Division. Washington, D.C.: U.S. Government Printing Office, January 1978.

Hassnick, Royal B. *Cowboys and Indians — An Illustrated History*. New York: Promontory Press, 1976.

Hazen, Charles D. *Modern European History*. New York: H. Holt & Co., 1917.

Herodotus. *The Histories*. Translated by Aubrey de Selincourt. Baltimore: Penguin Books, 1954.

IL5: A History of Convertible Roofs. Stuttgart, Germany: Institute of Lightweight Structures, 1973.

Jacobson, Cliff. "Consumer's Guide: Tents." *Camping Journal*, August–September 1977.

Kahn, Lloyd, ed. *Shelter*. Bolinas, Calif.: Shelter Publications, 1973.

Kemsley, William, and the editors of *Backpacker Magazine. Backpacking Equipment Buyer's Guide*. New York: Collier Books, 1977.

Laubin, Reginald and Gladys. *The Indian Tipi. Its History, Construction, and Use*. Norman, Okla.: University of Oklahoma Press, 1957.

LeGuin, Ursula K. *The Left Hand of Darkness*. New York: Ace Books, 1969.

Lippard, Lucy. "Body, House, City, Civilization, Journey." *Dwellings*, Institute for Contemporary Art, University of Pennsylvania, 1978.

McIntyre, James, and Richmond, I. A. "Tents of the Roman Army and Leather from Birdoswald." *Cumberland and Westmorland Antiquarian and Archaeological Society*, N.s.v.34. Transac. Kendal, 1934.

Mails, Thomas E. *The People Called Apache*. Englewood Cliffs, N.J.: Prentice-Hall, 1974.

Maxwell, Gavin. *Lords of the Atlas*. London: Longmans, 1966.

Meiss, Millard. *The Great Age of Fresco: Discoveries, Recoveries, and Survivals*. New York: George Braziller in association with the Metropolitan Museum of Art, 1970.

Nansen, Charles. "Comeback of the Canvas Camp." *Field and Stream*, April 1972.

National Geographic Society. *Vanishing Peoples of the Earth*. Washington, D.C.: National Geographic Society, 1968.

Nervi, Pier Luigi, gen. ed. *History of World Architecture*. Translated by Robert Erich Wolf. New York: Harry N. Abrams, Inc., 1978.

Nicolaisen, Johannes. *Ecology and Culture of the Pastoral Tuareg*. Copenhagen: National Museum of Copenhagen, 1963.

Oliver, Paul, ed. *Shelter in Africa*. London: The Overlook Press, 1971.

Otto, Frei. *Tensile Structures*, vols. 1 and 2. Cambridge, Mass.: MIT Press, 1973.

Peterson, Harold Leslie. *Arms and Armor in Colonial America*. Harrisburg, Pa.: Stackpole Books, 1956.

Peterson, Harold Leslie. *The Book of the Continental Soldier.* Harrisburg, Pa.: Stackpole Books, 1968.

Petrus, Jerzy T.; Piatkiewicz-Dereniowa, Maria; and Piwocka, Magdalena. *The Orient in the Wawel Collections.* Translated by Krystyna Malcharek. Wawel State Collections of Art, Poland.

Phillips, David F. "High Noon for the Empire." *Horizon,* Winter 1976, pp. 56–61.

Polo, Marco. *Travels.* Kansas City, Kan.: Haldeman & Julius, 1924.

Pritchard, James B. *The Ancient Near East in Pictures Relating to the Old Testament.* Princeton, N.J.: Princeton University Press, 1954.

Raswan, Carl R. *Black Tents of Arabia (My Life Among the Bedouins).* New York: Creative Age Press, 1947.

Rhodes, Godfrey. *Tents and Tent-Life.* London: Smith, Elder and Company, Cornhill, 1858.

The Rubáiyat of Omar Kháyyám. Translated by Parichehr Kasra. Delmar, N.Y.: Scholars' Facsimiles and Reprints, 1975.

Rudofsky, Bernard. *The Prodigious Builders.* New York: Harcourt Brace Jovanovich, 1977.

Schanche, Don A. "Tentmaking: A Collapsing Craft." *International Herald Tribune,* Oct. 20, 1978.

Sheehy, Gail. *Passages: Predictable Crises of Adult Life.* New York: E. P. Dutton and Company, Inc., 1974.

Sisson, Charles Jasper, ed. *William Shakespeare: The Complete Works.* New York: Harper & Row, 1953.

Tents. Tangents XX: Twentieth in a series of discussions from Koppers for the building design profession. Pamphlet by Koppers Architectural and Construction Materials. Pittsburgh: Koppers Company, Inc., 1978.

Soderstrom, Neil. "Tents for Family Camping." *Consumer's Research Magazine,* August 1977, pp. 7–13.

Tuchman, Barbara. *A Distant Mirror: The Fourteenth Century.* New York: Alfred Knopf, 1978.

Welch, Stuart Cary. *A King's Book of Kings: The Shah-Nameh of Shah Tahmasp.* New York: Metropolitan Museum of Art, 1976.

Welch, Stuart Cary. *Persian Painting: Five Royal Safavid Manuscripts of the 16th Century.* New York: George Braziller, Inc., 1976.

Williams, Neville. *Henry VIII and His Court.* London: Sphere Books, 1973.

Yule, Sir Henry. *The Book of Ser Marco Polo.* London: J. Murray, 1929.

INDEX

AAA Tent & Awning Co. *See*
  Kirkham's Outdoor Products
Abraham, 5, 8
Afghani nomads, 95–97
A-frame, 168, 169
Agora of Athens, 114
Air-supported structure, 116–137;
  defined, 117
Akcha, the, yurts of, 103
Alaarba tent, 92
Alaska Tent & Tarp, Inc., 194
Alexander I, Tsar, 30
Alexander the Great, 96; World Tent
  (Cosmic Tent) of, 10, 11
Ali Baba Goes to Town (film), 156
American Revolution, 41, 42
Anchor Industries, 130, 131, 193
Anchoring, 181, 182
Apache Indians, 69, 70; puberty
  ceremony, 4, 71
Arabian Nights (film), 157
Arapaho Indians, 63
Architecture, materials used: Roman,
  113–116; radomes, 118; modern,
  123, 126, 127, 132, 134
Arctic expeditions: and England, 40;
  and USSR, 40
Arup Associates, 122
A16 Wilderness Camping Outfitters,
  194
Assyrian, 10
Athalon Products, High Lonesome,
  195

Backpacking tent, 168; entries, 184;
  windows and vents, 185, 186;
  zippers, 186, 187
Baker tent, 174
Bakhtiari, 93, 94
Baluchi, 84, 97
Bangladesh, refugee camp in, 38
Baskervill and Son, and University of
  Virginia field house, 120, 121
Basque sheepherders, in U.S.A., 74
Basseri, 93
Bean, L. L., Inc., 191, 196
Bedouin, 5, 82–89, 92, 96, 106, 108;
  construction of, 83, 88, 89
"Bells of arms," tents, 41
Bell stretcher, 57
Ben-Hur (film), 154
Berber, 84, 89–93, 98
Berger, Horst, 120, 121, 127, 131, 134,
  135
Bethab (traveling litter), 88
Biblical women's tents, 5
Big top. *See* Circus
Bird, Walter W., 118
Birdair Structures, Inc., 118, 122, 124,
  125, 127, 128, 133, 136
Bishop's Ultimate Outdoor
  Equipment, 196
Black desert tent, 5, 16, 81–100; as
  tension structure, 82, 92; Eastern
  (Persian), 82; men's section, 89;
  Western (Arabic), 82; women's
  section, 5, 88, 89, 95, 100

Bonus Expeditionary Army, 55, 56
Boy Scout Jamboree, 59, 60
British army, 14, 15, 25, 31, 32, 34
Breathability. *See* Fabric
Brush arbors. *See* Squaw coolers
Buffington, Leroy S., 116
Bullock's department store (Menlo
    Park, Northern California), 134
Burford, Byron, 148, 149
Burgundy, dukes of, 29
Burton, Sir Richard, tomb of, 9

Cabin tent, roof-truss and yoke-type
    designs, 172
C & O Canal boat, tents atop, 42
Cabledome,™ concept, 124; *See also*
    Cable-net structure
Cable-net structure, 118–124, 126, 128,
    129, 132, 133
Cady, Sam, 148, 149
Caesar, Julius, 13
Camping tents: books and magazines
    about, 232; color choices for, 187;
    construction of, 179–187; designs
    for, 167–175; estimating size of, 166,
    167; fabric for, 175–178; floors in,
    183, 184; framing of, 179, 180;
    manufacturers of, 225–229; rental
    of, 222–225
Camp meetings, 42, 43
Cannondale Corporation, 197
Care of tent, 188–190
Car-top tent, 189
Carry on Camping (film), 162
Carulli, Diana, 144
Cascade Shelter, 231, 232
Cecil B. DeMille, Camp, 153
Charney, Len, 231, 232
Chautauqua Institution, 43, 45
Chemical Fabrics (Bennington,
    Vermont), 127
Ch'ien Lung, 24, 25
Chinese: emperor's, 23–25; military,
    23, 24; Temple of Heaven, 24
Christo, 150
Chuckchi Eskimos, 76
Circus, 49–55, 148, 149
Cities. *See* Tent cities
Civil War, 44
Cleopatra (film), 153, 160
Clothing loops, 187
Cody, William F. ("Buffalo Bill"), 45
Coleman Co., Inc., 198
Colosseum, the, 113, 114
Computer method of design, tension
    structures, 127, 130–132
Conestoga wagon, 42

Conical tent, 26, 31, 32, 34; Lapp, 78;
    in Palestine, 39; *tente conique*, 34;
    tente conique a muraille, 34; Sibley,
    43; tipi, 62–73
Contractor, The (play), 161
Cook holes, 186
Coperthwaite, William, and Yurt
    Foundation, 227, 231, 232
Coronation Durbar (1911), 34–37
Cosmic Tent. *See* Alexander the
    Great, World Tent of
Cottage tent, 175
Cotton. *See* Fabric
Cox, Chuck and Laurel, 226, 231, 232
CPAI-84 flammability standard, 178,
    179
Crimean War, 31, 32
Cro-Magnon, 3, 4
Crow Indians, 64
Crusaders, 26
Crusades, The (film), 155

Darius, 10, 11
Darkroom tent, 33
DeMille, Cecil. *See* Cecil B. DeMille,
    Camp
Denver Tent Company, 199
Depression, Great (1929), 55
Dew cloth. *See* Tipi, lining of; Fabric
Dome tent, 38, 75, 170
Duck. *See* Fabric
Dulles International Airport (Virginia),
    118–120
DuPont (Teflon). *See* Fabric
Dutch doors, 187
Duval County office building
    (Jacksonville, Florida), 134

Early Winters, Ltd., 200
Earthquake, San Francisco (1906), 55
Eastern Mountain Sports, Inc., 201
Edelson, Mary Beth, 142, 143
Edward II, 25
Elmer Gantry (film), 160
EMS. *See* Eastern Mountain Sports,
    Inc.
Entries, tent, 184, 185
Environmental Structures, Inc., 125
Eritrea (Ethiopia), 98, 101
Eskimo, 62, 75, 76; summer tent, 75,
    77; winter tent, 75, 76
Eureka! Tent, Inc., 202, 203
Exoskeleton tent, 170
Expedition tent, 169, 170
Explorer tent, 174

Fabric, of camping tents, 175–178;
    breathability of, 175; cotton, 175,

177, 179; drill, 177; duck, 177; DuPont (Teflon), 126–127, 134; of early tents, 4; featherweight nylon, 176, 178, 179; fire-retardant treatment of, 178, 179; Gore-Tex, 170, 177, 178–179; nylon taffeta, 178; polyethylene-coated polyethylene, 178; polyprophlene, 176; poplin, 177; ripstop nylon, 177; for tipi lining, 68; twill, 177; vinyl-coated nylon, 178; waterproofing treatment of, 178, 179; water-repellency of, 175
Family tents: entries, 184; windows and vents, 185; zippers, 186
Feigenbaum, Harriet, 138, 139, 146
Ferrer, Rafael, 150
Field house, University of Virginia, 120, 121
Field of the Cloth of Gold, 27, 28, 116
Fire-retardants. *See* Fabric
Fires, tent, 53, 178
Flathead Indians, 63
Fly tent, British, 33, 35
Folklife Pavilion (Philadelphia Bicentennial), 128
French, 26, 27, 29, 31, 32, 34
Fuller, Buckminster, 170, 189

Garden tent, Victorian, 33
Geiger-Berger Associates, P. C., 119, 121, 124, 126–130, 132–135
Geiger, David, 124, 126, 127
Genghis Khan, 15, 101
Genghis Khan (film), 159
George V, coronation durbar of, 34–37
Ger, 103; *see also* Yurts, nomadic
Gerry Co., 204
Gandhi, Mahatma, 38
Gibson, Richard, 27, 28, 116
Glenn, Tom ("Tent Tom"), 192
"God houses." *See* Yurts, ceremonial
Godfather, The (film), 161
Golden Horde, 101
Goldsmidt, Nicholas, 134
Goodwin-Cold Tentmakers, 226
Gore-Tex. *See* Fabric
Government Services Administration (Denver, Colorado), 137
Grand Vizir, Constantinople, 21
Great Adventure Amusement Park (New Jersey), 131, 132
"Greatest Show on Earth," 49, 54, 55; *see also* Ringling Brothers and Barnum & Bailey Circus
Greek, 10, 11

Gustavus III of Sweden. *See* Haga, Sweden, metal tents
Guy lines, 29, 35, 95, 181, 182
Gypsies, French, 30

Haga, Sweden, metal tents of, 115, 116–117
Hamites, 98
Hampton Roads Coliseum, 121
Healy, Anne, 143
Hebrew tribes, 5–7
Hemenway, Audrey, 146, 147
Henry V, 157
Henry VIII, 27, 28
Hera, 144, 145
Herodotus, 5
High Lonesome. *See* Athalon Products
Hirsch-Weiss /White Stag, 204–206
Holofernes, 9
Holubar Mountaineering, Ltd., 206
Holy of Holies, 7
Hospital Tents, 48, 56, 57, 59
Howdah, 88
H2C2 (architects), 128

IBM, Havant Plant of, 122
Ice-fishing tent, 173
Igloos, 75, 76
Independence Mall Pavilion (Philadelphia Bicentennial), 128
India, 17th-century hunting tents in, 22, 23
Inflated structure, defined, 117
Ingalls, Davis S., Hockey Rink (Yale University), 118
Iranian nomadic tent, 93, 94
Isimkheb, Princess, 3

Jacob, 5
Jael, 9, 10
Jansport, 207
Japanese-American detention camp, 58, 59
Jeddah International Airport (Saudi Arabia), 7, 116, 136, 137
Johnson, Philip, 121
Jones Mayer Associates, Inc., 135
Judith, 9
Julius Caesar (film), 158
Jumbo (film), 151, 154

Kaaba (Mecca), 7, 8, 137
Katz, Leandro, 148, 149
Khan, Batu, 101
King Richard and the Crusaders (film), 159
King Solomon's Mines (film), 158
Kiowa Indians, 73

Kirkham's Outdoor Products, AAA
    Tent & Awning Co., 208
Kits, tent, 230
Klondike Gold Rush camps, 46, 47
Kublai Khan, 15, 101
Kurds, 84, 93–95

L. L. Bean, Inc. See Bean, L. L., Inc.
Laacke & Joys Co., 209, 210
"Lady with the Unicorn" (tapestry), 27
Lapps, 4, 62, 77–81; Forest, 77, 78, 80;
    Mountain, 77, 78, 81; Sea, 77;
    summer tent, 78; tent transport, 81;
    winter tent, 79, 81
LaVerne College Student Center
    (LaVerne, California), 127
Lawrence of Arabia (film), 159
Le Sacre du Printemps (ballet), 151,
    152
Lineless tent, 169
Longest Walk (1978), 60, 73
Lot, 5
Lundy, Victor, 120, 121
Lurs, 93, 94

Maho Bay Camps, Inc., 135
Mahomet IV, Sultan, 17
Mary, Queen, coronation durbar of,
    36, 37
Mat and skin tents, 97, 98, 100, 101;
    frame systems, 97
Meg 2. See Government Services
    Administration
Metal tents. See Haga, Sweden
Migrant workers camps, 55, 57, 58
Mirrors (ballet), 151, 152
Modesty curtains, 187
Mohammad Rezi Shah Pahlavi, 93
Mongols, 16, 62, 101–104, 107
Moorish black tent, 84, 93
Morgan, William, 134
Moroccan, 20, 84, 89–92
Moses, 6
Moss, Bill, 190–192; Moss Tent Works,
    Inc., 210

Nadir Shah, 17
Napoleon I, 30
National Indoor Stadium (Tokyo), 120,
    122
Nero, Emperor, 13, 113, 116
Net tent, 174, 175
New Harmony, Indiana, Philip
    Johnson's dome in, 121
New York City Marathon, 59
Nikolais, Alwin, 151, 152
No-see-um-proof netting, 187
Noah, 5, 6

Nomads, tents of, 61–109; see also
    individual nomadic tribes
North Face, The, 189, 211, 212
Nowicki, Matthew, 118
Nylon. See Fabric

Odell, Jr., and Associates, A. G., 121
Old Testament, 5, 6, 9, 81
Olympiapark (Munich), 124
One-person shelter, 168
Open-air theater (Bad Hersfeld, West
    Germany), 124
Otto, Frei, 122–124, 130
Outdoor Venture Corp., 213
Owens-Corning Fiberglas Corp., 126,
    127, 134, 136

Palestine, refugee camps in, 39
Papilio, 12, 13
Paul, Saint, 15
Pegs. See Stakes
Pentadome-A, 118
Persepolis. See Persian Empire, 2500th
    anniversary of
Persian Empire, 2500th anniversary of,
    40
Persian tents, 15–17
Petzoldt, Paul, Wilderness Equipment,
    214
Piegan Indians, 64
Pinto, Jody, 144, 145
Poles, 179–180
Polyethylene-coated polyethylene.
    See Fabric
Polyprophlene. See Fabric
Pompeii, amphitheater in, 113, 114,
    116
Poor People's Campaign (1968), 59, 60
Prehistoric tents, 3, 4
Ptolemy II, 116
Pup/scout tent, 168
Pyramid tent, 43, 173, 174

Qashqai, 93, 94
Queeny, Edgar M., Park, 135

Radomes, 118, 122
Raleigh arena, 118, 119
Ramadas. See Squaw coolers
Recreational Equipment, Inc. See REI
    Co-op
Recreational vehicles, 229–230
REI Co-op/Recreational Equipment,
    Inc., 215
Renters, tent. See Camping tents,
    rental of
Revival meetings. See Camp meetings
Richard II (Shakespeare), 155

Ridge-pole tent, 103, 109
Ringling Brothers and Barnum & Bailey Circus, 49, 52–55
Rivendell Mountain Works, 216
Riyadh, University of (Saudi Arabia), recreational facility at, 133
Roman, 11–14
Rooge, Cornelius, 148
Rubruquis (Franciscan friar), as first travel writer, 101
Rudolph, Paul, 132

Saarinen, Eero, 118, 119
Samaritans, 39
San Francisco earthquake (1906), 55
Sauk and Fox Indians, 69, 70
Scout tent, See Pup/scout tent
Screen tent, 174, 175
Scythians, 5
Sea World (Orlando, Florida), 134
Seams, tent, 182, 183
Seattle Tent and Fabric Co., 217
Severud, Fred M., 118–121
Shah of Iran. See Mohammad Reza Shah Pahlavi
Sharon, Miriam, 140, 141
Shaver Partnership, 127
Sheldahl Company, 120
Shiek, The (film), 153
Shizuoka Convention Hall, 120
Sibley, Henry Hopkins, 43; and Civil War tent (Sibley tent), 43, 44, 58
Sierra Designs, 218
Silverdome (Pontiac, Michigan), 116, 126, 132, 134
Sioux Indians, 64; Oglala Dakota Sioux, 65
Skidmore, Owings, and Merrill, 137
Skin tents, See Mat and skin tents
Sisera, 9, 10
Snow tent, 169
Soap-film model, tension structure design, 131, 132
Sokolnikoff, Katherine, 140, 141
Solomon, King, 5
Somali, 101
Spanish-American War, 48
Squaw coolers, 69, 70
Stackhouse, Robert, 146, 147
Stakes, 181, 182
Stanley, Mildred, 143, 145
Stanley and Livingston (film), 156
Storey, David, 161
Stress points, 183
Stromeyer, 122
Stuttgart Institute of Lightweight Structures, 123
Succoth tents, 40

"Super tube." See Tube tent, modified
Sweat tent, 71, 74, 75

Tabernacle, 6, 7
Takamatsu Prefectural Office, 120
Tange, Kenzo, 120, 122
Tarp tent, 167
Tatars, 23, 101, 103
Teda (Sahara desert dwellers), 98
Teflon (TFE-coated Beta Fiberglas). See Fabric
Temkin, Merle, 144, 145
Temple of Heaven. See Chinese tents
Ten Commandments, The (film), 153
Tension structures, 118–137; defined, 118
Tent (ballet), 151, 152
Tent cabin, 44
Tent cities, 7, 8, 34, 37–40, 55, 59, 60, 99, 108
Tent house, 117
Tent hut, 86, 97
Tente d'abri, 10, 23, 31, 34, 48
Tente de troupe, 34
Tibetan, 106–109; construction of, 108, 109
Tipis, 62–73; child's, 64; construction of, 66–68; cooking, 69; four-pole, 66; lining of, 68; materials of, 66, 68, 70; painting of, 63–66, 73; smoke flap system, 64, 67, 68; symbolism of, 62–64, 68, 71; transport of, 62, 66, 68, 69, 72; three-pole, 66, 67; variations, 43, 44; women responsible for, 66, 69, 74
Tipi makers, 230–231
Tokyo Bay, housing complex, 120, 122, 123
Tournaments, 27
Trailwise, 219
Trajan's Column, 12
Travois, 69, 72
Tree tent, 4, 5, 10, 64, 71
Tuareg, 97, 98, 100, 101
Tube tent, modified, 167, 168
Tunnel tent, 171
Turkish, 17; in Poland, 17–20
Turks, Altai, 4
Twill and drill. See Fabric

Ulm Medical Academy (West Germany), 122
Umbrella tent, 172, 173
Unitarian Church (Hartford, Connecticut), 120, 121

United States Pavilion: Expo '70, 124, 126; Expo '74, 129
Ute Indians, 4, 64

Valentino, Rudolph, 153
Vela, 113–116
Vela /Future Tents, Ltd., 130–132, 134
Venetian, 29
Vents, 185, 186
Vestibule, 184, 185
Victoria, Queen, 32
Victoria Regina (play), 151, 155
Voelker, Betty. See Hera

Wall tent, 40, 41, 46, 48, 55, 70, 74, 171, 172
Washington, George, 41, 42
Waterproofing. See Fabric
Water-repellency. See Fabric
Wawel Museum (Poland), Turkish tents in, 18, 20
"Wedge" tent, 171
Wenzel Company, The, 220, 221

West German Pavilion, Expo '67, 123
White Stag. See Hirsch Weiss
Wickiups, 69, 70, 74, 86
Wild West shows, 45
Wilderness Equipment. See Petzoldt, Paul, Wilderness Equipment
Windows, tent, 185, 186

Xerxes, 116

Yalter, Nil, 139, 140, 146
Yurt, nomadic, 4, 15, 16, 23, 62, 101–107, 120, 121; ceremonial, 109; construction of, 102, 103, 106; materials of, 101, 105–107; symbolism of, 103, 106, 107; wagons, erected on, 101, 103
Yurt Foundation, 227, 231, 232
Yurts in America, 231, 232
Yuruks (Turkish sheepherders), 99

Zippers, 186, 187
Zucker, Barbara, 140